A Hermeneutic of *Imagination*

"How refreshing to read a book that endorses imaginative and creative readings of Scripture! Heim and Oetter have given us renewed justification to look for the strange, the abnormal, and even the fantastical in the pages of the Bible and to celebrate the human mind's ability to endlessly explore fresh possibilities of interpretation. They allow us to escape from narrow and constrictive readings and embrace humor, use of metaphor, and conflicting alternatives while firmly building on the imaginative contours of Scripture itself. This is a life-affirming, imaginative book that deserves a key place on your theological bookshelf!"

—**Katharine Dell**, University of Cambridge

"Nobody told me that we need imagination to read the Scriptures. The stress was on thinking logically. Using our imagination might lead us astray. Yet failing to use our imagination might lead us just as far astray. So this is a really useful book to enable us to work out the vital role of imagination in the study of the Scriptures. It's good on the theory, and it has lots of useful examples."

—**John Goldingay**, Fuller Seminary (emeritus)

"Heim and Oetter articulate a persuasive case for why reading the Bible with imagination is essential for faithful biblical interpretation. Significantly, they demonstrate that interpretation is inseparable from the act of imagination. Their work makes an important contribution to the field, offering fresh insight and refining existing interpretive paradigms. Grounded in relevant interdisciplinary theories and shaped by a deep reverence for Scripture, this book builds bridges between academic and ecclesial interpretive practices with clarity and conviction. Relevant to a broad audience—from students to academics and beyond—this work opens new avenues for unlocking Scripture's full potential."

—**Cami Brubaker**, Bethel University

"The work of Heim and Oetter brings together the best of both literary and theological readings of the biblical text in an illuminating hermeneutic of imagination. While these usually separate strands of biblical interpretation have produced some insightful work, they have often been posed as alternative ways of reading. The brilliance of this work is the case made that imagination, wielded in a variety of modes, is the necessary ingredient for fully understanding the wide literary range of texts intended and handed on as theological witness. Imagination is convincingly argued as the needed quality through which literary texts intended as sacred witness can reveal their full power."

—**Bruce C. Birch**, Wesley Theological Seminary (emeritus)

"By exploring the Bible's literary quality, figurative language, affective dimensions, and humorous capacity, the authors unveil the hermeneutic of imagination's impact on translation theory and practice, the intellectual and theological enrichment of the academic study of the Bible, and the embodiment of Scripture's moral imagination, thus enabling Scripture's readers to excavate its power to transform. Persuasive and compelling, this book is a must-read for all who employ their imaginative capabilities to authentically unlock the Bible's imaginative nature."

—**Madipoane Masenya** (**Ngwan'a Mphahlele**), University of South Africa, Unisa (emeritus)

A Hermeneutic of *Imagination*

UNLOCKING SCRIPTURE'S FULL POTENTIAL

Knut M. Heim
with Jeffrey R. Oetter

Baker Academic
a division of Baker Publishing Group
Grand Rapids, Michigan

Published by Baker Academic
a division of Baker Publishing Group
Grand Rapids, Michigan
BakerAcademic.com

Printed in the United States of America

Library of Congress Cataloging-in-Publication Data
Names: Heim, Knut Martin, author. | Oetter, Jeffrey R., 1983– author.
Title: A hermeneutic of imagination : unlocking scripture's full potential / Knut M. Heim with Jeffrey R. Oetter.
Description: Grand Rapids, Michigan : Baker Academic, a division of Baker Publishing Group, [2025] | Includes bibliographical references and index.
Identifiers: LCCN 2024059105 | ISBN 9781540969101 (paperback) | ISBN 9781540969170 (casebound) | ISBN 9781493450039 (ebook) | ISBN 9781493450046 (pdf)
Subjects: LCSH: Imagination—Religious aspects—Christianity. | Hermeneutics—Religious aspects—Christianity. | Spiritual formation.
Classification: LCC BR115.I6 H456 2025 | DDC 220.601—dc23/eng/20250324
LC record available at https://lccn.loc.gov/2024059105

Scripture quotations labeled AT are the author's translation.

Scripture quotations labeled KJV are from the King James Version of the Bible.

Cover painting: *Mary and the Infant Jesus*, Ole Kandelin / Artvee

Baker Publishing Group publications use paper produced from sustainable forestry practices and postconsumer waste whenever possible.

25 26 27 28 29 30 31 7 6 5 4 3 2 1

We dedicate this book to our students at Denver Seminary
in gratitude for their valuable feedback

Contents

Preface

My (Knut's) students are the most important stimuli that inspired the formation of a hermeneutic of imagination. First and foremost, I had the privilege of supervising Jeff Oetter's PhD research on the so-called psalms of vengeance, which culminated with his imaginative interpretation of Psalm 58. Second, at Denver Seminary I have the privilege to teach a survey course on the Old Testament covering the materials from 1 Samuel to Esther and from Isaiah to Malachi. In this course, I have the opportunity to read the biblical materials with imagination. It is Jeff's work on the psalms and the enthusiasm with which the students in this course have embraced imaginative reading strategies that have helped our hermeneutic of imagination take shape.

For me (Jeff), a hermeneutic of imagination began with my work on the psalms of vengeance. Toward the end of my PhD dissertation, as I was applying the fruits of my research to a fresh reading of Psalm 58, there came a moment when I realized that imagination played a sizable role in my work. I still remember, while drafting my interpretation of Psalm 58:5, first entertaining the idea that—perhaps—the psalmist was making a joke. I did not dare put this idea in my draft submission for my supervisor, but I did muster the courage to mention that possibility in our supervision meeting when we discussed the verse. Sadly, as I had feared, the idea was summarily dismissed. It is therefore with not a little satisfaction that as we revisited Psalm 58:5 upon having completed our chapter on humor, said gentleman has now admitted the error of his ways and admits that—yes, indeed—the verse is funny.

We are grateful for the encouragement and professional support we have received from Baker Academic, especially Brandy Scritchfield and Jim Kinney from the acquisitions team and Eric Salo from the editorial team, who have helped us sharpen our argument and present it well.

Last but not least, we are deeply grateful for the expert input of Peter Perry (assistant affiliate professor of New Testament and pastor of St. John's Lutheran Church in Glendale, Arizona) and Cami Brubaker (professor of Old Testament and Hebrew, Bethel University). Dr. Perry read chapter 5 on the humorous dimension of Scripture and made important suggestions to improve it, and Dr. Brubaker's encouragement and enthusiasm for the project have been invaluable. She has read the foundational chapters on imagination and figurative language and contributed numerous comments and suggestions that have helped us sharpen our wits and fine-tune our reasoning and presentation of ideas. We truly appreciate her generous investment in our undertaking.

We hope that a hermeneutic of imagination will kindle curiosity to explore the Bible's treasures anew. We hope that it will ignite a deeper passion to discover its wisdom at the grassroots level as well as the highest academic levels. We hope that—above all—it will inspire a no-holds-barred love for God, a proper love for self, and loving care for our neighbors, including those who are quite different from us. We hope that it will unlock the Bible's full potential to become an inspiration for life and a powerfully transformative resource for ministry. And we hope that it will bring fun, excitement, and a sense of adventure as we read.

CHAPTER ONE

Imagination and What It Has to Do with the Bible

As a combination of creative mental imaging and sensory perception, imagination helps us construct as accurate an interpretation of the Bible as possible, despite the various constraints that limit our understanding. The aim of this book is to explain why imagination is vital to reading the Bible and avoiding misinterpretation. We are proposing not a new *method* of biblical interpretation in the sense of a particular technique for analyzing texts but a *critical hermeneutic of engagement* with the Bible. Consequently, our imaginative approach builds on existing methods of biblical scholarship in ways that are interdisciplinary, imaginative, theological, and practical.

Walter Brueggemann's influential *The Prophetic Imagination*, published in 1978, first brought the importance of imagination to the attention of biblical scholars. Ten years later, Luis Alonso Schökel's *Manual of Hebrew Poetics* (1988) famously claimed that "what has been written with imagination must be read with imagination,"[1] a dictum that he repeated ten years later in his *Manual of Hermeneutics* (1998). Fifteen years after that, Knut Heim's *Poetic Imagination in Proverbs* (2013) applied Alonso Schökel's motto to an analysis of Hebrew poetry that demonstrated the importance of imagination in the composition and interpretation of proverbial parallelism.

1. Luis Alonso Schökel, *A Manual of Hebrew Poetics*, Subsidia Biblica 11 (Pontificio Istituto Biblico, 1988), 104.

In the nearly fifty years since Brueggemann's trailblazing work, significant developments in adjacent fields have prepared the ground for an interdisciplinary approach to biblical studies that considers recent progress in fields as diverse as neuroscience, metaphor theory and cognition, translation theory, the affective sciences, humor studies, and the interdisciplinary study of imagination itself. These disciplines have the power to enrich biblical studies in ways that were beyond the purview of earlier generations. *A Hermeneutic of Imagination* is the first book-length study that takes the Bible's imaginative nature seriously and integrates insights from these disciplines into the academic study of the Bible. This is our attempt to prove both parts of Alonso Schökel's dictum: the Bible was written with imagination, so we must read it with imagination.

The main hypothesis we seek to demonstrate in this volume is that to read the Bible well, we need to employ our imagination. Throughout the book, we hope to demonstrate how a hermeneutic of imagination does not dispense with existing exegetical methods; it builds on them. By doing so, it enriches the scholarly discourse on biblical hermeneutics, introduces fresh applications of existing methods, and offers insights into the meaning of biblical texts that have until now escaped scholarly attention.

In this introductory chapter, we will explain what imagination is and why it is so central to the task of reading the Bible. Crucially, reading the Bible with imagination is not a fanciful approach. Rather, imagination helps us to correct misperceptions that tend to arise when we trust only what we perceive with our sense organs without interpreting such input imaginatively to identify how what we perceive fits with reality. Additionally, imagination helps us to problem-solve purposefully and to engage in creative labor in the service of beauty, truth, and wonder.[2]

We acknowledge that imagination's capacity to generate new ideas that depart from accepted conventions can make those who exercise it look suspect—even dangerous—in the eyes of their peers, but we will demonstrate in this volume how we can apply imagination to the reading of Scripture in ways that develop genuinely biblical ideas to help the people of God revise erroneous cultural and religious assumptions.

Subsequent chapters will explore aspects of the Bible that reveal its profoundly imaginative nature to develop the contours of a hermeneutic of imagination. These include its exquisite literary quality (chap. 2), its powerful figurative language (chap. 3), its affective dimensions (chap. 4), and its humorous

2. Anna Abraham, ed., *The Cambridge Handbook of the Imagination* (Cambridge University Press, 2020), 3.

capacity (chap. 5). The remaining chapters will apply this hermeneutic of imagination to translation theory and practice (chap. 6), develop how it can enrich academic study intellectually and theologically (chap. 7), explore how it can inspire us to embody Scripture's moral imagination (chap. 8), and demonstrate how it can unleash the Bible's transformative power (conclusion). These chapters furnish the crucial building blocks for accurate biblical interpretation because imagination is not a free-floating enterprise that relies on nothing but the interpreter's creative genius. Rather, a hermeneutic of imagination builds on the imaginative contours of Scripture itself, and so these chapters will provide subject-specific knowledge about these imaginative aspects by presenting essential information to build imaginative interpretive competence.

Imagination: A Definition and Defense

As noted by Anna Abraham in her magisterial introduction to *The Cambridge Handbook of the Imagination*, the Oxford English Dictionary currently attributes five meanings to the word *imagination*. Three of these are relevant for identifying how we envisage the use of imagination in reading the Bible:

1. The power or capacity to form internal images or ideas of objects and situations not actually present to the senses, including remembered objects and situations, and those constructed by mentally combining or projecting images of previously experienced qualities, objects, and situations. Also: the power or capacity by which the mind integrates sensory data in the process of perception.
2. The tendency to form ideas which do not correspond to reality; the operation of fanciful, erroneous, or deluded thought. Also: an individual's fanciful, erroneous, or deluded thinking.
3. The mind's creativity and resourcefulness in using and inventing images, analogies, and so on; poetic or artistic genius or talent. Also: an individual's poetic or artistic genius or talent.

There are three main insights we can gain from these meanings attributed to imagination: (1) imagination is part of the process by which we *interpret what we experience with our senses*; (2) reading the Bible with imagination is *not fanciful thinking in the sense of the Oxford English Dictionary's definition*; and (3) imagination is the ability to be *creative*. Abraham offers a captivating paraphrase of these meanings that can help us appreciate just how amazing the human imagination is:

> Our imaginations aid our perception of the current external reality as perceived through our sense organs. Our imagination allows us to conceive of our former external realities. Our imaginations render it possible to fabricate alternative realities and fictional realms that we have never experienced in quite the same manner before. Our imaginations facilitate our ability to reconstruct events from the real past, the counterfactual past, and the potential future. Our imaginations enable us to fantasize aimlessly and problem-solve purposefully. Our imaginations impel us towards creative labor in the service of beauty, truth, and wonder. Through our imaginations, we can savor the fruits of creative labor.[3]

First, then, imagination helps us to interpret our sensory perceptions and experiences. As we will discuss below, not everything is precisely as we experience it with our senses, and imagination is in fact crucial for correcting misperceptions that would constantly arise if we trusted only what we perceive with our sense organs, without interpreting such sensory input imaginatively to ensure that what we perceive fits with reality. In the words of the Oxford English Dictionary quoted above, imagination is "the power or capacity to form internal images or ideas of objects and situations *not actually present to the senses*." In other words, it is the capacity to engage in creative thought about objects and circumstances that are not present to our physical senses.

Second, Abraham notes that our imagination helps us to fabricate alternative and fictional realities that we have not experienced before. Humans use their imagination to interpret reality as well as construct counterfactual ideas and realities. This is an aspect of the imagination that causes suspicion for many Bible readers, on two fronts.

On the one hand, readers may question whether imaginative reading produces interpretations that are fantastical. A phrase from Scripture itself heightens these concerns. In the evocative translation of the King James Version, a phrase from Jeremiah 13:10 describes the people of Judah as "this evil people, which refuse to hear my words, which walk *in the imagination of their heart*, and walk after other gods, to serve them, and to worship them" (emphasis added). Here imagination is associated with disobedience and idolatry, with a refusal to obey God's words, and with the worship of gods other than the God of the Bible.

3. Abraham, *Cambridge Handbook of the Imagination*, 3.

However, the normal Hebrew word for imagination in the sense of a delusion is *maśkiyt*.[4] This word is used in Psalm 73:7 ("Their hearts overflow with follies") and Proverbs 18:11 ("The wealth of the rich is their strong city; in their imagination it is like a high wall"). Jeremiah 13:10, however, uses the Hebrew word *šərîrût*, which means "stubbornness,"[5] and the phrase *bišrirût libbām* literally means "in the stubbornness of their hearts." Consequently, the New Revised Standard Version translates the phrase with "who stubbornly follow their own will," a rendering that better reflects the meaning of the original.

Similarly, verse 51 in Mary's triumphant claim in the Magnificat (Luke 1:46–55), which the KJV translates with "he hath scattered the proud in the imagination of their hearts," translates a Greek word, *dianoia*, which refers to thinking in general. Consequently, the NRSV translates "he has scattered the proud in the thoughts of their hearts." Therefore, with a more accurate translation, the Bible does not raise apprehensions about the imagination leading individuals astray.

On the other hand, readers might question whether reading the Bible with imagination plays into the hands of those who already believe it to be "not real." Scripture constantly talks about spiritual realities. The Bible engages a spiritual dimension that many modern Western people consider counterfactual. For them, the God of the Bible is not real, and they do not believe that many of the events described in the Bible actually happened. The contents of the Bible seem fantastical to them; they consider its spiritual claims as fabrications of a religious clique. The often-repeated claim "I believe only what I can see with my own eyes" captures this skeptical sentiment well.

Ironically, it is imagination that helps us to identify beings and events as true and real even when we cannot see with our own eyes and when we do not have sensory access to them. Christian and Jewish believers are convinced that the God of the Bible is not a fabrication of their own or the biblical authors' minds. When we imagine God, we do not conjure up a counterfactual reality. Rather, we imagine what the God of the Bible is like even though we likely have not seen this God with our eyes, touched this God with our hands, or heard this God with our ears. In fact, the prohibition against creating physical images of God (Exod. 20:4–5; Lev. 26:1; Deut. 5:8–9) explicitly prevents us from creating artifacts that would allow a sensory engagement with physical

4. Ludwig Koehler, Walter Baumgartner, and Johann J. Stamm, *The Hebrew and Aramaic Lexicon of the Old Testament: Study Edition*, trans. and ed. Mervyn E. J. Richardson, 2 vols. (Brill, 2001), 1:641; Herbert Donner, ed., *Gesenius: Hebräisches und aramäisches Handwörterbuch über das Alte Testament*, vol. 18 (Springer, 2013), 747.

5. Koehler, Baumgartner, and Stamm, *Hebrew and Aramaic Lexicon of the Old Testament*, 2:1658; Donner, *Gesenius*, 18:1413.

material designed to represent God. Since we cannot normally experience God with our physical senses, then, we cannot fathom what God is like unless we use our imagination to create mental images, based on what we read *about* God from the Bible, such as the idea that God behaves toward humans like a father to his children (e.g., Ps. 68:5; Isa. 63:16) or like a shepherd toward his sheep (e.g., Ps. 23). There is, then, nothing wrong with the human imagination per se. There is no need to qualify imagination with adjectives like "faithful" or "sanctified," as if it were in need of redemption.

Third, Abraham mentions that imagination helps us to "problem-solve purposefully" and that it encourages us "towards creative labor in the service of beauty, truth, and wonder,"[6] enabling us to enjoy the fruits of our creativity. This observation is also relevant for reading the Bible. As we consciously engage our imagination, we consider the kinds of obstacles and challenges that the biblical characters encounter and learn from their triumphs and tragedies how we can tackle similar problems today. As the biblical characters encounter beauty, truth, and wonder, we too experience with them those same qualities in our own lives. As we encounter creativity and imagination in the literary quality of the biblical texts, we use our own imagination to match that of the texts that we read: "What has been written with imagination must also be read with imagination."[7] While Alonso Schökel made this comment specifically with reference to the poetic literature of the Bible, this is also applicable for the rest of the biblical texts, as almost all of Scripture is of a high literary caliber and its composition demanded the use of its authors' imaginations throughout. We'll talk about this more in chapters 2–3.

Imagination Is Essential for Progress and New Ideas

Imagination is fundamental to human progress. Without it, human cultures would not be possible. The human capacity to employ imagination is and has been essential for the creation of new artifacts, the emergence of new ways of thinking, and the development of new forms of human conduct. Writing in 1930, Belarusian psychologist Lev Vygotsky captured this fundamental insight:

> Imagination is the basis of all human activity and an important component of all aspects of cultural life. Absolutely everything around us that was created by the hand of man, the entire world of human culture, as distinct from the

6. Abraham, *Cambridge Handbook of the Imagination*, 3.
7. Alonso Schökel, *Manual of Hebrew Poetics*, 104.

world of nature, all this is the product of human imagination and of creation based on this imagination.[8]

Imagination is not simply a by-product of individual human genius; it is essential to who we are as human beings. It is a sociocultural phenomenon that arises from all spheres of human experience. Building on Vygotsky's insights, Tania Zittoun, Vlad Glăveanu, and Hana Hawlina claim that imagination is "a process as well as an experience, it is highly contextual, develops over time, mediates action and is, at once, mediated both by culture and its various social, material, and symbolic resources."[9]

More recently, a book-length study by Jennifer Gosetti-Ferencei of how imagination affects human life comes to similar conclusions, aiming at "an encompassing and multifactorial grasp of major modes of imaginative cognition that define human thinking and being. These include inner imaging, seeing-as and related modes of interpretive perception, hypothetical or counterfactual thinking, pretense, and creativity, which makes use of the other modes."[10] In other words, Gosetti-Ferencei understands imagination as "a cognitive power."[11]

Vygotsky, who has influenced current debates, saw imagination as a product of "higher psychological functions" that "help us achieve distance from the immediate stimulations and constraints of the environment." Or, put slightly differently, one of its core characteristics and central functions is that it enables "a departure from the immediate situation" and "gives us a degree of freedom from the constraints of an immediate situation."[12] Vygotsky's observations have radical implications for social attitudes to imaginative thinking as well as for modern academic discourse and the interpretation of Scripture.

This freedom from immediate constraints also works on the sociocultural level, in that it fosters independence from the social constraints of what people around us think, what the commonly accepted solution to a given problem is. It is this social freedom that makes imagination such a controversial and

8. Lev S. Vygotsky, "Imagination and Creativity in Childhood," *Journal of Russian and East European Psychology* 42, no. 1 (1930): 4, quoted in Tania Zittoun, Vlad Glăveanu, and Hana Hawlina, "A Sociocultural Perspective on Imagination," in *The Cambridge Handbook of the Imagination*, ed. Anna Abraham (Cambridge University Press, 2020), 143.

9. Zittoun, Glăveanu, and Hawlina, "Sociocultural Perspective on Imagination," 146. They claim that this view "diverges from contemporary cognitive or neuroscientific accounts" (146). However, this need not do so in principle. Rather, it complements those latter views by adding the important insight that imagination has both an individual and a sociocultural dimension.

10. Jennifer Anna Gosetti-Ferencei, *The Life of Imagination: Revealing and Making the World* (Columbia University Press, 2018), 5.

11. Gosetti-Ferencei, *Life of Imagination*, 9.

12. Zittoun, Glăveanu, and Hawlina, "Sociocultural Perspective on Imagination," 146.

contested human trait. Imagination is the pathway to new ideas, *and it makes those who exercise it look suspect—even dangerous—to the social groups to which they belong*. This is also true for imaginative readings of the Bible. They at times produce fresh insights and new interpretations that can challenge long-standing cultural assumptions. The rest of this book will demonstrate that, even so, such readings develop genuinely biblical ideas that can get us closer to the meaning intended by the Holy Spirit and the original authors' intentions than more traditional interpretations.

The Bible Requires Interpretation, and *Good* Interpretation Requires Imagination

When we read the Bible, we read an extraordinarily rich and rewarding human-divine collection of classical literature, an entire library of amazing compositions inspired by the Holy Spirit. We read texts that come to us from God, written in different languages, originating from different times (preceding us by at least nineteen hundred years), from a different geographical region (unless we happen to be reading the Bible in the Middle East, in countries like modern Israel, Egypt, Lebanon, Syria, Iraq, Jordan, or Iran), and from different cultures. We cannot read an artifact as rich and wonderful as the Bible unless we also *interpret* it.

There are some who insist that interpretation is not necessary for reading the Bible. Their position is often expressed in something like this: "I believe in the inspiration of the Bible. Therefore, I take it literally." Common as it is, the idea of associating inspiration with literal meaning is wildly off the mark. Others will express a contrasting position: "Everything in the Bible must be interpreted, and nothing can be taken literally." Equally common as the first position, it is equally flawed. However, an analysis of both positions reveals that people across the theological spectrum tend to take those passages that they like or agree with literally while they interpret those passages that they disagree with. In the final analysis, no interpretation is also an interpretation, though rarely a good one. By contrast, when we read the Bible with imagination, we interpret everything, whether we like or dislike what we read. And this is a more honest approach to reading the Bible.

Reading the Bible with imagination differs, at least in part, from other approaches to the Bible, especially when we compare it with some Protestant approaches that emphasize the clarity of Scripture.

In a pointed departure from the Roman Catholic idea that a proper understanding of the Bible needed to be mediated through the church's tradition, relayed to lay Christians by trained experts, the priests, the theologians of the Reformation argued for the *clarity* of Scripture (*claritas Scriptura*). They insisted that the Bible can and should be read by everybody in their own languages and that nonspecialist laypeople are, at least in principle, able to understand the Bible.

Where we agree with the Reformation idea of the clarity of Scripture is reflected in Mary Warnock's insistence that interpretation can be "common to everyone, and in this sense ordinary," that imagination can "enable us to recognize things in the world as familiar."[13] Yes, some contents in the Bible we do recognize as familiar because human nature is remarkably constant and the experience of people from another place and time can be remarkably like our own. We share a huge amount of similarities in our bodies and emotions and ways of thinking. Even so, it is our imagination that helps us to see the similarities in spite of time gaps, cultural differences, and so on. Our imagination helps us to identify what we have in common despite our differences.

When we read the Bible, even at the simplest level, we use our imagination to interpret the sensory perception of lines of black marks on a white background to identify these marks as letters, we use our imagination to identify sequences of such letters as words, we use our imagination to identify sequences of such words as phrases and sentences, and we use our imagination to identify sequences of such phrases as stories and poems. When we read the word *donkey* in John 12:14 and Matthew 21:7, our imagination helps us to recognize that the passages in which the two words appear refer to one and the same incident in the life of Jesus and to identify that the two instances of the word refer to one and the same domestic animal, despite differences in detail. Without conscious effort, our imagination even helps us envisage what that donkey two thousand years ago might have looked like.

Where we disagree with the Reformation idea of the clarity of Scripture, however, is reflected in Warnock's claim that imagination "is also necessary if we are to see the world as significant of something *unfamiliar*."[14] Warnock's observation about the need for imagination in our experience of the world in general is also and especially valid for our reading of the Bible. Despite the similarities we have already talked about between us and the biblical characters, there are also numerous and significant differences. It is here where our imagination helps us again to recognize novelty and dissimilarity. We recognize that certain words and phrases, certain objects and customs, and so on are so unfamiliar that we cannot understand them unless we seek further

13. Mary Warnock, *Imagination* (Faber & Faber, 1976), 10.
14. Warnock, *Imagination*, 10 (emphasis added).

background knowledge and then use our imagination to integrate that additional background information into our interpretation of the biblical texts.

A Definition and Illustration of the Imaginative Process

As we shall see, artists have a take on the relationship between the imagination and sensory perception that differs from that of scholars in the humanities and the sciences.[15] This artistic perspective is particularly helpful for understanding why imagination is vital for reading Scripture. Artists integrate imagination and sensory perception. For example, renowned cellist Yo-Yo Ma teaches "how music can be a source of meaning, connection, imagination, and understanding." In his master class, he emphasizes several key components that also feature prominently in an imaginative reading of the Bible: meaning, imagination, and understanding (interpretation). He notes, "If we think of music as, of sound, as what is around us, we are constantly receiving information, and at the same time we are constantly interpreting this information." He highlights how our senses are connected to our creative imaginations, saying "we use our imagination by using all of our senses."[16]

This statement is crucial for our own understanding of imagination and how to use it in our reading of the Bible. Imagination kicks in not only when sensory input is lacking or limited. It also operates as and when we do receive sensory input. In fact, imagination is what helps us to process all the sensory information we receive in a more integrated and holistic way. Imagination enhances our ability to experience input from several sensory modalities (sight, sound, touch, taste, and scent) *all at once* and integrate that input creatively into an extraordinarily rich and rewarding experience.

Incorporating the above artistic perspective, we are now at the point where we can restate our own definition of imagination as we employ it in our reading of the Bible against the background of the more holistic perspective we have explored so far:

> As a combination of creative mental imaging and sensory perception, imagination helps us construct as accurate an interpretation of the Bible as possible, despite the various constraints that limit our understanding.

15. The academic discourse on the imagination has been shaped by scholars whose fields are in the humanities and the sciences, and even though the production and appreciation of art sometimes feature in their work, the perspectives of artists themselves rarely enter the debate. Here we aim to redress the balance, if ever so slightly.

16. Yo-Yo Ma, "Yo-Yo Ma Teaches Music and Connection," MasterClass, accessed June 15, 2022, https://www.masterclass.com/classes/yo-yo-ma-teaches-music-and-connection.

This definition entails three important claims:

- Imagination helps us transcend the constraints that limit our experience of reality.
- Imagination combines sensory perception and creative mental imaging.
- Imagination helps us construct a more accurate interpretation of the world.

The first claim acknowledges an important insight into how humans perceive the world around them. Most, perhaps all, significant encounters of humans with the world around them demand interpretation. To illustrate this, let us engage in a thought experiment, using the example of cats partially occluded behind a fence.

Figure 1.1

We may not see all of a cat when it is partially obscured by a fence. We may not hear every sound made in the performance of a piece of music when background noise drowns out part of it. We may not feel all parts of a glass when our fingers touch only a relatively small portion of its surface. The principle behind these examples is true already when we consider simple realities like physical objects. We will use a sequence of drawings by Jennifer Bunge that we commissioned for this purpose to illustrate this point. Figure 1.1 illustrates this incomplete perception of reality, an example of the frequent times our direct experience of reality is limited in the sense of being partial or incomplete.

We see a cat through the broken lattice of a fence. Parts of the fence obscure parts of the cat from sight, but as we contemplate those parts of the cat that we see, our capacity to imagine enables us to complete the picture, a mental process that philosopher Bence Nanay calls "amodal completion."[17] In our mind we can envisage what the whole cat looks like, how big the invisible parts of the cat's body are and what color they will likely have. And indeed, once we can see all of the cat, it looks just as we had imagined it would look (see fig. 1.2).

Figure 1.2

Nanay defines amodal perception "in terms of the lack of sensory stimulation."[18] However—and here we disagree with Nanay and other scholars of the imagination—partial gaps in sensory perception are in fact particularly strong instances of sensory stimulation. Our imagination automatically evokes an expectation of the whole. The visual gap prompts a spontaneous and automatic, almost instantaneous, reconstruction. Partial perception stimulates the completion of the sensory input into a restored, interpreted whole, and it is our imagination that enables this process of amodal completion. This human capacity operates all the time, even when we are not aware of it. Imaginative reading, then, does not *add* something to the biblical texts. Rather, it helps us perceive accurately what is actually there, including those parts of the text that are understated or implicit and thus less prominent and perhaps only partially visible.

Importantly, however, this simple illustration does not suggest that the solution to a correct perception of experienced realities is the removal of obstacles to our sensory perception, because many if not most perceived realities are partially obscured in this sense. It would simply be impossible to follow this solution in all instances.

17. Bence Nanay, "Perception and Imagination: Amodal Perception as Mental Imagery," *Philosophical Studies* 150 (2010): 239–54.

18. Nanay, "Perception and Imagination," 241.

More complex realities demand even more interpretive work. For example, what does the Bible say about whether women should be allowed to preach and teach in church services? An initial approach to answering this question is to gain as much information as possible about what the Bible says about the topic, to read all the relevant statements.

Several passages from the New Testament come to mind, such as 1 Timothy 2:12 ("I do not permit a woman to teach or to have authority over a man; she is to keep silent") and 1 Corinthians 14:34–35 ("Women should be silent in the churches. For they are not permitted to speak, but should be subordinate, as the law also says. If there is anything they want to learn, let them ask their husbands at home. For it is shameful for a woman to speak in church"), to mention the most important examples. For many, these two passages alone settle the issue and provide what they consider "clear" guidance on the matter. For them, the answer to the question of whether women may preach or teach is no. In our illustration, the biblical evidence supporting this answer may be represented with a *white* cat.

However, there are other passages in Scripture that seem to suggest otherwise, such as Romans 16:7 ("Greet Andronicus and Junia, my fellow Israelites who were in prison with me; they are prominent among the apostles, and they were in Christ before I was") and Luke 24:9–10 ("And returning from the tomb, they told all this to the eleven and to all the rest. Now it was Mary Magdalene, Joanna, Mary the mother of James, and the other women with them who told this to the apostles").[19] Here are passages that suggest that Junia, a woman,[20] was considered a prominent apostle, one of the highest offices in the early church, and that the earliest witnesses to the resurrection of Jesus were women. For many, these two passages settle the issue differently, providing equally clear guidance to the effect that the answer to the question is yes. In our illustration, the biblical evidence supporting this answer may be represented with a *black* cat.

We are now left with sensory evidence that suggests the presence of two cats in Scripture, one white and one black. How should we process the sensory stimulus, especially in the light of the inspiration of Scripture and various hermeneutical guidelines and doctrinal commitments, such as the unity of Scripture and the principle that we should use Scripture to interpret Scripture, or the idea that there should be no contradiction in the Bible?

19. Cf. also the prominent role of Priscilla according to Rom. 16:3–4 and Acts 18:26.

20. A compelling argument for the name being a female name rather than a male is presented in Ulrich Wilckens, *Der Brief an die Römer (Röm 12–16)*, Evangelisch-Katholischer Kommentar zum Neuen Testament VI/3 (Neukirchener Verlag, 1989), 135–36.

An initial response would be to say that there must surely be only one cat, a cat that looks *white* when we focus on passages like 1 Timothy 2:12 and 1 Corinthians 14:33–35 but also looks *black* when we focus on passages like Romans 16:7 and Luke 24:9–10. The information that is presented in the two sets of passages, however, makes the cat look unusual, to say the least. It may be presented visually as in figure 1.3.

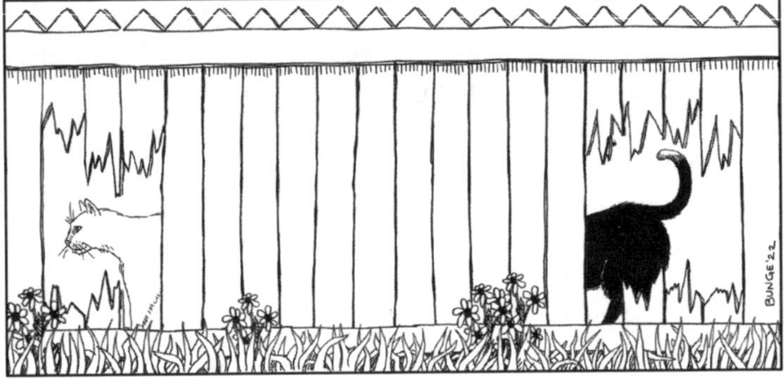

Figure 1.3

This image represents visually what an interpretation that only pays attention to sensory input—what we see written in Scripture, without interpretation—looks like. However, this cat looks rather unusual. For one, its color scheme is unusual. While cats with mixed-color coats of black and white are common, the color distribution on this cat—only white at the front and only black at the back—looks abnormal. What is more, its sausage-like body shape is unlike any normal cat. It is here that the indispensable role of imagination comes into view, for it allows us to mistrust our sensory perception and conclude that there must in fact be two cats in Scripture, one white and one black, as in figure 1.4.

Figure 1.4

At the level of our cat illustration, then, we use our imagination to correct an interpretation of the sensory input we receive that would mislead us into thinking that we are looking at a biological monstrosity—a cat whose coat displays an unnatural color scheme and whose body is grotesquely long. Our imagination permits us to correct misleading sensory input and interpret what we see as two normal cats, not one fanciful one.

At the level of biblical interpretation, we use our imagination even more constructively. First, we give ourselves permission to admit that the Bible contains statements that are in tension with one another. One set of passages seems to permit women to teach, while another set of passages does not. There really are two cats, not just one. Second, while this initially creates the impression of a contradiction at the literal level, our capacity for imagination allows us to keep in mind that these statements appear in Holy Scripture, a body of texts that is not only penned by human authors but also inspired by the Holy Spirit. An unimaginative reading would mislead us to conclude that here Scripture contradicts itself and therefore contains an error. In reality, this insistence to take all statements on the topic literally amounts to a refusal to *interpret* the biblical passages, and it is this refusal to engage our imagination that undermines the credibility of Scripture. Ironically, it is again the lack of imagination that leads to fanciful readings.

Imagination as an Aid to a More Accurate Interpretation of Reality

Imagination, then, is a cognitive process by which we combine the mental capacities of remembering the past and anticipating the future with our various physical sense perceptions to construct meaningful and accurate representations of reality. This is especially important when we are confronted with more complex phenomena, such as those we often encounter in Scripture, that are more interesting than simple objects or events.[21]

Our sensory perceptions alone cannot enable us to understand what we experience. This has already been noted by philosopher Nigel J. T. Thomas:

> Imagination is what makes our sensory experience meaningful, enabling us to interpret and make sense of it, whether from a conventional perspective or from a fresh, original, individual one. It is what makes perception more than the mere physical stimulation of sense organs. It also produces mental imagery,

21. A close relationship between imagination and memory has been proposed so regularly by scholars in a variety of academic disciplines that we can justifiably call it a consensus view. Abraham, *Cambridge Handbook of the Imagination*, 5.

> visual and otherwise, which is what makes it possible for us to think outside the confines of our present perceptual reality, to consider memories of the past and possibilities for the future, and to weigh alternatives against one another. Thus, imagination makes possible all our thinking about what is, what has been, and, perhaps most important, what might be.[22]

Reality is almost always richer and more interesting than the limited sensory information that we receive through our sense organs alone. And imagination also has consequences in the real world; it also happens "inside the world, rather than inside the head, achieved through processes of creative material engagement." Drawing on material engagement theory and enactive cognitive science, anthropologists Maria Koukouti and Lambros Malafouris explain how potters use their imagination: In a "*hylonoetic* process" the potter anticipates and partially visualizes "possibilities of form-making that lie beyond the reach of the immediate here and now of the potter's perception. Whatever the final form of that vase might be, it was absent (as a real material object) during those early imaginary stages."[23]

Above we noted that imagination is the capacity to engage in creative thought about objects and circumstances that are not present to our physical senses. This is also true for our interpretation of most biblical texts. Narratives, including biblical ones, can never include all the relevant background information of events that happened elsewhere in the past. We have to rely on our imagination to fill in the gaps. Poems, including biblical ones, will not spell out all the emotions that the poet experienced when composing their piece, even though the poet may in fact want to evoke these same emotions in the poem's readers. We need to draw on our imagination to deduce what the author may have felt when he or she composed the words we now see on the page. In other words, we fill in the picture, we imagine the sounds, we simulate what the poet might have felt at the time in order to empathize with the poet, and perhaps even with other readers of the poem.

The cat analogy we used above illustrates this complex function of the imagination in our experience of the world around us, including biblical texts. When we observed a partially visible cat on one side of the fence, we experienced the cat as a whole and effortlessly reconstructed what the cat looked like even though part of its body was hidden by the fence. We used our

22. The quoted section does not appear in the online version of Thomas's "Mental Imagery" entry in the Stanford Encyclopedia of Philosophy (https://plato.stanford.edu/entries/mental-imagery); rather, the quote is from a citation of an earlier version of his article in Abraham, *Cambridge Handbook of the Imagination*, 5.

23. Maria Koukouti and Lambros Malafouris, "Material Imagination: An Anthropological Perspective," in Abraham, *Cambridge Handbook of the Imagination*, 42.

imagination to construct a mental image of the cat that accurately interpreted the incomplete visual stimulus we had received. That is, we engaged in a *cognitive* process that corrected the limited and thus potentially misleading sensory input, an imaginative activity that Nanay designates as amodal completion.

As we contemplated those parts of the cat that we saw, our capacity to imagine enabled us to complete the picture. In our mind we could envisage what the whole cat looked like, how big the invisible part of the cat's body was, and what color it had.

Conversely, our imagination also helped us to avoid trusting our physical senses when they might have misled us.[24] Take for example the incident where we saw the front half of a cat behind an open space in the fence while its back half was partially obscured by two vertical planks in the fence. Prior knowledge reminded us of the normal size of a cat's body and its proportion, but to our astonishment we saw that the hind part of the cat was still visible. The shape of the cat did not concur with what we expected, and our curiosity was aroused. Yet, even without moving to peer behind the fence, we could imagine two scenarios. One was a cat that was shaped like a dachshund, having a sausage-shaped body. Such cats of course do not exist in the real world. What our eyes misled us to see was counterfactual and fantastical. Our imagination helped us remember that such cats do not exist, so we deployed our imagination to arrive at another interpretation of the puzzling visual stimulus we had received: We concluded that there must be two cats behind the fence, and what we saw was the front half of the first cat and the hind part of the second. And when we checked, it turned out that our imagination had helped us to avoid a misinterpretation of the visual stimulus we had received.

The scenario in this thought experiment illustrates crucial benefits that arise from the use of our imagination in many spheres of life, not least in biblical interpretation. Since we read the Bible in a confessional context, with a set of fundamental beliefs that guide our interpretation (equivalent to our knowledge of the normal body shapes of cats in the illustration above), when we now encounter a statement like Psalm 82:6 ("I say, 'You are gods,

24. We have not found this aspect in the literature, but we believe it is a very important function of our capacity to imagine. Gosetti-Ferencei comes close: "Objective thought that would exclude imagination would be severely limited, for imagination enables engagement of the possible involved in any significant study of reality. . . . Just as we are sometimes misled by imagination, we may on other occasions fail to understand complexities because we fail to adequately imagine how things could be or might otherwise be" (*Life of Imagination*, 254). This is why our imagination helps us to surpass existing knowledge, to go beyond what is already known in ways that are inspirational and transformative (255). Consequently, "as an inextricable dimension of human thinking, imagination's multifactorial engagement is essential for understanding ourselves, our forms of life, and our future possibilities" (252).

children of the Most High, all of you'"), we do not take this statement literally and conclude that God is speaking to rival gods. Rather, we interpret the passage appropriately. The refusal to use our imagination would have led to a misinterpretation.

So imagination must emerge from a keen sense of normality. It needs to be aware of both what is "normal" and what is not, and it is our memory of previous experience that helps us decide. It is memory that draws on prior knowledge of what is considered normal that creates the framework of expectations that enables the use of imagination to accurately represent reality, and only against this background can imagination function constructively to help humans identify what is abnormal, new, or fantastical.[25]

It is the perception of something being *abnormal* that often stimulates creative, imaginative thinking, and as a result we arrive at an imaginative interpretation of abnormal phenomena as fantastical, or we may reinterpret some or all of the phenomena we observe to integrate them imaginatively into a new or different interpretation of reality that enables more mature reflection and new, deeper insights. This is especially important in Scripture, which is full of the *abnormal* and thus requires us to use our imagination. Details such as God living as a man, dying, and rising from the dead are easier to place into the category of abnormal, and we give them great attention because of their theological significance. Other examples, such as a talking donkey, while just as easy to discern as abnormal, are given less attention due to the lack of theological claims built upon them. Throughout this book, many examples will be given that illustrate the elements in Scripture that many find odd and thus require imagination to understand, as well as the elements that are odd and require imagination to understand but are often overlooked for a variety of reasons.

Overview of the Book

By this point, we hope you have a better idea of what we mean by imagination, how it works, and how it can be useful for readers of the Bible. In the following chapters, we will explore these concepts in more depth by examining key developments in adjacent disciplines, such as metaphor theory and human cognition, the affective sciences, and humor theory.

25. Even the abnormal or fantastical, however, can of course be construed as "normal" in an imaginative event that seeks to create a new imaginary "world" that exists only in the mind of the imaginer, a world that can even be communicated to others in words and pictures. Crucially, both the imaginative creator of such a domain and his or her audience will remain aware that the new realm or reality that has been created in this way is a fanciful, counterfactual entity that does not exist in the real world.

As we already mentioned above, these chapters will explore aspects of the Bible that reveal its profoundly imaginative nature. Accurate biblical interpretation is not a free-floating enterprise arising from the interpreter's imaginative ingenuity.[26] Rather, it must build on the imaginative contours of Scripture itself, and so these chapters will provide subject-specific knowledge about these imaginative aspects. Consequently, the following chapters are foundational building blocks for reading Scripture with imagination because they present information essential for building imaginative interpretive competence. They will be filled with practical examples that focus on difficult or problematic texts to illustrate the impressive contributions that reading with imagination can make, especially when it comes to complex interpretive, ethical, and theological problems. They will also include practical examples that demonstrate how a hermeneutic of imagination can transform academic study of the Bible into aesthetically inspiring, intellectually stimulating, emotionally rewarding, theologically rich, and spiritually transformative adventures of the mind that contribute to problem-solving and human flourishing.

In chapter 2, we will highlight the literary artistry of the biblical texts, which necessitates careful observation to ensure accurate interpretation. We will show how the skillful authors of the biblical texts often included subtle rhetorical signals that shape meaning, and how imaginative reading encourages careful attention to these signals to encourage deeper engagement and richer interpretations. For example, traditional interpretations often fail to detect nuance or humor because of the impulse to explain away unexpected details to make the text fit with preconceived ideas, and so what is truly interesting, intriguing, and rewarding tends to be missed because it appears to be an obstacle for understanding. By contrast, reading with imagination intentionally focuses on problematic content as opportunities for deeper understanding and new insights—as opportunities for discovery, growth, and transformation. Consequently, imagination encourages us to adjust our interpretations to fit the texts rather than adjusting the texts to fit our expectations.

In chapter 3, we will explore the figurative aspects of the Bible and how imagination helps us recognize and understand them. Texts of a high literary caliber like the Bible contain numerous figures of speech that are not just ornamental but essential as means for shaping and communicating meaning: The way we know through language is essential for cognitive progress. While

26. Creative imagination cannot be reduced either to "mystifying" accounts of imagination that ascribe it to the genius of exceptionally gifted individuals or to accounts that describe it exclusively as the product of "combinatory skills" that simply blend what is already known. Gosetti-Ferencei, *Life of Imagination*, 252.

we will focus on metaphors in this chapter, we will argue that most if not all of our discussion applies equally to other kinds of figurative language.

In chapter 4, we will examine how the Bible evokes emotions, both intentionally and unintentionally, and how imagination plays a role in responding to those emotions. We will first rehabilitate the value of emotions and demonstrate their importance for how the Bible, and all literature, influences how we as readers behave. Even when emotions appear in understated fashion, imagination helps us experience characters as three-dimensional human beings to whom we can relate. We begin to understand their actions, and their inner lives can now inform how we think, feel, and act today. By contrast, the Bible can also invite unintended emotions that alienate modern readers. When ethically suspect actions receive no or little censure, the texts appear to endorse them for those who read without imagination and miss subtle rhetorical signals.

In chapter 5, we will survey how the Bible uses humor to communicate important truths. We will argue that humor is everywhere, in all cultures and in all significant expressions of those cultures. And while the type of humor can vary across cultures, humor can be understood cross-culturally, at least in principle. And we believe that imagination, yet again, plays a crucial role in cross-cultural explorations of humor, including that found in Scripture. A main hypothesis of this chapter is that humor in the Bible is much more frequent and beneficial than has previously been acknowledged. Imaginative reading of the Bible will help us detect more potentially humorous texts than before because it encourages us to pay special attention to textual clues that prompt the inference of nonlinguistic markers in the performance of texts, especially where reported speech occurs.

In chapter 6, we will examine how modern translations have obscured the foreign and odd nature of Scripture, and how this often prevents us from engaging our imagination, which is important when reading the Bible. Translations often hide indications of the Bible's origin from a different time and place and from a different culture and language. They smooth out oddities and try to remove unusual features of the text that may have been intended by the authors to communicate something. Therefore, we advocate for "foreignizing" translations that consciously reproduce what might be considered oddities in the original and draw readers' attention to these features rather than obscure them. What sounded funny or strange in the original should feel and sound equally unusual, vague, or funny in the modern translation. In short, imaginative translations will enable readers in the target language to experience how a contemporary native speaker may have experienced the text when first hearing or reading it. They will reproduce the poetic artistry of the original as well as its potential for oral performance. They will reflect all the imaginative components that went into the original composition so that what was written with imagination can be read with imagination.

In chapter 7, we will discuss how imagination helps us merge academic and theological study of the Bible. The study of the Bible from an academic perspective independent of faith commitments does not have to be in competition with its study from a theological point of view within the Christian faith tradition. We will argue that each perspective has relative strengths and weaknesses and that studying the Bible from both perspectives at once has important advantages. Reading the Bible with imagination encourages us to undertake our scriptural reading with more academic rigor and our academic study with more spiritual vigor. As a result, a hermeneutic of imagination can enrich the church, the academy, and society at large.

In chapter 8, we will argue that a hermeneutic of imagination harnesses the moral imagination of the Old and New Testaments and puts it to work. If the supreme goal of Scripture is to promote love for God and neighbor, then that love needs to find an outlet in practical Christian living that goes beyond the care for the victims of injustice and leads to contending proactively for justice by helping potential victims before perpetrators can harm them, and by contending with potential perpetrators if necessary. To achieve this, we need nothing short of a full-scale reorientation of our reading perspectives.

In the conclusion, we will first explore the transformative power of Scripture. Here we will argue that the Bible is designed by the Holy Spirit to make God present to those who read it and to exert a transformative power upon them. This enables readers to experience God's presence as a positive dynamic reality that inspires them to grow in love for God and their neighbors. The Bible is and remains an active agent that makes the divine realities of which it speaks present to those who read it. It contains divine revelation and has the power to mediate it. Reading the Bible with imagination enables us to adopt a posture that opens us to experience this reality inductively, through the effects that the Bible has on us as we read. Reading the Bible, we come face-to-face with the living God, and a hermeneutic of imagination helps us to become aware that Scripture is more than a static artifact. It emanates dynamic and ongoing revelation. Reading the Bible with imagination thus creates a space where the veil between the supernatural and the natural world becomes transparent.

We then will turn to an interpretation of Psalm 23, with special focus on verse 2. Here we will illustrate what changes when we apply a hermeneutic of imagination to one of Scripture's most well-known and most thoroughly studied poems. We will discover that reading the verse with imagination facilitates a more accurate interpretation that leads to a transformative engagement with the text that is at once theologically rewarding, intellectually compelling, emotionally liberating, and personally transformative. This example will thus make a credible case for the potential of a hermeneutic of imagination to inspire our reading of all of Scripture.

CHAPTER TWO

A Hermeneutic of Imagination Allows Us to Enjoy the Literary Quality of Scripture

Various labels have been assigned to methods that prioritize the literary quality and rhetorical impact of biblical texts. These include "close reading," "literary readings," and so on. Early patristic authors called it *akribeia*, "accurate attention" to the details of the text.[1] There is much overlap between what we call "careful observation" and rhetorical criticism or new literary criticism, whose role in a hermeneutic of imagination we explore in chapter 7.

Such "close" reading will "involve probing beneath a surface reading of the text."[2] This is true as far as it goes. However, drawing the distinction like this is also somewhat misleading because it does not go far enough. Even here, a tacit and perhaps unconscious assumption is made that a "surface" reading is a neutral kind of reading, as if it were acceptable to produce surface readings of the Bible. However, if the biblical texts were written with the intention to produce *deeper* levels of meaning, then "surface" readings are misreadings.

The biblical texts are of such a high literary caliber that surface readings that bypass their nuanced literary and rhetorical details are, by definition,

1. Margaret M. Mitchell, "Rhetorical and New Literary Criticism," in *The Oxford Handbook of Biblical Studies*, ed. J. W. Rogerson and Judith M. Lieu (Oxford University Press, 2006), 629.

2. J. Richard Middleton, *Abraham's Silence: The Binding of Isaac, the Suffering of Job, and How to Talk Back to God* (Baker Academic, 2021), 165.

*mis*readings. The authors have frequently left indirect clues in their literary artifacts. Hence, "surface" readings that fail to observe these clues or deliberately overlook them are not just superficial; they are wrong. Imaginative readings that pay attention to these indirect clues are the result of careful observation, paying attention to every detail related to the form and content of the text as such. They are not an extra step that may or may not be added to "normal" readings that remain at the surface.

We are contending that imaginative reading is not an optional extra; rather, it is essential for reading the biblical texts if we want to understand them as they were intended to be understood by their authors, human and divine. In this we follow a string of biblical interpreters in recent decades.[3] Many have observed that much of what is most important for discerning the meaning of the biblical texts is presented in an understated fashion. Erich Auerbach, for example, drew a contrast between the Homeric epics (which have shaped Western expectations regarding literature of high quality), which are characterized by "fully externalized description," and the quality of Hebrew narrative, which is "fraught with background."

Similarly, Robert Alter observed in his classic volume on the artistic quality of Hebrew narrative that it is characterized by "a certain indeterminacy of meaning, especially in regard to motive, moral character, and psychology."[4] Since questions of motive, moral character, and psychology are among the most relevant aspects of the biblical texts if we want to read them to inform Christian faith and practice, the careful observation of understated clues left by the narrators to inform us of such matters is crucial. We are meant to draw "reasonable inferences" from the clues that the biblical authors have left behind. We are expected to follow the trail formed by the breadcrumbs that our authors have intentionally left behind—scattered at just the right places to prompt imaginative engagement but not so obvious and frequent that no effort at all is required—to make the "hunt" more intriguing, enjoyable, and rewarding.

Commenting on the scarcity of information regarding the interior life of Abraham and Isaac in Genesis 22, for example, Shai Held observes that "the narrator's silence invites us in, opens the door for us to imagine the thoughts and feelings that were undoubtedly swirling inside Abraham on that fateful climb."[5] The paucity of direct information about more complex matters, such

3. Some of the following comments draw on Middleton's defense of his imaginative reading of the Aqedah (the binding of Isaac) in Gen. 22. Middleton, *Abraham's Silence*, 166–67.

4. Robert Alter, *The Art of Biblical Narrative* (Basic Books, 2011), 12.

5. Shai Held, "A Response to My Respondents," *Canadian-American Theological Review* 9, no. 1 (2020): 53.

as emotional states, moral evaluations, or spiritual nuances, have all too often encouraged surface readings of the texts that resulted in apparently straightforward conclusions regarding their meaning and significance.

However, such superficial interpretations are being exposed as simplistic by the "rhetorical signals" that the skillful authors of the biblical text have intentionally left behind. Imaginative reading encourages careful attention to these signals, signals that complicate simplistic interpretations and encourage deeper engagement and richer interpretations. These signals include which details authors chose to include or omit, elements that seem unusual or incorrect upon first reading, seemingly problematic content, and intentionally ambiguous or vague language.

Imagination and Minor Details

What is being selected for inclusion and what is being omitted in biblical texts, especially narratives, can be of fundamental importance for their meaning and theological significance. This principle operates across all parts of the biblical canon, as an important editorial note near the end of the Gospel of John illustrates: "But there are also many other things that Jesus did; if every one of them were written down, I suppose that the world itself could not contain the books that would be written" (John 21:25). We will illustrate the importance of what may often look like minor details with a case study from the Old Testament.

The account of the reign of King Omri in 1 Kings 16:21–28 is extremely short. Its brevity suggests that Omri was a minor king. In reality, however, Omri was an important and influential king, as his attestation in various extrabiblical inscriptions (the Mesha Stele or Moabite Stone, the Black Obelisk of Shalmaneser III) and the Assyrian Annals demonstrates.[6] The Assyrians, at the time among the most powerful nations in the region, recognized him as the founder of a dynasty, and the nation of Israel flourished under his twelve-year reign. Its borders were expansive and secure. Even so, the account of his reign is a mere eight verses long. It is characterized by *omission*. A large amount of information about his reign has been omitted, not because the biblical writers had no knowledge about it but because they did not consider it to be *theologically* significant.

6. William Brown, "Moabite Stone [Mesha Stele]," *Ancient History Encyclopedia*, February 11, 2019, https://www.ancient.eu/Moabite_Stone_[Mesha_Stele]; and A. L. Oppenheim, "Babylonian and Assyrian Historical Texts," in *Ancient Near Eastern Texts Relating to the Old Testament*, ed. J. B. Pritchard (Princeton University Press, 1969), 284, 285.

The terseness of the account of his reign is cast into even sharper relief when we compare it to the excessively long account of his successor, his son Ahab. By comparison, this account is characterized by *inclusion*. Even though King Ahab was likely not as influential and successful a ruler, he is more famous than his father for events in his life like his marriage to Queen Jezebel, a foreign princess from Sidon who encouraged him to engage in idolatry (1 Kings 16:31–32), doing "more to provoke the anger of the Lord, the God of Israel, than had all the kings of Israel who were before him" (16:33).

Ahab is also well-known for his theft of the vineyard of his neighbor Naboth, an incident that led to murder when Naboth refused to sell the property (1 Kings 21:1–16). The combination of idolatry and social injustice that was so prominent during Ahab's reign made him much more important to the biblical authors because of the theological significance of these offenses, and so the account of Ahab's reign, in marked contrast with that of King Omri, occupies *seven* chapters (16:29–22:40), 209 verses in all. The narrative for Ahab is more than *twenty-six* times as long as the account of the reign of his father Omri!

Consequently, it comes as something of a surprise that Omri's account includes two apparently random and unimportant pieces of information: that he paid "two talents of silver" to the owner of a hill on which he built his new capital city, and that he named the city Samaria, "after the name of Shemer, the owner of the hill" (1 Kings 16:24). Why were these seemingly minor details selected for *inclusion*?

The answer lies in an important theological conclusion that the biblical narrators wanted to drive home in a fashion that is all the more compelling for its subtlety, at least for those who read these chapters with imagination because they pay close attention to such details in the texts. While Ahab, with the help of his queen, stole the vineyard of Naboth after having him killed, Omri, evil as he was (1 Kings 16:25) acquired the real estate of Shemer legally by paying for it and then honored the original owner by naming the city he built on the land after him.

Imagination Allows Us to Make Sense of Unusual Texts Without Changing Them to Fit Our Expectations

When we encounter unexpected or unusual content in the Bible, our response should not be to "fix" the apparent problem. Rather, we need to adjust our interpretations to fit the biblical texts. Readings that adjust the biblical texts to fit our expectations concerning what the meaning of the texts should be are not interpretations but rather intrusions into the biblical texts that often obscure important theological points and consequently undermine their authoritative nature. They are *mis*interpretations.

A good example to illustrate what we mean can be found near the beginning of the account of the reign of Israel's first king. The Hebrew of the account of Saul's reign includes two curious pieces of information related to the age of Saul when he began to reign as well as the length of his reign: "Saul was *a year old* when he began to reign, and he reigned *two* years" (1 Sam. 13:1 AT). The numbers in this verse do not match other information about Saul that we find in the Bible. Earlier in 1 Samuel we read that Saul was already a young man before he became king (9:2). So how could he have been one year old at his accession to the throne? And Acts 13:21 informs us that Saul ruled for forty-two years, confirming the information in 1 Samuel 12–31 that Saul ruled for many decades. So how is it that this verse informs us that he ruled for only two years?

The two numbers in italics appear in the Hebrew but are rarely included in modern translations. The NIV 2011 has: "Saul was *thirty* years old when he became king, and he reigned over Israel *forty*-two years." The translators of the NIV recognized the discrepancy and adjusted the text to make it fit with other biblical data. Assuming that the Hebrew text has two gaps, they first followed a few late manuscripts of the Septuagint, which have the number "thirty." They then followed Acts 13:21 and added the number "forty." The translators of the NRSV also noted the discrepancy and presented their assumption that the Hebrew text lacked the expected numbers by indicating two gaps with ellipsis dots. The Jewish Study Bible also uses ellipsis dots for the first number and notes that "the precise context of the 'two years' is uncertain." An interesting case is the translation in the ESV. It reads as follows, retaining the numbers as preserved in the Hebrew but connecting the words with different syntactical arrangements, including the syntactical connection to the following verse: "Saul lived for *one year and then* became king, and when he had reigned *for two years* over Israel . . . , Saul chose three thousand men of Israel" (1 Sam. 13:1–2). We commend this attempt to make sense of the text through an interpretation that aims to reflect the wording of the actual text as it appears. The translators of the ESV indeed adjusted their interpretation to fit the text. However, the syntactical constructions that they developed cannot easily be explained from the grammar and the sequence of the Hebrew words of these verses in the original. While the numbers and the words are preserved here, it is the grammar and syntax that are adjusted.

An imaginative interpretation, by contrast, can make sense of the text as it stands. In anticipation of our detailed examination in chapter 5 of how imagination helps us to detect and interpret biblical humor, a case can be made that the Hebrew words and their most natural syntax make sense, if we adapt our interpretation to include the possibility that the expression was meant to be humorous. The text makes sense and does not contradict other parts of the Bible when the expression is taken to be sarcastic. It is a dig, right at the beginning of the account of Saul's reign, on the immature nature of his rule. When the text says that he was "a year old" when he began his reign, it is implying that Saul conducted his duties "like a baby." When the text says that he ruled "for two years," it is implying that he continued how he started, fulfilling his responsibilities "like a toddler." The Douay-Rheims Bible translates it as, "Saul was a child of one year when he began to reign, and he reigned two years over Israel," which comes from an original Latin text that still reflected the Hebrew in all its awkwardness. It is the only translation into English we could find that retains this foreignizing element. The added "was a child of" permits and perhaps even encourages the imaginative interpretation we propose. Once the text is taken seriously as it stands, we can engage it creatively in a fashion that honors the text's integrity while arriving at an imaginative interpretation that is theologically meaningful and aesthetically rewarding, even entertaining. Imaginative reading not only helps us here but also reveals that humor plays a crucial role in numerous other passages throughout the Bible.

Consequently, when complex decisions must be made about the meaning of biblical texts, we need to adjust our interpretations to fit the evidence, not the other way around. Traditional scholarship has, at times, given a priority to what "seems to fit," especially when the text is obscure. Rather than declaring the text corrupt and offering emendations, we can read the Bible with imagination and arrive at an interpretation that is both faithful to the text as presented and, at the same time, robust and meaningful. Interpretations that adjust the biblical texts to fit our expectations are intrusions that tend to obscure intriguingly rich aspects of the texts and neglect important theological points that the divine and human authors built into the biblical material to evoke more imaginative engagement in readers.

Imagination Helps Us See Problematic Details in Scripture as Opportunities for Deeper Understanding and New Insights

Most biblical texts include at least some unusual and difficult content. These difficulties can be of a textual nature—for example, rare or unusual words, new and different grammatical or syntactical expressions, or metaphors and other figurative language. Other potentially obscure parts of biblical texts include allusions to events or objects or customs that were well-known to the original audience but are not as well-known today. Such difficulties can also be of a historical, moral, or theological nature. Texts contain information that surprises us because they mention something we do not expect in the Bible. For example, Psalm 95:3 informs us that "the LORD is a great God, and a great King above all gods." This violates our theological expectations because the Judeo-Christian faiths are monotheistic.

Another example is the demand of God that Abraham kill his son Isaac as a sacrifice in Genesis 22, a demand that is in direct opposition to biblical texts such as Exodus 13:11–13; 34:19–20; Leviticus 27:26–27; Numbers 3:11–13; 8:1–20; 18:13–18; and Deuteronomy 15:19–23, all of which stipulate that the firstborn of humans, while belonging to the Lord, should be "redeemed" by offering substitutes. What are we to make of this?

Similarly, Micah 6:6–7 records an inquiry: "With what shall I come before the LORD, and bow myself before God on high? Shall I come before him with burnt offerings, with calves a year old? Will the LORD be pleased with thousands of rams, with ten thousands of rivers of oil? Shall I give my firstborn for my transgression, the fruit of my body for the sin of my soul?" Many interpreters take this inquiry to be made by a "concerned citizen" who is convicted by the words of the prophet Micah and wants to repent. Consequently, they feel compelled to make this offer to sacrifice their firstborn child sound more acceptable than it is.[7] So, is child sacrifice really an acceptable way of approaching God? There are scholars who think that it was at the time, for some at least.[8] In our view, this is not the case at all, as we will demonstrate through imaginative interpretations of the two passages elsewhere in this book.

More traditional ways of reading the Bible often fail to detect nuance (as in the Gen. 22 passage) or humor (as in the Mic. 6 passage; see the full discussion in chap. 5). Rather, if something is unusual, difficult, or problematic, the interpretive instinct is to explain it away so that the text is made to fit with what people already believed and expected before they encountered the problem in the biblical text. So often, what is truly interesting, intriguing, and rewarding—the real jewels in the text—are swept under the carpet.

7. Francis I. Andersen and David Noel Freedman, *Micah: A New Translation with Introduction and Commentary*, 1st ed., The Anchor Bible 24E (Doubleday, 2000), 523–24; and Ralph L. Smith, *Micah–Malachi*, Word Biblical Commentary 32 (Word, 1984), 50–51.

8. Heath D. Dewrell, *Child Sacrifice in Ancient Israel*, Explorations in Ancient Near Eastern Civilizations 5 (Eisenbrauns, 2017), 99–108.

By contrast, imaginative interpretation considers problematic content in the Bible not as obstacles or hurdles but as opportunities for deeper understanding and new insights, as opportunities for discovery, growth, and development.

Imagination Helps Us See Intentional Ambiguity as Productive

Texts can have several intended meanings all at once. Many readers of the Bible are not comfortable with that. For them, ambiguity is a setback, not an asset. For them, the ambiguity of biblical passages is a problem that needs to be resolved, because for them, ambiguity threatens one of the doctrines of the Reformation, the clarity or perspicuity of Scripture (*claritas Scripturae* in Latin). Admittedly, ambiguity can be a problematic textual feature. "Where it is unintentional, a vague or equivocal expression occurring when precision and particularity of reference are needed leads to misunderstanding. Where intentional, an oblique or evasive expression can be misleading and even deceptive."[9] However, intentional ambiguity can also be productive as

> a deliberate poetic device, usually marked as such in the context. The use of a single word or expression to signify two or more distinct references, or to express two or more diverse attitudes or feelings, makes it possible to say much with few words (Abrams, 10–11). Polysemy can hint at the complexity and multivalence of apparently simple ideas, and homonymy can signal connections between apparently unrelated ideas.[10]

The history of the interpretation of many biblical passages, where several possible meanings have been entertained for centuries, attests to the reality that many passages are and will forever remain ambiguous. More often than not, then, biblical ambiguity is intentional. When ambiguity occurs, Paul Raabe observes,

> very often there will be disagreement among the commentaries. Each commentary will choose only one of the possibilities and then vigorously defend its choice. The net result is a stalemate. Each rendition can be defended. This tendency to choose only one of the possibilities seems to be caused by two factors. First, the task of translation inevitably forces one to choose. Very rarely

9. Knut M. Heim, "Wordplays," in *Dictionary of the Old Testament: Wisdom, Poetry and Writings*, ed. Tremper Longman III and Peter Enns (IVP Academic, 2008), 925.

10. Heim, "Wordplays," 925, citing M. H. Abrams, *A Glossary of Literary Terms*, 7th ed. (Heinle & Heinle, 1999), 10–11.

> can such ambiguity be captured in the target language. Second, the need for scientific precision contributes to the pressure.[11]

As a consequence, Raabe contends, "sometimes, maybe more often than we think, a word, phrase, or sentence could be understood in two (or more) ways because both were intended, it is deliberate ambiguity."[12]

And since we are convinced that the Bible we have is the Bible that God wants us to have, this means that most of its ambiguities are intentional. They are purposefully created by the Bible's authors. In fact, even on the rare occasions when it is possible to demonstrate that a given ambiguous passage was not intended to be so by its human author, the Holy Spirit has nonetheless allowed it to be so, and therefore even then we can consider such passages to be inspired in their ambiguous form.

We are convinced that this is not a drawback. Rather, biblical ambiguities reflect the wonderful complexity of God's creation, the interesting quality of the divine handiwork in all its beauty and wonder. Ambiguity "can surprise, amuse, delight, invite curiosity and prompt active reader involvement while communicating serious, complex and significant information,"[13] and it can do so in words that entertain and inspire imaginative engagement. Polysemantic puns, for example, express two meanings through the same occurrence, giving "two meanings for the price of one" and so adding "density and richness of significance."[14]

As do authors of other literary works of a high caliber, the biblical writers employ intentional ambiguity as a literary device to create multiple layers of meaning.[15] This adds depth to the Word of God; it creates room for interpretation with a wonderfully dynamic flexibility when intentionally ambiguous biblical texts are related to various real-life situations. Ambiguity conveys complex ideas and topics in subtle perspectives and invites readerly imagination. It encourages us to draw dynamically on the Word of God to inspire fresh ideas and conclusions that become our own because we invest interpretive energy in them. Intentional ambiguity allows for more than one way of reading Scripture faithfully. The Word of God reflects reality and confirms that we live in a wondrously interesting world with rich complexity and numerous opportunities.

11. Paul R. Raabe, "Deliberate Ambiguity in the Psalter," *Journal of Biblical Literature* 110 (Summer 1991): 213.

12. Raabe, "Deliberate Ambiguity in the Psalter," 213.

13. Heim, "Wordplays," 926.

14. Geoffrey N. Leech, *A Linguistic Guide to English Poetry*, English Language Series (Longman Harlow, 1973), 212.

15. See Jamie A. Grant, "Determining the Indeterminable: Ambiguity and the Historical Titles of the Psalms," *Tyndale Bulletin* 54, no. 1 (2003): 63–88.

There are different kinds of ambiguities. The following drawing is an intentionally ambiguous image.

Peter Hermes Furian / Shutterstock

Figure 2.1 *Rubin's Vase*, a picture of two identical faces framing a vase

This illustration reflects a highly stylized and obvious, even contrived form of ambiguity. A fitting biblical example is Philippians 1:3, which can be translated "I thank my God every time I remember you" as well as "I thank my God every time you remember me." The ambiguity is obvious in the Greek and reflects that Paul wants to express both sentiments at once.

Ambiguity in the next drawing is less stylized and more complex but equally intentional.

Figure 2.2 *My Wife and My Mother-in-Law*, by William Ely Hill, a picture of what can be seen as an elegant young lady and an old haggard woman

The ambiguity in this illustration is less obvious by far, and many viewers tend to see one woman or the other, while finding it difficult to see the alternative. Even so, the ambiguity is deliberate, and those who engage in its visual interpretation until they can see both will be rewarded. A fitting biblical example to illustrate this is the episode we already mentioned above, Micah 6:6–7. We will demonstrate the importance of identifying the humor in this passage in more detail in chapter 5. A summary in anticipation of that discussion will illustrate our point.

On the one hand, the passage appears like a sincere inquiry as to whether God would accept a repentant sinner's sacrifice of his firstborn child. This is how the passage has traditionally been read. On the other hand, our imaginative reading opens the possibility for a humorous interpretation, namely that the one who asks this question is vexed with the prophetic indictment in the preceding verses and sarcastically asks Micah what else God may want, beyond what he thinks he is doing already to please God. In this reading, the offer is insincere and highly offensive, intentionally insulting the prophet and the God who sent him. The ambiguity is far from obvious, and the two possible interpretations could not be more different. Both are intended, but one reflects a falsely positive attitude, while the other presents an accurate yet ugly attitude toward God. Here the ambiguity demands intense effort, but the effect is powerful and impressive, as we will demonstrate in chapter 5.

Intentionally ambiguous language can have immense benefits. First, ambiguity demands attentiveness. Genre expectations (e.g., in humorous performances or extended jokes) and the presence of ambiguity near the beginning of a discourse raise the anticipation of more ambiguity. Even when readers settle into a more cursory reading routine, ambiguity makes reading more difficult. The problem in the text stirs readers out of complacency and engages their imaginations. Ambiguity slows down the reading process and prompts deeper reflection in order to process the passage. Second, ambiguity can change readers' perceptions of the world. This can happen in two ways. It can make readers aware of previously unrecognized connections between ideas. Or it can make readers aware of the multivalence and complexity of ideas that had previously been thought to be simple or one-dimensional. Third, ambiguity can surprise, amuse, delight, invite curiosity, and prompt interest and active reader involvement while communicating serious, complex, and significant information. Consequently, ambiguity encourages readers to view apparently ordinary things and concepts in more imaginative ways. In short, ambiguity can infuse a sense of surprise and discovery, fun and curiosity.

It can alert readers to deeper connections. It can turn them into engaged and involved readers.[16]

The next kind of ambiguity is so distinct that we will present it under its own subheading.

Imagination Helps Us Fill the Gaps in Underdetermined Language

The designation *underdetermination* is a technical term normally used in the philosophy of science.[17] It is popular in complex scientific theories like general relativity or quantum mechanics to describe situations where different theories (interpretations) of reality can be supported by the evidence.[18] I (Knut) have coined the designation "underdetermined language" as a technical term to describe expressions that result from the strategies of indirection employed in the book of Ecclesiastes, by Agur in Proverbs 30, and by many modern stand-up comedians, where the language is intentionally vague so that it will be understood differently by different audiences. In situations where speakers or writers are critiquing those who are more powerful than they, it is advisable not to fix the meaning of what they are saying—to purposefully suppress what they really mean to create plausible deniability. The powerless deploy an art of resistance via hidden transcripts that mask what they really mean behind multiple possibilities.[19]

Ambiguity in the next drawing illustrates this well. It shows two identical faces, at once a face that looks straight at the viewer as in a passport photograph and also a face in profile. Both meanings are equally prominent, and

16. The benefits listed here are slightly adapted from my exploration of the benefits of punning in Heim, "Wordplays," 928–29. Similar benefits are listed in Raabe, "Deliberate Ambiguity in the Psalter," 226–27. There is a direct and strong link between ambiguity, imagination, and creativity: "Imagination may be most essential, and most productively manifest, in just the kinds of experiences that are singular, in which the way is off-piste, the procedure yet to be discovered, and wherein the inspiration comes without instructions." Consequently, such creativity requires "some tolerance for ambiguity, uncertainty, the not-yet known, and for divergence, enabling cognitive play." Jennifer Anna Gosetti-Ferencei, *The Life of Imagination: Revealing and Making the World* (Columbia University Press, 2018), 12.

17. For a fuller discussion of the phenomenon, see Knut M. Heim, *Ecclesiastes*, Tyndale Old Testament Commentaries 18 (InterVarsity, 2019), 5–8; and Knut M. Heim, "Of Leeches, Lizards, and Lions: The Humorous Function of Animal Talk in Proverbs 30," in *Human Interaction with the Natural World in Wisdom Literature and Beyond: Essays in Honour of Tova L. Forti*, ed. Mordechai Cogan, Katharine J. Dell, and David Glatt-Gilad, The Library of Hebrew Bible/Old Testament Studies 720 (Bloomsbury T&T Clark, 2023).

18. Ian McDiarmid, "Underdetermination and Indeterminacy: What Is the Difference?," *Erkenntnis* 69 (2008).

19. James C. Scott, *Domination and the Arts of Resistance: Hidden Transcripts* (Yale University Press, 1990).

while the underdetermined image shows one and the same face, that face looks in a different direction, depending on which perspective we adopt.

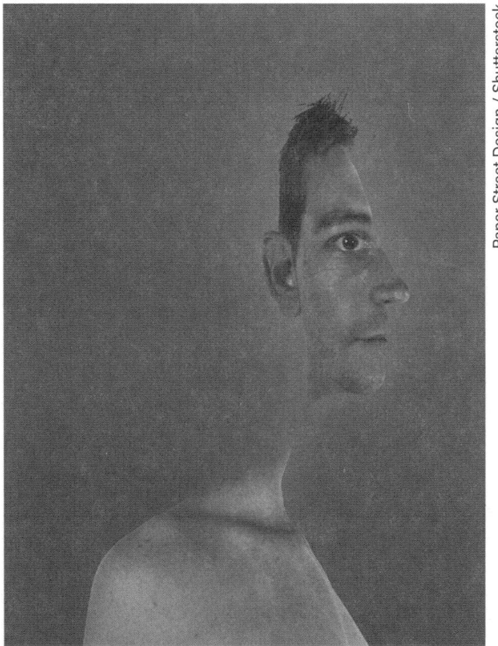
Paper Street Design / Shutterstock

Figure 2.3 Face in portrait and profile

The ambiguity in this illustration is obvious, and it is easy to switch from one to the other interpretation. The ambiguity is deliberate, and the visual interpretation of the image is aesthetically pleasing. Fitting biblical examples appear throughout the book of Ecclesiastes and throughout the performance of Agur in Proverbs 30. Traditional interpretations have continued to describe both texts as difficult, enigmatic, even obscure. Our imaginative reading opens the possibility for humorous interpretations that have explanatory power because they also account for the power dynamics in which the two texts operate.

Conclusion: A Case Study from Ezekiel

The book of Ezekiel includes a brief but disturbing scene. Actually, it includes quite a few disturbing passages, but the one we want to focus on here is perfect for illustrating how important imagination is for carefully observing the literary and rhetorical signals in the Bible that we've been discussing in this chapter. Here is the text:

> The word of the Lord came to me: Mortal, with one blow I am about to take away from you the delight of your eyes; yet you shall not mourn or weep, nor shall your tears run down. Groan quietly; make no mourning for the dead. Bind on your turban, and put your sandals on your feet; do not cover your upper lip or eat the bread of mourners. So I spoke to the people in the morning, and at evening my wife died. And on the next morning I did as I was commanded. (Ezek. 24:15–18)

Why is this disturbing? God tells his faithful servant, the prophet Ezekiel, that he—God himself!—will let his wife die so she can serve as a "sermon illustration." On top of that, God seems to forbid Ezekiel to mourn for his departed wife—at first sight, at least. Stunningly, and perhaps even more disturbingly, the episode ends with a brief report that what God had predicted and demanded did happen. In the morning Ezekiel told the people around him that God had informed him that his wife would die, in the evening of that same day she did die, and the very next morning, Ezekiel informs us, "I did as I was commanded." As simple as that. As simple as that?!?

Traditional interpretations do not know what to make of this episode. So disturbing is this incident that many students who are assigned the task to summarize the book of Ezekiel simply omit the entire passage, as if it were not even there. We will come back to the reason for this shortly.

Others include the passage in their summary but simply do not know what to make of it. Their summaries reflect bewilderment, disorientation, and discomfort. Interestingly, almost all students are so taken up with the main challenge of the passage, the calculated killing of Ezekiel's wife at the hand of God, that they become distracted from observing important details in it.

Here is what happens, almost without exception. Students report that God forbids Ezekiel to mourn for his wife. However, this is not in fact true. Rather, God forbids Ezekiel to mourn his wife *publicly*. The suppression of the culturally expected mourning rites (not wearing one's turban, walking barefoot, covering one's upper lip [beard], and eating the bread of mourners) confronts the exiles around Ezekiel with the impending shock of Jerusalem's destruction and God's prohibition for them to follow the customary mourning rites when they experience the national disaster that God is about to inflict on them. Ezekiel is, nonetheless, encouraged to mourn the loss of his wife in private: "Groan quietly" (Ezek. 24:17)! We will come back to this important detail too.

The episode that comes next reports the impact of Ezekiel's failure to mourn his wife publicly:

> Then the people said to me, "Will you not tell us what these things mean for us, that you are acting this way?" Then I said to them: "The word of the Lord came to

> me: Say to the house of Israel, Thus says the Lord God: I will profane my sanctuary, the pride of your power, the delight of your eyes, and your heart's desire; and your sons and your daughters whom you left behind shall fall by the sword. And you shall do as I have done; you shall not cover your upper lip or eat the bread of mourners. Your turbans shall be on your heads and your sandals on your feet; you shall not mourn or weep, but you shall pine away in your iniquities and groan to one another. Thus Ezekiel shall be a sign to you; you shall do just as he has done. When this comes, then you shall know that I am the Lord God." (Ezek. 24:19–24)

The brutally bright spotlight that the text shines on the apparently callous killing of Ezekiel's wife acts like a shiny object that diverts readers from observing what is most important regarding the entire episode and its wider context. It was the failure of Ezekiel to mourn *publicly* that prompted the people's inquiry as to the reasons for his strange behavior.

What is more, in the direct speech from God that Ezekiel reports in his answer, God reveals that he himself—in permitting the destruction of Jerusalem and the third wave of exile—had lost his own wife, his people, and God himself abstained from mourning the loss of his beloved one. What was going to happen to the people of God is reflected in Ezekiel's loss of his beloved wife, and Ezekiel's loss reflects God's own loss and pain, which, even though not publicly displayed—"and you shall do as *I* [God!] have done" (Ezek. 24:22)—was as acute and heart-wrenching for God himself as the loss felt by Ezekiel and the loss felt by the people as a whole. When God took away the delight of Ezekiel, this represented the terrible truth that God allowed his own wife—the people of Israel—to be taken from him.

We now return to the observation made earlier, that many are so disturbed by the episode's challenging nature that they simply ignore it. Why? Because the actions and intentions of God in this incident do not match their theological beliefs and assumptions about the life of faith. Here is one student's reflection upon realizing the importance of what she had missed:

> Ezekiel's personal engagement with Israel's suffering seems unparalleled in the Old Testament. Besides Job or possibly Jeremiah, I can't think of anyone who suffered more intensely. Take for instance Ezekiel's wife dying and his inability to publicly mourn her. I was initially so perplexed by such a tragedy that I inadvertently left out the death of Ezekiel's wife in my summary of the book.[20]

A few semesters later, the same student reflected on the long-term impact of her experience: "That is *still* one of the formative moments for me in

20. Kelly Minter, "Ezekiel Portfolio, Part 4" (Denver Seminary, 2020), 3.

seminary—that I completely missed such a significant part of summarizing Ezekiel because I subconsciously couldn't handle, or make sense of, what had happened to him. That was a learning moment for me, for sure."[21] Our case study illustrates just how important our imagination is for interpreting challenging biblical content. The difficult nature of the text demands that our imagination help us cope with its challenging content. We cannot understand or process texts like this without it. Only with imagination can we resist the temptation to ignore or neglect difficult content like this and discover its transformative potential.

21. Kelly Minter, personal communication, February 7, 2023.

CHAPTER THREE

A Hermeneutic of Imagination Reveals the Theological Power of Scripture's Figurative Language

We have shown above that understanding the literary caliber of the Bible enables us to both appreciate and examine the text in a much deeper way. We have shown several examples of how small and seemingly insignificant details are used as the crux of many different stories. This same phenomenon can be examined on a much more particular level as well. In this chapter, we will examine the role of imagination in figurative language.

Figurative language has had a bad reputation for a very long time, and this has become even more prominent since the Enlightenment, as the following words of philosopher Francis Bacon illustrate: "For all that concerns ornaments of speech, similitudes, treasure of eloquence, and such like emptinesses, let it be utterly dismissed."[1] Comments Malcolm Guite:

> Instead of acknowledging, as many thinkers do now, that the *way* we know, *the language through which we know*, may be an essential and helpful part of knowledge itself, some philosophers of the enlightenment thought that image

1. Francis Bacon, *The Philosophical Works of Francis Bacon*, ed. J. M. Robertson (Routledge, 1905), 403.

> and imagination simply clouded and obscured the pure dry knowledge that they were after.[2]

We will argue precisely this point, that the *way* we know through the language that we use to think is essential for human understanding. The neglect of figurative language in biblical interpretation has been a serious mistake. By contrast, we aim to demonstrate that the imaginative use of figurative language is essential for cognitive progress.

Figurative expressions are commonly grouped together under the three terms *figures of speech*, *poetic imagery*, and *figurative language*, and these are often used interchangeably. In this chapter, we use *figurative language* as the umbrella term for all three classifications, preferring to use *poetic imagery* with regard to figurative language in poetic texts and *figure(s) of speech* for figurative language in prose texts.

More than anything else, it is figurative language that makes the Bible such an impressive example of imaginative literature. Consequently, if we want to read the Bible on its own terms, we need imagination to help us understand its figurative language well.

We will concentrate on metaphors, but figurative language includes other types of imaginative expression, such as simile, metonymy, synecdoche, and many more.[3] Such expressions are similar to but also distinct from metaphors, but the distinctions amount to differences in degree rather than in kind. William Brown's comparison of metaphors and similes illustrates this well:

> The simile represents a form of analogical language that *may* relieve the ambiguity and narrow the interpretative possibilities provoked by the metaphor, but not necessarily. . . . It is best, then, to classify the simile as a form of metaphor, one that makes explicit the object of comparison, but in so doing *can* limit the range of association.[4]

While the simile, like the metaphor, conveys understanding of one thing in terms of another, it nonetheless sometimes "hedges its bets—it makes a

2. Malcolm Guite, *Faith, Hope and Poetry: Theology and the Poetic Imagination*, Routledge Studies in Theology, Imagination and the Arts (Routledge, 2017), 2.

3. For an extended discussion of the relationship between metaphor and metonymy, see George Lakoff and Mark Turner, *More Than Cool Reason: A Field Guide to Poetic Metaphor* (University of Chicago Press, 1989), 100–106. For the role of conceptual metonymies in human language, see the groundbreaking work of Jeanette Littlemore, *Metonymy: Hidden Shortcuts in Language, Thought and Communication* (Cambridge University Press, 2015).

4. William P. Brown, *Seeing the Psalms: A Theology of Metaphor* (Westminster John Knox, 2002), 7.

weaker claim" than the metaphor.[5] When the comparative statement in the simile is about more complex and multifaceted phenomena, however, the assertion is much more evocative and comprehensive, bringing it closer to metaphor in that regard. And the same is true for other kinds of figurative language.

This chapter will explore how recent progress in our understanding of metaphors highlights the importance of imagination, with special emphasis on conceptual metaphor theory, sometimes also called structural metaphor theory. The chapter has five parts. First, we will expose the limitations of traditional metaphor theories. Second, we will demonstrate how important imagination is in conceptual metaphor theory. Third, we will introduce the role of imagination in embodied simulation. Fourth, we will explore the role of figurative language in modern visual art and its significance for reading with imagination. Fifth and finally, we will combine the insights we have gained from those considerations into a meta-metaphoric description of metaphors and related figurative language that demonstrates the importance of imagination in reading the Bible for all its worth.

Traditional Metaphor Theories Inhibited Imaginative Interpretations

Below we will show that modern metaphor theories demonstrate the crucial role of imagination for understanding figurative language well. Here we highlight that traditional theories have inhibited imaginative interpretations of metaphors and other figurative language. Most humans are competent users of their native language and regularly and competently employ metaphors in daily life. Nonetheless, metaphors have until recently been poorly understood by philosophers and scholars of literature. The following summary from Mike Abrams's *A Glossary of Literary Terms* from 1999 paints a sobering picture:

> After twenty-five centuries of attention to metaphor by rhetoricians, grammarians, and literary critics—in which during the last half-century they have been joined by many philosophers—there is no general agreement about the way we identify metaphors, how we are able to understand them, and what (if anything) they serve to tell us.[6]

Abrams's verdict is even more stunning in view of the fact that the questions of how we identify, understand, and apply metaphors were the actual

5. Brown, *Seeing the Psalms*, 7–8, quoting Lakoff and Turner, *More Than Cool Reason*, 133.
6. M. H. Abrams, *A Glossary of Literary Terms*, 7th ed. (Heinle & Heinle, 1999), 155.

foci of inquiry in metaphor studies of the first three-quarters of the twentieth century. Here is George Lakoff and Mark Johnson's summary of the main tenets of metaphor studies before 1980:

1. Metaphor is a matter of words, not thought. Metaphor occurs when a word is applied not to what it normally designates, but to something else.
2. Metaphorical language is not part of ordinary conventional language. Instead, it is novel and typically arises in poetry, rhetorical attempts at persuasion, and scientific discovery.
3. Metaphorical language is deviant. In metaphor, words are not used in their proper senses.
4. Conventional metaphorical expressions in ordinary everyday language are "dead metaphors," that is, expressions that once were metaphorical, but have become frozen into literal expressions.
5. Metaphors express similarities. That is, there are preexisting similarities between what words normally designate and what they designate when they are used metaphorically.[7]

Lakoff and Johnson, whose positive contribution to metaphor theory we will explore shortly, have highlighted major drawbacks of the various traditional theories of metaphor. Among other things, the designation of conventional metaphorical expressions as "dead" has led to a neglect in the study of the vast majority of metaphoric expressions in human communication.

It also led to a misguided concentration on the study of one particular type of metaphoric expression, the so-called bold metaphor, a concentration that perforce led to fundamental misunderstandings of the phenomenon of metaphors as a whole.

In addition, most earlier studies of metaphor failed to distinguish between metaphoric expressions on the one hand and their underlying metaphoric idea on the other. For example, a phrase like "they were hunting us down in packs" is a metaphoric expression that draws on the underlying metaphoric idea of the conventional metaphor "MAN IS A WOLF." (Here and throughout we employ a convention introduced by Lakoff and Johnson to represent conventional metaphors in capitals, with the slight change of using small capitals and capitalizing the weightier words in the representation.)

7. George Lakoff and Mark Johnson, *Philosophy in the Flesh: The Embodied Mind and Its Challenge to Western Thought* (Basic Books, 1999), 199.

Also, customary treatments of metaphors have analyzed them as somehow being composed of "tenor and vehicle" (I. A. Richards), "primary subject" and "secondary or subsidiary subject" (Max Black), or "occasion" and "image" (Paul Avis), and so have prioritized the reconstructed "meaning" of a metaphor over the actual metaphoric expression. As a consequence, "the distinction sets up an unnecessary hierarchy of classification: in hermeneutical practice, the 'tenor' easily takes precedence over the 'vehicle,' which is, thereby, considered secondary or derivative of the 'tenor.'"[8] (We will come back to Richards's nomenclature in our conclusions near the end of this chapter.)

In the final analysis, then, "such designations fail to indicate the kind of interaction that takes place between the metaphorical image and its referent or underlying subject in a given communicative context."[9] The metaphoric expression as it occurs in real human interactions and actual literary texts was thereby sidelined and considered superfluous, and the main work of interpreting metaphors became an effort to get rid of them by paraphrasing them in literal, nonfigurative language. Since they only ornamented what, it was assumed, could also have been said better in literal fashion, the task of metaphor interpretation became an exercise in substituting the metaphoric expression with what was considered a literal equivalent.

Imagination and Conceptual Metaphor Theory

Conceptual metaphor theory informs reading with imagination. Sometimes also called structural metaphor theory, it was developed by Lakoff and Johnson in their landmark volume *Metaphors We Live By*, published in 1980, and revealed a close connection between metaphor and cognition.[10] This discovery has exposed some of the limitations of more traditional theories, which we have already considered.

Lakoff and Johnson have exercised a profound influence on the development of metaphor theory. In their book, they make the following programmatic affirmation, which at first sight does not look so different from previous descriptions of metaphor:

> The essence of metaphor is understanding and experiencing one kind of thing in terms of another.[11]

8. Brown, *Seeing the Psalms*, 5.

9. Brown, *Seeing the Psalms*, 5.

10. George Lakoff and Mark Johnson, *Metaphors We Live By* (1980; repr., University of Chicago Press, 2003).

11. Lakoff and Johnson, *Metaphors We Live By*, 19.

This statement may seem unassuming and noncontroversial, but the way they develop it has massive consequences for metaphor theory. They identify two realms of meaning: one is closer to our experience, while the other is what we are exploring with the help of a metaphoric expression. This distinction inaugurated an increasing scholarly focus on the *cognitive* aspects of metaphor.[12]

Furthermore, the reference to "understanding and experiencing" in this definition implicitly rejects the notion that metaphors are simply ornamental, one of the tenets of traditional theories. Rather, metaphors contribute to *understanding*, and they do so by helping us not only to reflect on what is being said but also to *experience* it. There is a *multisensory and cognitive* aspect to metaphor that connects it directly to the human imagination.

In collaboration with Mark Turner, Lakoff then published a follow-up volume entitled *More Than Cool Reason* in 1989. Here key insights from the earlier work were developed and refined in significant ways. Lakoff and Turner concluded that most if not all metaphors are "conceptual" in that they belong to a complex and highly structured system of conventional metaphors. And novel metaphors arise naturally from this system:

> The major point to take away from this discussion is that metaphor resides for the most part in this huge, highly structured, fixed system, a system anything but "dead." Because it is conventional, it is used constantly and automatically, with neither effort nor awareness. *Novel metaphor uses this system, and builds on it, but only rarely occurs independently of it.* It is most interesting that this system of metaphor seems to give rise to abstract reasoning, which appears to be based on spatial reasoning.[13]

The growing influence of Lakoff, Johnson, and Turner on subsequent thinking about metaphors can be traced through the three editions of *The Cambridge Handbook of Metaphor and Thought*.

The first edition of *The Cambridge Handbook of Metaphor*, then still with the title *Metaphor and Thought*, was edited by Andrew Ortony. It appeared in 1979, one year too early for Lakoff and Johnson's breakthrough

12. The work of Lakoff and Johnson and Lakoff and Turner is "among the most widely recognized and discussed in the field," according to Raymond W. Gibbs Jr., "Metaphor and Thought: The State of the Art," in *The Cambridge Handbook of Metaphor and Thought*, ed. Raymond W. Gibbs Jr. (Cambridge University Press, 2008), 5.

13. Lakoff and Turner, *More Than Cool Reason*, 227–28 (emphasis added). Spatial reasoning underlies our proposal for a meta-metaphorical model to describe the cognitive power of metaphors (see chap. 3 below under "Previous Meta-Metaphorical Talk About Metaphor" for more on spatial reasoning).

monograph. Even its second edition, fourteen years later in 1993, made only passing reference to *Metaphors We Live By*, although that second edition at least had a contribution by Lakoff, who was by then beginning to be recognized as a player in the field.

It was not until 2008, when the third edition of *The Cambridge Handbook* edited by Raymond Gibbs appeared, that the full impact of the work done by Lakoff, Johnson, and Turner came into full view. Their influence could now be felt on almost every page and from the hand of every contributor to the volume—Lakoff and Johnson's *Metaphors We Live By* was finally recognized for what it was. That work and its follow-up *More Than Cool Reason* together defined the state of the art in metaphor studies.

The third edition of *Metaphor and Thought*, published in 2008 as *The Cambridge Handbook of Metaphor and Thought*, thus signaled a paradigm shift in metaphor studies. Gibbs rightly claims in his introduction to the volume that it is the "most comprehensive collection of essays in multidisciplinary metaphor scholarship ever published." He notes that "there is now a huge body of empirical work from many academic disciplines that clearly demonstrates the ubiquity of metaphor in both everyday language and specialized language," both in abstract thought and in people's emotional experiences. We are now in a position to describe more fully and more realistically the essential contribution that metaphor makes to human cognition, communication, and culture. In particular, empirical study of metaphor reveals its importance for theories of mind and meaning, showing the prominence of metaphorical thought in everyday life. Gibbs notes the "marvelous interaction between basic and applied scholarship, such that findings on the ways that metaphors are employed in real-world contexts offer important constraints on general theories of metaphor."[14]

There is now a growing consensus that metaphor provides an essential component of the larger system of human cognition and communication, leading to a growing conviction supported by ever-increasing evidence that verbal and nonverbal metaphor does not require extraordinary human effort to be produced and understood. "Metaphor arises from the interaction of brains, bodies, languages, and culture," and is prevalent in other domains of human experience, including gesture, art, and music.[15]

These comments by Gibbs stand in contrast with traditional reflection on metaphor (including most of the first edition and much of the second edition of *Metaphor and Thought*), which focused on how people understand

14. Gibbs, "Metaphor and Thought," 3–4.
15. Gibbs, "Metaphor and Thought," 4, 5.

novel metaphorical language, "with the implicit assumption that the creation of these poetic figures was attributed to special individuals with significant artistic talents."[16]

Attention to how metaphors are used by real human beings in natural contexts reveals what Gibbs called the "paradox of metaphor," that metaphors are simultaneously ordinary and spectacular: "Metaphor is creative, novel, culturally sensitive, and allows us to transcend the mundane while also being rooted in pervasive patterns of bodily experience common to all people."[17]

Metaphor has the power to reshape our imagination. It can "create new modes of understanding often accompanied by special aesthetic pleasures," while creative, poetic metaphors can at the same time be "extensions of enduring schemes of metaphorical thought and not necessarily created de novo." Research that focuses on the "conceptual and embodies grounding for metaphorical thought" can draw "connections between what is simultaneously ordinary and spectacular about metaphor."[18]

In short, the introduction to the third edition of *The Cambridge Handbook of Metaphor and Thought* signals a growing consensus that all the main tenets of metaphor studies from before 1980 that we listed above in Lakoff and Johnson's summary have now been abandoned and replaced with new ideas that are proving immensely fruitful for human thought in general as well as for the interpretation of high-caliber literature like the Bible.

These new findings have led to an exciting interdisciplinary stage in metaphor studies, and the way we read the Bible with imagination draws enthusiastically on these new insights. One of these is the discovery of the embodiment of the human mind, an insight that has become possible through combining conceptual metaphor theory with technological advances that make the measurement of sense perceptions and brain activities possible.

Imagination: Embodied Simulation of Figurative Language

In understanding language, literal and figurative, we create simulations in our minds that fill in gaps and create a rich world of background information relevant to the verbal information we receive.[19] Meaning is more than just knowing definitions of words or even rules about their combination. "In

16. Gibbs, "Metaphor and Thought," 4.
17. Gibbs, "Metaphor and Thought," 5.
18. Gibbs, "Metaphor and Thought," 5.
19. Benjamin K. Bergen, *Louder Than Words: The New Science of How the Mind Makes Meaning* (Basic Books, 2012).

understanding language, our brains engage in a creative process of constructing rich mental worlds in which we see, hear, feel, and act."[20] The crucial component in the interpretation of language involves the imagination, and nowhere is this more true than in the interpretation of figurative language.

In the book *Louder Than Words*, a wide-ranging study of how the mind makes meaning, Benjamin Bergen documents how new technology measures and shows the correlation between sensory perception and brain activity. The evidence he discovered demonstrates that we use our perceptual and motor systems to run embodied simulations when we undertake to understand language. This, the embodied simulation hypothesis, is the central idea of the book.[21]

Bergen's evidence confirms what we have already observed in chapter 1, that we employ our imagination to accurately interpret what we perceive with our sense organs. The claim that we use our perceptual and motor systems to run embodied simulations when we interpret the world around us is another way of saying that we employ our imagination.

This is also true for how humans understand abstract concepts, such as faith, hope, love, justice, truth, beauty, happiness, grace, God, forgiveness, learning, thinking, or meaning.[22] Bergen's examination of talk about meaning and understanding as it occurs in ordinary human language revealed that such language is mostly metaphorical. Such metaphorical language enables the *simulation of abstract concepts* along similar lines to concrete things: "Metaphorical language provides a hint about how we might be able to understand language about things that don't look like anything."[23] In conclusion, not only do we *talk* about abstract concepts as if they were concrete things, but we also *think* about them in that way.

Bergen took this idea further by proposing a "*metaphorical simulation* hypothesis,"[24] and he developed from this hypothesis the theory that it is metaphorical language and thinking that enables human understanding of abstract concepts. We engage in embodied simulations of the metaphors that we use to speak about those concepts. The theory postulates that the cognitive processing of abstract concepts is accomplished using the *same* embodied simulations that we perform to understand concrete things.

Good illustrations for what happens when humans interpret metaphorical idioms about abstract concepts such as confidentiality or pride are phrases

20. Bergen, *Louder Than Words*, from the blurb.
21. Bergen, *Louder Than Words*, 195.
22. Bergen, *Louder Than Words*, chap. 9.
23. Bergen, *Louder Than Words*, 196.
24. Bergen, *Louder Than Words*, 198.

like "spill the beans" and "swallow your pride." Here "the language metaphorically describes abstract things (secrets or pride) as though they were physical objects that can be spilled or swallowed." The hypothesis predicts that we interpret metaphorical language in quasi-literal fashion, "rendering the concrete things and actions it describes in embodied simulations that you use in understanding the actual abstract concepts."[25] This prediction can indeed be verified empirically.[26]

Relevant experiments show not only that *performing* an action speeds up understanding of a subsequent matching metaphorical phrase[27] but also that merely *simulating* an action helps us understand a phrase faster if it metaphorically describes that same action. Bergen concluded that this "suggests that understanding metaphorical language involves embodied simulations of the specific details of the metaphorical language, like the concrete actions that it describes abstract activities in terms of."[28]

Bergen has demonstrated that humans *simulate bodily experiences* when they perceive and process cognitive information. This is another way of saying that we use our imagination to interpret what we experience, whether it is through human conversation or when we read books like the Bible. We interpret what we read by imagining what it would be like to be one of the characters in a story.

For example, we *engage in embodied simulation* to help ourselves understand what David felt and thought when he learned about the humiliation of the Israelite military at the provocation of Goliath in 1 Samuel 17.

Similarly, when we read Psalm 51, we engage our imagination to understand how David must have felt when the prophet Nathan confronted him in 2 Samuel 12:1–15 about his adultery and murder (2 Sam. 11). We *construct embodied simulations* as we read the various descriptions of his interior life in Psalm 51 to imagine the guilt he felt when he admitted his sin in 2 Samuel 12:13. Here imagination is all the more necessary because the story and its aftermath are conveyed to us in translation from a different culture with a different language that reaches us from a different time and place. "To speak and understand a language, you have to think, and languages, to some extent, dictate what things you ought to think, what things you ought to pay attention to, and how you should break up the world into categories."[29]

25. Bergen, *Louder Than Words*, 199.
26. Bergen, *Louder Than Words*, 199–203.
27. Bergen, *Louder Than Words*, 199–200.
28. Bergen, *Louder Than Words*, 201.
29. Bergen, *Louder Than Words*, 192.

Cross-cultural differences determined by different languages influence cognition and communication, even in translation. We need to employ our imagination. "When two people's backgrounds are different, whether it's within or across cultures, the words they use will evoke different embodied simulations in their respective minds," and this leads to different interpretations. It is likely that such differences will lead to miscommunication and misunderstanding. Nonetheless, we can employ our imagination to help us remain aware of such cultural and linguistic differences and correct possible misinterpretations. This is precisely what we hope to achieve with this volume.

In conclusion, the combination of conceptual metaphor theory with new measuring technologies has made it possible to measure how closely sense perceptions and brain activities are related. This has led to a transformation in our understanding of the crucial role that imagination and metaphor play in human cognition. "There is a revolution going on, a revolution in our understanding of what it is to be a human being. At stake is nothing less than the nature of the human mind."[30]

> For centuries, we in the West have thought of ourselves as rational animals whose mental capacities transcend our bodily nature. In this traditional view, our minds are abstract, logical, unemotionally rational, consciously accessible, and above all, able to directly fit and represent the world. Language has a special place in this view of what a human is—it is a privileged, logical symbol system internal to our minds that transparently expresses abstract concepts that are defined in terms of the external world itself.[31]

This means that "thought is carried out in the brain by the same neural structures that govern vision, action, and emotion. Language is made meaningful via the sensory-motor and emotional systems, which define goals and imagine, recognize, and carry out actions."[32] This is true also for how we read the Bible with imagination, as William Brown's comment on the interpretation of figurative language in the Psalms illustrates:

> To read the psalms is to *hear* their rhythms; to hear them is to *behold* the rich imagery they convey; to behold the psalms is to *feel* them in all their pain and promise; and to feel them is, ultimately, to "taste and see that the Lord is good" (Ps. 34:8a).[33]

30. George Lakoff, foreword to Bergen, *Louder Than Words*, ix.
31. Lakoff, foreword to Bergen, *Louder Than Words*, ix.
32. Lakoff, foreword to Bergen, *Louder Than Words*, ix.
33. Brown, *Seeing the Psalms*, 2.

Brown thus draws attention to the fact that poetic imagery in the Psalms can be experienced through audial, visual, and tactile sensory perception, and he hints at the sense perception of "taste" as well by means of the quotation from Psalm 34. "In the event of a metaphor, two or more modes of perception become juxtaposed and fused."[34]

In conclusion, then, figurative language like metaphors, similes, metonymies, and synecdoches are the essential building blocks for human thought and communication, including in the Bible. Figurative language provides us with the means to verbalize mentally how our bodies through our brains process what our senses perceive in the world around and within us. Imagination is essential for interpreting the rich figurative language in the Bible because the prominence of figurative language in Scripture reveals how much imagination has gone into its production. The Bible has been written with imagination. And it deserves to be read with imagination.

Figurative Language Is an Essential Part of How the Bible Communicates Meaning: An Example from Picasso

Two examples from Pablo Picasso's art, *She Goat* and *Bull's Head*, illustrate the importance of imagination for human language and cognition. As we shall see, his work was considered an extreme use of metaphor because it challenged traditional views. *She Goat*, *Bull's Head*, and other works appeared so extreme at the time because they challenged contemporary views of figurative language, especially views about metaphors and metonymies. Picasso's work focuses our attention on the essential role of the metaphoric element in human language and cognition and on the importance of our imagination for true cognitive progress.

There are many ways in which figurative language has been used in the visual arts, but here we focus on metaphors. Cubism and surrealism are the art movements that have used metaphors most prominently. They make use of metonymy and metaphor in ways that highlight metaphors more directly than other streams of visual artistic expression. In cubism, the depicted object is metonymically fragmented into its constituent parts; in surrealism, the depicted object is represented through different objects that metaphorically represent it or its parts.[35]

34. Brown, *Seeing the Psalms*, 6.

35. Roman Jacobson, "Der Doppelcharakter der Sprache und die Polarität zwischen Metaphorik und Metonymik," in *Theorie der Metapher: Studienausgabe*, ed. Anselm Haverkamp (Wissenschaftliche Buchgesellschaft, 1983), 170.

Picasso's *She Goat* (Vallauris, 1950, cast 1952) provides a particularly powerful illustration of the phenomenon. It is a life-size bronze assemblage composed of a wicker basket for the goat's body, a palm leaf for the back, two ceramic flowerpots for the udder, as well as other metal elements. Most of the objects apparently were salvaged by Picasso from fields near his Vallauris studio.[36] Explains Picasso: "My sculptures are plastic metaphors. It is the same principle as in painting."[37] Picasso used tangible objects—such as old baskets, pipes, vases, parts of bicycles—for his sculptures instead of employing traditional materials such as gypsum. Picasso did this to show

> that in aesthetic perception and in its objects metaphor becomes more visible, that it becomes more overtly perceived and valued through compositions whose parts consist of objects with an identity and name of their own, rather than formless gypsum, which does not form anything of its own until it is shaped into something else which can be identified according to its resemblance.[38]

Picasso draws on conventional metaphors that are built based on similarity. For example, in using a wicker basket to depict the chest of *She Goat*, the goat's rib cage *is* a wicker basket that one needs to *see as* the goat's chest. In reverse, while looking at the shape of the goat's body, one can see the goat's rib cage as a wicker basket.[39] The result is a composite metaphor with a dual line of sight. By contrast, if the goat's chest were made of gypsum, the view would go in only one direction. Picasso explains further:

> One could say the rib cage resembles a woven wicker basket. I move from the basket back to the rib cage: from the metaphor back to reality. I make you see reality because I used the metaphor. The form of the metaphor may be worn-out or broken, but I take it, however down-at-the-heel it may have become, and use it in such an unexpected way that it arouses a new emotion in the mind of the viewer, because it momentarily disturbs his customary way of identifying and defining what he sees. It would be very easy to do these things by traditional

36. A picture and description can be found at "The She Goat, 1950 by Pablo Picasso," https://www.pablopicasso.org/she-goat.jsp.

37. Françoise Gillot and Carlton Lake, *Life with Picasso* (New York Review Books, 2019), 296–97.

38. Virgil C. Aldrich, "Visuelle Metapher," in *Theorie der Metapher: Studienausgabe*, ed. Anselm Haverkamp (Wissenschaftliche Buchgesellschaft, 1983), 144 (our translation). In this analogy, the use of gypsum is comparable to the now obsolete traditional metaphor theories considered above, while Picasso's art anticipates modern metaphor theory in the wake of Lakoff's work.

39. The metaphoric transformation is even more intuitive in German. The German equivalent for *rib cage* is *Brustkorb*, lit. "breast *basket*," which aligns nicely with the sculpture's wicker *basket* (see the discussion in Aldrich, "Visuelle Metapher," 145).

> methods, but this way I can engage the mind of the viewer in a direction he hadn't foreseen and make him rediscover things he had forgotten.[40]

This quote draws attention to two aspects of Picasso's art that are relevant to imagination and figurative language.

First, Picasso's reference to the "down-at-the-heel" state of metaphors is his way of referring to those metaphors that traditional theorists considered "dead" metaphors, and his art not only revives them but also shows that they were never dead in the first place.

Second, Picasso's use of tangible objects rather than gypsum enables a more accurate interpretation by firing the viewer's imagination: "I make you see reality because I used the metaphor." This is precisely what figurative language does for human cognition. Conversely, the use of gypsum, by removing or at least reducing the need for imagination in the interpretive process, leads to an impoverished cognitive experience. And this is precisely what happens when figurative language is suppressed in our reading of the Bible. The less figurative language, the less interpretation is needed. A reduced need for interpretation makes imagination less important. The actual Bible we do have in the original languages is the equivalent of Picasso's *She Goat* and *Bull's Head*. Some of the Bible translations into modern languages like the English Good News Bible, which reduce or even eliminate figurative language with the aim to produce "language that is natural, clear, simple, and unambiguous" (according to its preface), are like goat's and bull's heads of gypsum.[41] The Bible helps us see reality because it uses figurative language. Attempts to remove it impoverish our perception of the spiritual realities it aims to reveal.

Françoise Gilot, Picasso's partner and muse, recalls memories related to another of his sculptures, *Bull's Head* (1942):

> About the time I first met Pablo, he had made a sculpture of a bull's head out of the seat and handlebars of a bicycle. He used to say that this sculpture was reversible. "I find a bicycle seat and handlebars in the street, and I say, 'Well, here's a bull,'" he explained to me. "Everybody who looks at it after I assemble it says, 'Well, there's a bull,' until a cyclist comes along and says, 'Well, there's a bicycle seat,' and he makes a seat and a pair of handlebars out of it again. And that can go on, back and forth, for an eternity, according to the needs of the mind and the body."[42]

40. Gilot and Lake, *Life with Picasso*, 298.

41. We will explore the detrimental impact of some modern Bible translations on imaginative biblical form and content more fully in chap. 6.

42. Gilot and Lake, *Life with Picasso*, 297. A picture and description can be found at "Bull's Head, 1942 by Pablo Picasso," https://www.pablopicasso.org/bull-head.jsp.

Bull's Head is an artwork created from found objects—the seat and handlebars of a bicycle—and since they are not disguised, the metaphoric components remain transparent. According to art critic Eric Gibson, this transparent quality makes it "an assertion of the transforming power of the human imagination," and we agree. This is what Picasso himself said about *Bull's Head* to visiting photographer George Brassai in 1943:

> Guess how I made the bull's head? One day, in a pile of objects all jumbled up together, I found an old bicycle seat right next to a rusty set of handlebars. In a flash, they joined together in my head. The idea of the Bull's Head came to me before I had a chance to think. All I did was weld them together. . . . *[But] if you were only to see the bull's head and not the bicycle seat and handlebars that form it, the sculpture would lose some of its impact.*[43]

The italicized words explain what this art reveals about the role of the imagination in human language and cognition. Picasso's visual art illustrates the cognitive power that metaphors can have in literature, including in the Bible. If we were to see only the decoded "plain" meaning (the bull's head in Picasso's visual analogy) and not the actual figurative language in the Bible that produces such meaning (the bicycle seat and the handlebars that form it in Picasso's analogy), the figurative language of the Bible would lose not only some of its impact but also *some of its meaning*.

Picasso's art really does help us understand and experience one kind of thing in terms of another, as Lakoff and Johnson have said.[44] It also illustrates powerfully how essential figurative language is for our ability to understand and be transformed, to experience and enjoy the power of God in his Word as the Holy Spirit fires our imagination to process not only the *content* of God's revelation but also its *beauty*.

Picasso's *She Goat* has the capacity "to force attention onto the metaphoric element."[45] However, sculptures like *She Goat* and *Bull's Head* can do that not because they are examples of "an extreme or expanded form of metaphor"[46] but because they help viewers, art critics, and metaphor theorists see the very realities that have been obscured by traditional theories of metaphor and figurative language. Unusual and revolutionary as they seemed when they were created, Picasso's sculptures only appeared that way because of theories that had restricted metaphors to ornamental and other trivial functions.

43. Pablo Picasso, quoted in "Bull's Head, 1942 by Pablo Picasso" (emphasis added).
44. Lakoff and Johnson, *Metaphors We Live By*, 19.
45. Aldrich, "Visuelle Metapher," 145.
46. Aldrich, "Visuelle Metapher," 145.

Picasso's capacity to demonstrate the metaphoricity of ordinary objects, including body parts of humans and animals, draws attention to the correlation between metaphor and human thought. Human cognition—naturally and of necessity—employs metaphors and other figurative language at every twist and turn. Picasso's method of *increasing the visibility of ordinary, everyday metaphors in the most mundane of circumstances* could seem "extreme" or "expanded" only in a time when metaphors had been relegated to the realm of trivial and derivative phenomena in human language.

In conclusion, Picasso's art recaptured a basic insight that had been lost to human reflection on language and cognition. His work challenged traditional views of metaphor. The extremity of *She Goat* lies in the challenge it represents to false ideas and misguided theories. The genius and true intellectual and artistic achievement of Picasso and artists like him are found in the fact that their work focuses our attention on the essential role of the metaphoric element in human language and cognition and on the importance of our imagination for true cognitive progress.[47]

How Imagination Helps Us Interpret Figurative Language in the Bible

As we have seen, the visual art of Picasso and others illustrates an important truth: The very ways in which we talk about human language and cognition are themselves metaphorical. And this is especially true in how we discuss metaphors and figurative language.

47. The imaginative energy in the fine arts is also explored in Jennifer Anna Gosetti-Ferencei, *The Life of Imagination: Revealing and Making the World* (Columbia University Press, 2018). Reflecting on Vincent van Gogh's painting *The Starry Night*, she notes: "The painter does not hide his labor, but makes his brushstrokes visible and vivid, rendering what can be imagined as the painter's intentionality forever present in the work; the viewer may feel touched by and through the physical medium of the painting. Far from sparing one the need for intense imagining . . . this work would ignite the viewer's imagination with its expressive exuberance, inviting new possibilities of seeing, stimulating a metaphorical or even narrative impulse toward the interpretation, or even production, of meaning. Aesthetic reception does not require passive submission, but provokes imagining, or concretization, of the attentive viewer" (20). Similarly, she describes Leonardo da Vinci's inventions "as experiences that involve inner imagining, hypothetical thinking, seeing-as, as well as material creativity" that "directly engage environmental interest and human concern" (21–22). She supports this claim with the observation that "Leonardo's studies of the flight of birds and the human body are, in his notebooks, enfolded together within his plans for flying machines, such as the ornithopter and helicopter" (22). In her view, da Vinci's work illustrates "the essential rather than merely contingent relation between imagination and creativity" (22), and we agree. In the final analysis, then, creativity is productive and useful in the real world for problem-solving and human flourishing: "The capacity to bring together ideas untethered to reality with the reality before us, in order to overcome the limitations of the latter, is an imaginative achievement" (22).

In the final part of this chapter, we will capitalize on this crucial insight. We will integrate the different parts of our discussion into a comprehensive model of human language and cognition that will build the foundation for how imagination helps us interpret the figurative language in the Bible. First, we will explore and critique the meta-metaphorical dimension of talk about language in the work of two influential scholars. Then we will develop our own model for talk about language and cognition.

Previous Meta-Metaphorical Talk About Metaphor

We begin with a biblical scholar's description of metaphor and then will consider how a philosopher of language from the beginning of the twentieth century described metaphors.

Our first example of meta-metaphoric language about metaphor comes from a well-known and popular description of metaphors by G. B. Caird, a respected biblical scholar, in his widely used *The Language and Imagery of the Bible*. He emphasizes the significance of metaphor by using the analogy of a lens:

> When we look at an object through a lens, we concentrate on the object and ignore the lens. Metaphor is a lens. It is as though the speaker were saying, "Look through this and see what I have seen, something you would never have noticed without the lens!"[48]

Despite its evocative quality and eloquence, this illustration is problematic because it is informed by the ornament theory of metaphor. While Caird correctly highlighted that metaphors enable a unique way of "seeing" the concept that would be impossible without the metaphor, the very choice of the metaphor—"metaphor is a lens"—he uses to explain the nature and function of metaphor is misleading: "When we look at an object through a lens, *we concentrate on the object and ignore the lens*." Yet the very statement "*Look through this and see . . . something you would never have noticed without the lens*" implies of necessity that the metaphoric expression itself is indispensable from and necessary for the cognitive process.

Caird's meta-metaphor is also misleading for other reasons. First, a metaphor is usually used not to describe something that one has never noticed before but to describe something that is known but not well understood. Second, most "lenses" that are useful for the purpose for which they were designed do nothing else but magnify and so only help us see what we have already seen without them, only bigger. We may see *smaller parts* of the object that are invisible

48. G. B. Caird, *The Language and Imagery of the Bible* (Duckworth, 1980), 152.

to natural sight, but that is all. And when a lens causes us to see something *differently*, it is usually a faulty lens that *distorts* the object we contemplate.

This flawed example of meta-metaphoric talk about metaphors reflects outdated theories of metaphors like the ones we have already considered above. It effectively represents those ornamental views, but the views themselves are flawed, and so the meta-metaphor to explain the nature and function of metaphors is flawed also.

Even so, Caird's failed attempt illustrates the points we made earlier in this chapter, that figurative language is essential for cognitive progress. As soon as we attempt to explain more interesting phenomena such as metaphors, we cannot do so but with recourse to figurative language.

Our second example of meta-metaphoric language about metaphor comes from philosopher of language Ivor A. Richards. In his influential volume *The Philosophy of Rhetoric*, published in 1936, he develops what has come to be known as an "interaction theory of metaphor."[49] Here, too, the theory is meta-metaphorical.

Richards explains: "When we use a metaphor we have two thoughts of different things active together and supported by a single word or phrase, whose meaning is a resultant of their interaction."[50] Richards describes the "interaction" between the two thoughts present in a metaphor through two technical terms: the *tenor*, or underlying subject of the metaphor, and the *vehicle*, the actual metaphor used to shed new light on it. (Theoretical treatments before Lakoff and Johnson's work appeared in 1980 rarely distinguished between actual metaphorical expressions in real language events and the metaphoric ideas, what we now call conceptual or structural metaphors, on which these expressions are based.)

Richards's technical terminology is a blend of metaphors from the language of transport (vehicle) and the language of music (tenor). It is meta-metaphorical and blends two metaphors from two different spheres of human experience to describe metaphors.

The first meta-metaphor, vehicle, describes the actual metaphoric expression itself.[51] It comes from the language of human transport, via the Latin noun *vehiculum*, "carriage" from the verb *vehere*, "to carry."

49. Ivor Armstrong Richards, *The Philosophy of Rhetoric* (Oxford University Press, 1936).

50. Richards, *Philosophy of Rhetoric*, 93, quoted in Soskice, *Metaphor and Religious Language* (Oxford University Press, 1989), 45. A German translation can be found in Richards, "Die Metapher (1936)," in *Theorie der Metapher: Studienausgabe*, ed. Anselm Haverkamp (Wissenschaftliche Buchgesellschaft, 1983), 34.

51. Actually, it describes what we call the metaphoric expression *as well as* its underlying structural metaphor, since Richards does not explicitly distinguish between the two.

The second meta-metaphor, tenor, describes the *meaning* or *significance* of the metaphoric expression.[52] It comes from the language of music, via the Latin verb *tenere*, "to hold." Richards's choice of the meta-metaphor of tenor reveals that he considers the *meaning* of the metaphor more important than the way it is expressed. This seems clear because in a musical performance it is usually the tenor that "holds" the melody—and thus the main sequence of sounds that conveys the "message" of the score, as opposed to the variations upon it in the harmonies.

In other words, the "interaction" between the "two thoughts of different things" is described in terms of transport from one spatial location to another, with the metaphoric expression being the "vehicle" and thus providing the means of transport, while the "tenor"—what the metaphoric expression is designed to describe—is imagined as the passenger. Ultimately, then, in this meta-metaphoric construct, a metaphor is not about the metaphoric expression, which is only the vehicle and thus only a means to an end. Rather, in Richards's meta-metaphoric model, a metaphor is about the passenger, the tenor, and thus the end for whose sake the metaphoric expression was created. For Richards, then, the vehicle is less important than the tenor.

By contrast, we are convinced that the vehicle matters, and this brings us back to a comment by Lakoff and Turner—one that we already presented above at the end of our extended quotation about the conventional and conceptual nature of metaphors—that "this system of metaphor seems to give rise to abstract reasoning, which appears to be based on spatial reasoning."[53] What Lakoff and Turner describe as "spatial reasoning" is one of the primary conceptual metaphors to help us understand human cognition. It is a meta-metaphor for progress in our thinking about the things that matter most to us as human beings. It is to this meta-metaphorical conceptual metaphor for human cognition that we now turn for the remainder of this chapter on the role of imagination and figurative language for reading the Bible, for it will inform our own proposal for a meta-metaphorical description of metaphors and other kinds of figurative language.

Imagination and Metaphoricity: The Metaphorical Nature of Human Language and Cognition and Its Significance for a Hermeneutic of Imagination

Our meta-metaphorical model to describe the cognitive power of metaphors is based on spatial reasoning. The way we use language shapes the

52. The word *tenor* refers to the pitch of a singing voice, higher than the baritone and thus the highest voice of the adult male range.

53. Lakoff and Turner, *More Than Cool Reason*, 228.

way we perceive the world, and it is essential for how we think.[54] And the way we use language about the way we understand the world suggests that abstract reasoning is based on spatial reasoning. We agree with this proposal by Lakoff and Turner. Human talk and thought about language and cognition are themselves metaphorical, and the underlying metaphoric idea, the conceptual or structural metaphor for cognition, is UNDERSTANDING IS PROGRESS ON A JOURNEY. We are talking about THOUGHT-TRAVEL, and this idea has immense explanatory power. Consequently, the structural metaphor METAPHORIC EXPRESSIONS ARE MEANS OF TRANSPORT FOR COGNITIVE PROGRESS accurately describes the nature and function of metaphors, and it can serve the same purpose for other kinds of figurative language. What do we mean by "MEANS OF TRANSPORT" when we talk about THOUGHT-TRAVEL? We are describing a "metaphoric field," in analogy with "semantic fields" in the study of word meanings.[55] Metaphors are MEANS OF TRANSPORT as a VEHICLE, and here we think of them as a TRAIN-OF-THOUGHT, in line with the underlying idea of spatial reasoning noted by Lakoff and Johnson and discussed earlier.

Metaphoric expressions and other kinds of figurative language, then, are the "VEHICLES" that propel human understanding on its progress toward learning. We use the meta-metaphor VEHICLE differently from the way in which Richards used it. In our model, the various metaphoric expressions and other types of figurative language that we use to articulate conceptual metaphors are the kinds of VEHICLES we choose as means of transport on our intellectual journeys. The meta-metaphoric expression VEHICLE is thus a collective designation for the various means of transport that we can choose to convey us from a given cognitive starting point to our cognitive destination.

And this conceptual meta-metaphor casts human interlocutors into the roles of active participants associated with the experience of human THOUGHT-TRAVEL. Those who use (coin or utter) metaphoric expressions in communication are the DRIVERS who offer the metaphor (the VEHICLE) to their interlocutors as a convenient way to reach a cognitive destination, while those who hear or read the metaphoric expression become its PASSENGERS.

A good example to illustrate this are the various metaphors the Bible uses for God. In Psalm 23:1–4, God is imagined as a shepherd. In Psalm 23:5–6, we

54. Philip Wheelwright, "Semantics and Ontology," in *Metaphor and Symbol*, ed. L. C. Knights and B. Cottle, Colston Papers 12 (Butterworth's Scientific Publications, 1960).

55. The idea of metaphoric fields is different from so-called metaphoric clusters, which, put simply, identify where in a text metaphoric expressions occur with significantly higher frequency than in the remainder of the text. For metaphoric clusters, see Mason D. Lancaster, *Hosea's God: A Metaphorical Theology*, Ancient Israel and Its Literature 48 (SBL Press, 2023), 16–27.

see him as our host. In Isaiah 6, he is portrayed as a king. In Exodus 4:22–23; Deuteronomy 1:31; 8:5; 14:1; 32:6; Isaiah 43:6; 63:8, 16; 64:8; and many other Old Testament texts, he is pictured as the father of Israel.[56] In Psalms 50:6; 75:8; 96:13, he is portrayed as a judge, and in Isaiah 33:22 he is painted in the persona of a judge *as well as a lawgiver and king* who will save. In Exodus 33:11 and Isaiah 41:8, he is depicted as a friend. In Isaiah 66:13, God compares himself to a mother, and in Deuteronomy 32:4 and Psalm 18:2 he is declared to be a rock. And this list is far from exhaustive, since there are many other metaphors for God in the Bible.

Consequently, metaphoric expressions and other kinds of figurative language will furnish different *modes* of transport for THOUGHT-TRAVEL. For example, some figurative expressions may be rather "pedestrian," offering slow but very flexible progress, while others may be comparable to a bicycle, a motorcycle, a car, a heavy-goods vehicle, a train, or an aircraft, differing in thought-processing speed and thought-processing flexibility. A bicycle is faster than progress on foot yet still offers much flexibility regarding route choices; cars are faster still but dependent on various existing road systems; trains can be very fast but need to follow predetermined tracks; aircraft are high-speed modes of transport, can fly almost anywhere on any route, but usually have to stick to their pre-authorized flight plans; and so on.

What this proposed meta-metaphor suggests, then, is that the VEHICLES we choose for the ways in which we think matter profoundly. It matters whether we envisage God predominantly as a judge or as a parent, as a king or as a shepherd. The underlying conceptual metaphors matter, and the numerous metaphoric and other figurative expressions that belong to them matter as well.

Alternatively, metaphoric expressions and other kinds of figurative language can also be envisaged as a TRAIN-OF-THOUGHT. In this way of modeling the cognitive journey, metaphoric and other figurative expressions belong to a hybrid type of VEHICLE as our MEANS OF TRANSPORT.

Here metaphoric and other figurative expressions are likened to a train. They invite the MIND-TRAVELER to come on board and take a journey of the imagination, one where the ideas and experiences associated with a given metaphoric or figurative expression are landmarks along the road. The metaphoric or figurative expression as TRAIN-OF-THOUGHT takes us on a journey of discovery on which our perception of and engagement with the entity that the metaphor or figure expresses is enriched.

56. Cf. Goran Medved, "The Fatherhood of God in the Old Testament," *Kairos—Evangelical Journal of Theology* 10, no. 2 (2016).

The object of contemplation that we hope to understand by means of the metaphor is JOURNEY'S END, the destination of our THOUGHT-TRAVEL. The ticket we have chosen is a return ticket. We can travel all the way to the TRAIN-OF-THOUGHT's final destination and back again. However, with the power to travel come added constraints, and our chosen mode of transport limits the range of destinations we can reach. If we imagine God *only* as our judge, this will impact how we experience our relationship with him. Our chosen TRAIN-OF-THOUGHT carries us along a trajectory, a track that is predetermined by the nature of the VEHICLE we have chosen. *This* TRAIN-OF-THOUGHT will get us only so far, and there will come a time when the landmarks become unfamiliar because the cognitive potential of the ideas and experiences associated with a given metaphoric or figurative expression has been exhausted. God is not only a person who is to be feared. If fear is all we experience when we think of God, a time has come when staying aboard *this* metaphor will carry us further away from our goal of understanding rather than closer to it. What should we do now?

This is where the cognitive potential of our TRAIN-OF-THOUGHT meta-metaphor really comes into its own. The beauty of THOUGHT-TRAVEL is that we are not compelled by physical constraints. We can disembark from our TRAIN-OF-THOUGHT at any point, but we do not have to before we really want to. For the sooner we do so, the less certain we will be as to whether we have come as close to our goal as *this* TRAIN-OF-THOUGHT can take us. Staying on longer is worthwhile and crucial for pushing the boundaries of our understanding. Only by going beyond the familiar landmarks that everyone recognizes instantly will we be able to reach new territory of the mind and thus gain genuinely new insights. Now we may realize that we need other metaphors for God, like God as father or mother, to help us rediscover that he also cares for us and longs to forgive us, as a good human parent does.

It is a win-win situation, for even when our train takes us beyond where we wanted to go, we can, in the imaginary world of metaphoric THOUGHT-TRAVEL, disembark instantly and retrace our journey by jumping straight back to where we now know we should have disembarked in the first place to catch another TRAIN-OF-THOUGHT, perhaps of God as a shepherd, a rock, or a potter.

Once we have realized that it is time to come off the train, we can, in an instant, hop back and onto another means of metaphoric or figurative transport to get us ever closer to our destination. *This* metaphoric or figurative expression, the VEHICLE we have chosen to become our TRAIN-OF-THOUGHT, has been right for a distance, bringing us closer to the destination of understanding, but the time has now come to change. *This* metaphoric or figurative expression has brought us to a mental relay station where we can catch a different VEHICLE, whether that is another TRAIN-LINE (another metaphor, like God as a shepherd), a REPLACEMENT BUS (a simile, like God as a mother), a TAXI (a metonymy, like God as a rock), or a RENTAL CAR (a synecdoche, like God's rod and staff in Psalm 23), that will bring us closer still. Note that all the VEHICLES in this meta-metaphor are *modes of public transport*, a conscious choice to emphasize that most metaphors are conventional and thus a *common* good.

Without imagination, by contrast, we may get stuck with only one predominant metaphor that ultimately distorts and impoverishes how we experience God, when all along the Bible imagines a rich kaleidoscope of ways for how God wants to relate to us and how he wants us to relate to him. We really do need an imagination to match the imaginative range of the biblical texts, and a thorough understanding of metaphor theory and figurative language will inform our imagination to do this well.

Conclusion

Our concluding remarks bring together the findings from the different parts of this chapter by drawing on insights from an important discussion on metaphor theory in a study of Psalm 18 in Alison Gray and Benjamin Bergen's discussion of embodied simulations that are prompted by imagining flying pigs.[57] Figurative language can set an entire scene "before our eyes" (as Aristotle put it).[58] In fact, it can do even more than that. Metaphoric and other figurative expressions can create entire worlds in the reader's or listener's imagination and invite them to inhabit those worlds. They can evoke the creation of entire scenes, landscapes not just filled with stationary figures but populated with real-life representations of people, animals, and other circumstantial data, such as time, temperature, lighting conditions, and so on. And it is our imagination that helps us experience the full transformative potential of the

57. "The basic understanding of metaphor in this thesis is that it is a particular kind of 'word-picture.' This definition is akin to Macky's description of metaphor as a 'photo-landscape symbol,' and resonates with Aristotle's explanation that metaphor sets 'the scene before our eyes.' The term 'analogical word-picture,' whilst emphasizing the nature of metaphor as a form of verbal art, distinguishes it from other types of verbal art by identifying analogy as the underlying basis of its modus operandi." Alison Gray, *Psalm 18 in Words and Pictures*, Biblical Interpretation (Brill, 2013), 9–10, quoting Peter Macky, *The Centrality of Metaphors to Biblical Thought: A Method for Interpreting the Bible*, Studies in the Bible and Early Christianity 19 (Mellen, 1990), 102–14; and Aristotle, *Art of Rhetoric*, trans. J. H. Freese (Harvard University Press, 2020), 399. Cf. Bergen, *Louder Than Words*, 17–20.

58. Aristotle, *Art of Rhetoric*, 399.

Bible's rich imagery, as we will demonstrate in our imaginative reading of Psalm 23:2 in the conclusion of this book.

These "imaginations" are embodied simulations that are created on the spot, creatively and constructively, as humans draw on prior experiences and merge them together to create not just a "scene" in the sense of a still life to be observed from a distance (as in a photograph or landscape painting) but an actual experience in which the observer plays an active participant role, for example through the simulation of ambient details, such as smells, sounds, flavors, and textures—and even emotions associated with these simulations. A hermeneutic of imagination encourages these kinds of intimate and transformative experiences that invite us into the presence of the God whom we encounter in the Bible's pages. We will explore more deeply in this book's conclusion how imagination helps us to experience the transformative power of the Bible.

CHAPTER FOUR

A Hermeneutic of Imagination Attunes Us to the Emotional Intentions of Scripture

Emotions play an important role in the Bible. This is readily apparent in poetic texts like the Psalms, the book of Job, and the Song of Songs, for example. In other text types like narratives, by comparison, emotions still have important functions but appear in more subtle ways that are frequently misunderstood or missed entirely in traditional readings. In this chapter, we will demonstrate the importance of emotions in Scripture. We will then explore how a hermeneutic of imagination helps us detect more subtle expressions of emotion and prevent misunderstandings. We will demonstrate the importance and value of emotions that are easily overlooked in narrative texts. And we will explore specific emotions whose importance becomes apparent when we apply a hermeneutic of imagination to their interpretation and their application in Christian practice. Most important among these is the supreme emotion that forms the goal of all Scripture, love for God, neighbor, and self.

Emotions Are Essential for Reading the Bible

In this chapter, again, we need to rehabilitate an important ingredient of imaginative reading from an undeserved poor reputation. Emotions have a bad reputation all around—in Western cultures at least. They are seen as uncontrollable drives that threaten the proper function of rational thought. They are considered fickle and unreliable. They are deemed dangerous. This is true in Western cultures in general, and in Western Christian circles in particular.[1]

Christian prejudices are, at least in part, influenced by Greek thought, which equates the heart with the seat of human emotions.[2] Consequently, warnings regarding the heart like Jeremiah 17:9 ("The heart is devious above all else; it is perverse—who can understand it?"), Proverbs 28:26 ("He that trusteth in his own heart is a fool: but whoso walketh wisely, he shall be delivered," KJV), and Matthew 15:19–20 ("For out of the heart come evil intentions, murder, adultery, sexual immortality, theft, false witness, slander. These are what defile a person.") are taken at face value and considered biblical denunciations that warn against the dangers caused by emotions. Given the interpretation of the heart as the seat of human emotions, then, it is no wonder that Christians consider emotions as irrational, sin-inducing, and evil.

However, this reading is based on a fundamental misunderstanding of biblical anthropology. In reality, biblical usage associates the kidneys, the liver, and other organs located in the abdomen with human emotions, while the heart is associated with the human intellect. Indeed, "biblical thought locates different emotions in the individual organs within the abdomen."[3] Consequently, when biblical texts indict the human heart, they confront the way humans tend to think, not how they feel.

Furthermore, recent developments in the humanities and in the sciences have contributed to a veritable rehabilitation of the damaged reputation of the emotions. The burgeoning new field of the affective sciences is discovering the importance and value of emotions, and the relationship between language and emotion has also received new interest. In their discussion of emotional intelligence, for example, Peter Salovey, Marja Kokkonen, Paulo Lopes, and John Mayer conclude that

> emotions often serve adaptive, purposeful, and helpful functions. . . . It is the emotional system, in this view, that focuses attention, organizes memory,

1. Some of the following comments draw on J. Richard Middleton's defense of his imaginative reading of the Aqedah (the binding of Isaac) in Gen. 22 in Middleton, *Abraham's Silence: The Binding of Isaac, the Suffering of Job, and How to Talk Back to God* (Baker Academic, 2021), 166–67.

2. Silvia Schroer and Thomas Staubli, *Body Symbolism in the Bible* (Liturgical Press, 2001), 41–55.

3. Schroer and Staubli, *Body Symbolism in the Bible*, 71.

> helps us to interpret social situations, and motivates relevant behavior. Accordingly, it makes little sense to place emotions in opposition to reason and rationality.[4]

Emotions are essential for human cognition and successful human relationships. And the ways in which we speak about and evoke emotions shape how others feel:

> Linguistic utterances express and name, evoke, intensify and constitute emotions and emotional dispositions. When we talk about specific emotions like fear or love, we encode emotional states by way of expressive verbal representations and in doing so we transmit thereby what is being felt internally as something that can be experienced by others.[5]

Consequently, how literature in general and the Bible in particular speak about and evoke emotions also influences how we as readers behave. If we ignore or neglect the affective dimension of Scripture, we will inevitably misunderstand it. We cannot read the Bible well unless we pay attention to the emotions mentioned in and evoked by the biblical texts, and to do this responsibly we need to read them with imagination. What is more, we need to train our imaginative capacities to engage appropriately with the emotions of biblical characters. We need to educate our imagination so we can learn to adopt those emotions that the biblical texts intend to evoke, to reject those emotions that some biblical texts inadvertently evoke due to misunderstanding, and to know the difference between the two.

A Hermeneutic of Imagination Helps Us Reflect on and Understand Emotions Found in and Evoked by the Biblical Texts

In the following paragraphs, we will explore how a hermeneutic of imagination helps us detect more subtle expressions of emotion and avoid misunderstandings, especially in narrative texts, where they are easily overlooked or misunderstood. We need imagination to attune us to the understated ways in which biblical narrators relate emotions—those of God, those of other characters in the stories, and their own. How else would we know what someone else feels,

4. Peter Salovey, Marja Kokkonen, Paulo N. Lopes, and John D. Mayer, "Emotional Intelligence: What Do We Know?," in *Feelings and Emotions: The Amsterdam Symposium*, ed. Antony S. R. Manstead, Nico Frijda, and Agneta Fischer (Cambridge University Press, 2004), 321.

5. Monika Schwarz-Friesel, *Sprache und Emotion*, 2nd ed., Universitäts-Taschenbuch (Francke, 2013), 365 (our translation).

whether they are the person right next to us or a character we encounter in the biblical texts?

A good case study to show this is 2 Samuel 13:1–20, where we learn about a young woman named Tamar (Absalom's sister) and her fate after her half brother Amnon had raped and then abandoned her.

Our example illustrates why we need imagination to discern emotions, especially when those emotions tend to be reported in understated fashion, as happens here. It demonstrates that we need an emotionally intelligent imagination to know which emotions the biblical texts *do* aim to evoke and which emotions they *do not* aim to evoke.

Information about the mental state of Tamar in the text is sparse, but what little is there matters. All we learn at the explicit level is that she "put ashes on her head, and tore the long robe that she was wearing; she put her hand on her head, and went away, crying aloud as she went" (2 Sam. 13:19); and after her brother Absalom had told her to be "quiet for now" and urged her to "not take this to heart," she "remained, a desolate woman, in her brother Absalom's house" (13:20). The emotions of the young woman Tamar are covered in a mere two verses. Yet her pain, felt acutely by her brother Absalom, triggers the dramatic, traumatically destructive events narrated in the next seven and a half chapters until 2 Samuel 20:22. If this passage is examined from only a narrow perspective, it would be easy to think that Absalom's actions were simply a matter of a young man's depraved ambition. Imagination, however, allows us to understand the emotions of many characters in the narrative and realize that, in reality, Tamar's pain led to a rebellion resulting in a civil war that almost tore the entire nation apart and nearly extinguished the two siblings' entire family.

The text's relative silence about Tamar's mental state after she had been raped has led many to conclude that her emotions did not matter to God, to the biblical authors, or to any of the other characters in these chapters—perhaps not even to her brother Absalom. And consequently, her pain was also largely neglected by many later readers of the text. Here a hermeneutic of imagination encourages "mental state reasoning," a technical term for the ability to analyze and understand what another person may be thinking or feeling.

Our imagination helps us to reflect on and understand emotions, our own and those of others. It facilitates mental state reasoning, which in turn helps us

> to develop an understanding of the mind's processes, make predictions about how people may behave, and form explanations for people's past and future behavior. Mental state reasoning is integral to the everyday navigation of a social

> landscape. Without this ability, humans would be unable to fully understand the actions of themselves and other people.[6]

Understood in this way, then, mental state reasoning is an important component of the human capacity to imagine how other people feel and why they behave in certain ways. Imagination helps readers of the Bible understand how various characters in the story behave; it helps us as readers to feel what was going on in Absalom's mind, to experience his seething hatred, and to comprehend why it lasted for no less than eleven years (2 Sam. 13:23, 38; 14:28; 15:7) and occupied eight chapters in the Bible (13:1–20:20).

And reading these chapters with imagination not only helps us to understand the emotions of the various characters but also enables us to understand their actions. It helps us to put ourselves in their shoes and see the world and the events that unfold in the text from their perspectives. It helps us infer what they may be thinking and feeling, and what drives their actions. The characters in the stories become three-dimensional human beings to whom we can relate and whose inner lives can inform how we think, feel, and act today.

Upon reflection, we are now more attuned to the fact that the biblical authors, too, were emotionally invested in the events they describe. We now notice that quality trumps quantity in how biblical authors, especially in narrative texts, relate emotions. The author of 2 Samuel was much more invested in how this young woman felt than the brief notes on her inner state suggest to readers who are not attuned to the understated ways in which biblical narrators relate emotions—those of God, those of other characters in the stories, and their own.

It is only now, also, that a hermeneutic of imagination helps us connect the emotional dots across biblical episodes. It is no coincidence that the rape of Tamar and the expansive narrative of its terrible human costs come so hard on the heels of the narrative about the rape of Bathsheba and the murder of her husband (2 Sam. 11:1–27), and the consequent confrontation between David and the prophet Nathan (11:27–12:15).

It is only now that the full weight of divine emotion behind the brief comment "But the thing that David had done displeased the Lord" in 2 Samuel 11:27 comes into full view. It is only now that the severity of the divine judgment "Now, therefore, the sword shall never depart from your house. . . . I will raise up trouble against you from within your own house" in 2 Samuel 12:10–12 can be fully grasped. It is only now that we can begin to comprehend

6. Paige E. Davis, "Imaginary Friends: How Imaginary Minds Mimic Real Life," in *The Cambridge Handbook of the Imagination*, ed. Anna Abraham (Cambridge University Press, 2020), 373.

why Absalom's seething hatred targeted not only the actual perpetrator, his half brother Amnon, but also his entire family, and especially his father. It was David's failure to punish his son Amnon appropriately ("When King David heard of all these things, he became very angry, but he would not punish his son Amnon, because he loved him, for he was his firstborn," 2 Sam. 13:21). It is only now that we may, quite appropriately, speculate that David's shame over his own, similar malfeasance in the previous chapter may have had something to do with his catastrophic failure as a father to Tamar, Absalom, Amnon—and all his children, for that matter.

So far, our case study has demonstrated why we need imagination to understand what drives the emotions of biblical protagonists, including God. We have also discovered how an emotionally intelligent imagination enables us to adopt emotions that the biblical text aims to evoke in us—despite its understated presentation—by feeling compassion for Tamar back then and for survivors of rape here and now. However, our example text can also help us to appreciate that we need imagination to resist the adoption of emotions that the text does *not* aim to evoke. We will remain with our case study to explore this further.

First, should we feel sorry for the ten concubines whom David left behind and who fell victim to public rape by one of the sons of their husband (2 Sam. 15:16; 16:20–22; cf. 12:11–12)? Were they not just innocent bystanders? Yes, we should. Here our sympathy is justified.

Second, what about David? It is tempting to feel sorry for him as well. Was he not also just an innocent bystander? In the case of David, the temptation is even bigger because other parts of the Bible, including 1 Samuel 13:14 and Acts 13:22, portray him as a hero of the faith. Yet when we read the story with imagination, we can recognize the culpability of David within the larger picture of the narrative. We can integrate the dark side of David into a more realistic evaluation of the man as a flawed human being that includes his strengths as well as his weaknesses to arrive at a more nuanced, realistic, and truthful evaluation that does justice to all the biblical witness—without distortion or bias and, most importantly, without ignoring what the eleven chapters from 2 Samuel 12 to 22 add to the interpretation of 2 Samuel 11.

Reading with imagination, then, encourages us to pay attention to all the emotions that appear in the texts, and it helps us to critically examine what kinds of emotions the texts aim to evoke in us as we read. In turn, a deeper appreciation for and understanding of emotions enables us to employ our imagination in emotionally intelligent ways to learn how to reject emotions that the biblical texts do not aim to evoke in us even when it may be tempting to do so, as for example in the common Christian tendency to inappropriately sympathize with David and ignore his culpability.

A good case to illustrate this are popular Christian readings that one-sidedly focus on divine grace ("Now the Lord has put away your sin; you shall not die," 2 Sam. 12:13) in response to David's repentance ("I have sinned against the Lord," v. 13). These are now exposed as unimaginative because they ignore the main point of the larger narrative that exposes the seriousness of God's words when the prophet Nathan announces to David that "therefore, the sword shall never depart from your house" (12:10). By contrast, an imaginative reading that focuses on the emotions of all the characters in the story becomes a rich, transformative resource to support modern rape victims in their trauma and inform better, more realistic care for rape survivors here and now. It shows that God cares for them too, just as he cared for the victims then. And it shows that God holds perpetrators of rape accountable, then and now. Finally, it demonstrates that, as Christian churches and as Christian believers, we should care in more practical ways for survivors of rape and that we should hold perpetrators accountable to the full extent of the law.

Among other misinterpretations, we will highlight readers' emotions, such as distorted emotional attitudes toward biblical characters (as, for example, in the case of King David) as well as toward the biblical texts themselves (as, for example, in the case of ethically suspect actions that appear to be endorsed by the biblical texts when they are read unimaginatively; see the episode in Ezek. 24:15–18 discussed above).

Since these unintended emotions lead to misunderstandings, they tend to alienate modern readers from the content of the biblical texts. Again, a failure to engage the texts with imagination frequently leads to misinterpretations. Imaginative reading will not ignore or suppress such emotions, nor will it explain them away in simplistic fashion. Rather, it will use them as prompts for intentional engagement and deep reflection.

A Hermeneutic of Imagination Unlocks the Significance of Specific Emotions

A hermeneutic of imagination draws our attention to the importance of emotions in the biblical texts. It highlights, in fact, the need for a substantial and comprehensive biblical theology of the emotions. A monumental undertaking like this is beyond the scope of this chapter, but in the following sections, we will focus on a small selection of emotions that are especially relevant for a hermeneutic of imagination, in the hope that our initial exploration here will inspire further work in this important area.

Among many emotions worth exploring, we have concentrated on three to illustrate their relevance for a hermeneutic of imagination: awe and wonder; divine wrath; and love for God, neighbor, and self. They exemplify emotions that Scripture reports on or seeks to evoke, beyond those we have considered above. As we shall see, a hermeneutic of imagination is indispensable for reading the relevant texts if we want to read them as the original authors and the Holy Spirit intended.

A Hermeneutic of Imagination Helps Us Experience the Sensations of Awe and Wonder That the Biblical Texts Aim to Inspire

One of the many imaginative aspects of Scripture is that it aims to evoke in us a sense of the grandeur of God and his creation. God's Word does this by stimulating our imagination.

In a volume entitled *Sacred Sense* and subtitled *Discovering the Wonder of God's Word and World*, Old Testament scholar William Brown notes, "Lamentably, whether in Sunday school or in seminary, not much is done in the way of treating Scripture as a source of transforming wonder."[7] In this section, we want to demonstrate that the sensation of awe and wonder stimulates imaginative engagement and promotes spiritual growth. For "without wonder, faith in a God who 'works wonder(s)' remains stuck and stagnant."[8] Conversely, imaginative reading attunes us to this important and fascinating feature of Scripture.

The wonder that Scripture evokes is transformative because it affects our whole being, our bodies, our emotions, our intellect, and our volition. In other words, it fires our imagination and builds our faith. The wonder that Scripture evokes in us helps us imagine a better world and motivates us to become different and better people who contribute to the welfare of others.

Common to all experiences of wonder is how they combine the experience of fascination with a sense of attraction. The experience creates a perception and appreciation of beauty and joy, it has an "affiliative power" that goes far beyond mere curiosity, it arouses a desire to discover more about what has caused it, and it arouses "our desire to venture forth in a new direction."[9] Wonder stimulates our imagination because it is a response to the discovery of something mysterious, and the fascination of it draws us into a journey of exploration and discovery. Frequently, the experience of wonder also evokes a

7. William P. Brown, *Sacred Sense: Discovering the Wonder of God's Word and World* (Eerdmans, 2015), 2.

8. Brown, *Sacred Sense*, 3.

9. Brown, *Sacred Sense*, 6.

spiritual response; it becomes a religious experience of human encounter with the divine, stirring the sensation of proximity with a being who is at once holy and wholly other. Rudolf Otto describes this experience in his groundbreaking study of "the holy" as a *mysterium tremendum et fascinans*, an experience of mystery characterized by both awe and fascination,[10] a sense of reverence more than fear (contra Brown).

There are different kinds of wonder. First, there is wonder that results from a new discovery that unsettles our prior understandings, values, and commitments.[11] This kind of wonder challenges us and encourages us to grow through an invitation to change that may not always be easy but always is rewarding. This "deep sense of wonder counters the 'prettiness' of superficial understandings that identify wonder only with what is pleasing."[12] Texts in Scripture frequently evoke this type of wonder to promote spiritual growth through genuine change in fundamental aspects of our value systems and core beliefs.

Second, there is wonder that arises from the experience of a "sense of perfection in the ordering of the world."[13] Brown describes various kinds of experiences that evoke this sense of wonder: "discovering a hidden pattern, finding a lost connection, or discerning a haunting melody from a seemingly random arrangement of notes."[14] It is the experience of beauty and order, whether in mathematics, science, or the fine arts. "It is what scientists yearn for, what artists strive for, and what the rest of us enjoy in planetariums, concert halls, galleries, and, perhaps best of all, nature."[15] Such experiences are akin to receiving a present, a precious gift.[16] They evoke a sense of being blessed and the sensation of being the recipient of grace.

As we reflect on how biblical texts can evoke in us the experience of wonder as imaginative readers today, it becomes clear that Scripture has the capacity to evoke wonder not only through content that relates sensational events, such as theophanies and miracles, but also through the power and beauty of words and images, and through details in its stories and poems that at first sight seem

10. Brown, *Sacred Sense*, 6n16, citing Rudolf Otto, *The Idea of the Holy: An Inquiry into the Non-Rational Factor in the Idea of the Divine and Its Relation to the Rational* (Oxford University Press, 1958), 12–40.

11. Brown, *Sacred Sense*, 5, citing Celia Deane-Drummond, *Wonder and Wisdom: Conversations in Science, Spirituality and Theology* (Darton, 2006), 1.

12. Brown, *Sacred Sense*, 5, quoting Cecilia González-Andrieu, *Bridge to Wonder: Art as a Gospel of Beauty* (Baylor University Press, 2012), 37.

13. Brown, *Sacred Sense*, 5.

14. Brown, *Sacred Sense*, 6.

15. Brown, *Sacred Sense*, 6.

16. Brown, *Sacred Sense*, 8.

mundane and down to earth. Wonder stimulates our imagination, and in turn our imaginative reading attunes us to Scripture's capacity to evoke wonder and awe at every turn. And when a hermeneutic of imagination attunes us to this wondrous quality of the texts, we will enjoy the experience more and more often. We will delight in Scripture more frequently and more joyfully.

There is a deeply emotional and imaginative quality to discovering how the Bible evokes wonder in us. We will more easily experience gratitude emerging from our growing sense of God's wondrous generosity; we will have a sense of privilege that in turn inspires in us a sense of obligation to match the wonder of divine grace with a more graciously loving attitude toward others. Wonder leads to awe before the God whom we encounter in our reading. "If wonder is what drives good science, if wonder is what inspires great art, perhaps wonder also lies at the heart of biblical faith."[17] And so, reading with wonder also inspires in us a desire to contribute to the common good: "Bible-inspired wonder is what drives many to commit themselves to lives of justice and mercy, wisdom and hope, joy and perseverance, charity and responsibility."[18] There is an intrinsic connection between imagination and wonder.[19] And reading with wonder also has a sensory dimension (Ps. 34:8), something that we already explored earlier in our discussion of imagination.[20]

Reading with wonder and reading for wonder are not extraneous things that we bring to the biblical texts from outside. Rather, the experience of awe and wonder is what inspired the authors of the biblical texts to write down what we now encounter in Scripture, and their sense of wonder can still be felt on almost every page. Each text is "thick with meaning and thin with transparency,"[21] and that is why we need to read with imagination if we want to experience their wondrous nature. The biblical texts do "more than simply recount certain wondrous encounters; they attempt through word and imagery to (re-)create something of an experience of wonder, to

17. Brown, *Sacred Sense*, 10.

18. Brown, *Sacred Sense*, 13.

19. "Reading with wonder is reading not for information . . . or even for answers to urgent questions. It is not a means to a specific end. . . . It is the kind of reading that lingers; it is reading with keen attentiveness, savoring every word and detail. It is reading with readiness for surprise and in the process raising . . . questions and ponderings that stir the imagination and generate thinking. . . . Reading with wonder is responding with wonder" (Brown, *Sacred Sense*, 11). In other words, then, reading with wonder is reading with imagination.

20. "Reading Scripture with wonder requires an openness to seeing, hearing, smelling, tasting and touching something new. Through its evocative use of language, the Bible engages the full range of the senses. Scripture is a full-bodied text that requires full-bodied engagement. 'Taste and see that the Lord is good,' invites the psalmist (34:8)." Brown, *Sacred Sense*, 13.

21. Brown, *Sacred Sense*, 14.

share it, to kindle the reader's imagination and desire."[22] And as we read the words of Scripture with imagination and encounter the care and kindness of God on its every page, we experience the mystery of God's grace anew and respond in kind as we, in turn, become caught up in wonder, love, and praise.

A Hermeneutic of Imagination Inspires a Fresh Perspective on Divine Anger

Anger usually leads to violence, and it is therefore often a negative emotion. However, this is not always the case. Righteous anger is a positive emotion in which God and humans are justifiably angry about what is evil and harmful. A hermeneutic of imagination helps us to see that divine anger in Scripture is always righteous and just, an emotion that grows out of God's love for his creation. God's love for humanity entails two essential expectations: that humans should love him and be devoted to him alone and that humans should love and care for each other. When one or both expectations are violated, God's righteous anger is kindled. Here is not the place for a full exploration of divine wrath, but we want to show how a hermeneutic of imagination helps us to avoid three common misunderstandings that tend to arise when biblical texts mention or describe God's anger.

First is the impression that God gets angry at the slightest provocation and about a wide range of issues. This sentiment is captured well in the early part of an entry on "anger" in a standard dictionary of Old Testament theology: "A large number of times rebellion against his will motivated Yahweh's wrath. . . . [God's] anger proceeds from the disregarding of his will."[23] While true in general, it is nonetheless misleading because it is too vague, as we shall see.

Second, divine anger seems unrestrained because it frequently appears to result in extreme measures, severe judgment, or death. A good example to illustrate how this misunderstanding has arisen appears in 2 Samuel 6:6–8: "When they came to the threshing floor of Nacon, Uzzah reached out his hand to the ark of God and took hold of it, for the oxen lurched. The anger of the Lord was kindled against Uzzah, and God struck him there, and he died there beside the ark of God." This example demonstrates how easy it is to arrive at such misunderstandings. In fact, the very next verse suggests that David, who witnessed the event, felt just like modern

22. Brown, *Sacred Sense*, 14.

23. Bruce Edward Baloian, ed., *New International Dictionary of Old Testament Theology and Exegesis*, vol. 4 (Paternoster, 1996), under "anger."

readers: "David was angry because the LORD had burst forth with an outburst upon Uzzah."[24]

Third, divine wrath is associated with an implacability that cannot be assuaged until God's desire for punishment has been satisfied. Even though the idea has been prominent in Christian theology at least since Augustine, it is most famously expressed in Anselm of Canterbury's book-length treatise *Cur Deus homo*.

A hermeneutic of imagination will help us to correct these misunderstandings. First, it helps us *identify more precisely what motivates divine wrath*. A survey of the Old Testament reveals that, with very few exceptions,[25] divine anger is kindled in response to two things: idolatry and social injustice.[26] In fact, the most frequent motivation for God's anger is his *compassion*, as a response to the maltreatment of fellow humans.[27] What is more, compassion for the oppressed also stirs God's rage when he wants people to intervene on his behalf but they refuse to obey; he also unleashes his anger against those who turn a blind eye and give way before the wicked, thus abandoning the vulnerable to their fate (cf. Prov. 24:10–12; 25:26; Isa. 1:16–17). Moses himself, in the first passage in the Old Testament that describes God as angry, illustrates this.[28] As David Lamb observes, divine anger effectively motivates

24. However, just a few verses later we read that David learned an important lesson from this incident. In his second attempt to retrieve the ark of the Lord, it was transported by pole bearers on foot, accompanied with the required sacrifices, in accordance with the divine decree rather than on a cart, as before. While the text is not explicit, imaginative reading helps us to infer that Uzzah likely did not belong to the personnel (priest and Levites) who were allowed to touch the ark, and that the casual way the ark was being transported contributed to Uzzah's unfortunate end.

25. The incident in 2 Sam. 6:6–8 mentioned above is one such exception. The provocation seems to have been a disrespect for God evident in the casual treatment of the ark.

26. Baloian has also recognized this. When texts include the reasons for God's wrath, almost all mention one of two reasons: social injustice, "the wickedness of human beings in their behavior towards one another," or idolatry, "pride, syncretism, or blatant idolatry" (Baloian, *New International Dictionary*, under "anger"). While there are other things that God considers wrong and thus sinful, it is these two that provoke God's anger.

27. David Lamb has demonstrated this in an analysis of the exodus (Exod. 2:23–4:17). In response to the maltreated Israelites in Egypt who cry out to him for help, God's anger is kindled and moves him to rescue them by pouring out his anger upon those who abuse them. See David Lamb, "Compassion and Wrath as Motivations for Divine Warfare," in *Holy War in the Bible: Christian Morality and an Old Testament Problem*, ed. Heath Thomas, Jeremy A. Evans, and Paul Copan (IVP Academic, 2013), 131–49.

28. In response to the divine call, "So I will send you to Pharaoh to bring my people, the Israelites, out of Egypt" (Exod. 3:10; note that Moses is commissioned to confront the powerful perpetrator to achieve this), Moses raises a series of objections (Exod. 3:11, 13; 4:1, 10, 13–14). With the fifth and final objection, when Moses attempts to outright refuse the divine commission—"O my Lord, please send someone else"—the Lord becomes angry (4:13), a sentiment that

Moses to action.[29] Such anger is a good anger, a "highly compelling" anger, and "even worthy of praise."[30]

Second and third, a hermeneutic of imagination reveals that God's punitive response to provocation tends to be nuanced and proportionate to the severity of the offense. In fact, God frequently refrains from punishing offenders to the full extent of the law and urges his people to do the same. Related to this, God tends to be patient and slow to anger, and his anger over sin subsides quickly (Ps. 103:8–9). We will explore this with an analysis of the self-revelation of God's "name" in Exodus 34:5–12, part of the aftermath of the golden calf incident (Exod. 32:1–6), which provoked God's wrath: "Now let me alone so that my wrath may burn hot against them and I may consume them, and of you I will make a great nation" (32:10).

Reading the divine injunction "now leave me alone so that my wrath may . . . consume them" with imagination, we note intentional similarities with God prompting Abraham to intercede against God's express intention to destroy Sodom and Gomorrah in Genesis 18. Comments Yochanan Muffs, "If God is determined to destroy these sinful cities, why does He at the last moment have second thoughts and tell His prophet? Surely He realizes that Abraham might begin to pray, and that a battle of words and unpleasant bargaining is liable to develop."[31] It is easy to imagine that the same sentiments motivated God to volunteer his destructive intentions here. He wanted to motivate Moses to intercede for his people.

After Moses achieves the divine purpose to change God's mind, however, the plot thickens. Moses asks the Lord to show him his glory (Exod. 33:18), and the Lord agrees. He promises, "I will make all my goodness pass before you and will proclaim before you the name, 'The Lord,' and I will be gracious to whom I will be gracious and will show mercy on whom I will show mercy" (33:19). And in the morning, God indeed revealed himself as "a God merciful and gracious, slow to anger, and abounding in steadfast love and faithfulness . . . yet by no means clearing the guilty" (34:6–7).

Moses would have perceived from the tone of voice in which God gave the following instructions (4:14–17), since he stops objecting and obeys.

29. "Yhwh's call to Moses is connected to [the Israelites'] cry for help (Ex 3:23). Moses' unwillingness to help deliver his own relatives provokes a strong response of anger from God. Yhwh was angry that Moses was unwilling to participate in his act of compassion. Yhwh was not willing to let Moses' lack of compassion prevent him from delivering Israel from Egyptian bondage." Lamb, "Compassion and Wrath," 135–36.

30. Lamb, "Compassion and Wrath," 149.

31. Yochanan Muffs, *Love and Joy: Law, Language, and Religion in Ancient Israel* (Jewish Theological Seminary of America; Harvard University Press, 1992), 10.

A hermeneutic of imagination helps us to see that God's anger is not in competition with his love. Both are essential to who he is. It is *love* that motivates the divine anger, as the prominent place of this self-revelation throughout the Old Testament demonstrates. Acquiring the quality of a creedal statement, it expresses the heartbeat of the Old Testament.[32] In God, love for the vulnerable and anger against their oppressors belong together. Psalm 103:8–9 also illustrates the point: "The Lord is merciful and gracious, slow to anger and abounding in steadfast love. He will not always accuse, nor will he keep his anger forever." The phrase "nor will he keep his anger forever" is a litotes, a rhetorical figure that emphasizes something by denying its opposite. Reading with imagination helps us to see that not only is God slow to anger, but he is also quick to let go of his anger. For God, anger and love are of a piece.

A Hermeneutic of Imagination Helps Us Embody the Love of God, Neighbor, and Self That the Biblical Texts Aim to Inspire

As far as we know, the double love of God and neighbor as the supreme goals for reading the Bible was first proposed by Saint Augustine, who was inspired by Jesus's identification of love of God and neighbor as the two greatest commandments (Matt. 22:37–40). Jesus explained that "on these two commandments hang all the Law and the Prophets" (22:40). Jesus builds his response on two key passages from the Old Testament: Deuteronomy 6:5, where Moses reminds the people of God to love their God passionately, and Leviticus 19:18, where God urges his people to love their neighbors, even in the face of provocation. The reference to "all the Law and the Prophets" is shorthand for the Scriptures that formed the Bible in Jesus's day.

Crucially, the two commandments are said to be the hooks on which all of Scripture hangs, a visual metaphor that prioritizes love for God and neighbor as the supreme goal that God had in mind when he inspired all the books in the Bible through the Holy Spirit. A hermeneutic of imagination thus alerts us to a sobering truth: Readings of the Bible that do not aim for love of God and neighbor or that fail to reach these goals fail to understand the express will of God.[33] Thus, it inspires in us a passionately intimate love for God and a deep affection and fondness for all human beings.

32. Mark J. Boda, *The Heartbeat of Old Testament Theology: Three Creedal Expressions*, Acadia Studies in Bible and Theology (Baker Academic, 2017).

33. As Brown notes, "The ultimate test of exegetical 'correctness,' which for Augustine begins with the literal sense, is whether one's interpretation 'contribut[es] to the reign of charity.'" William P. Brown, *Seeing the Psalms: A Theology of Metaphor* (Westminster John Knox, 2002), 12, quoting Augustine, *De doctrina christiana* 3.15.23.

Any reading of the Bible that does not inspire love for God and love for our neighbor is a misreading of the Word of God. All texts in the Bible promote love for God and love for our neighbor. Only readings that promote love for God and love for our neighbor are accurate interpretations of the Bible. And it is reading with imagination that helps us to arrive at such interpretations.

Many Christians think that they cannot properly love God unless they sometimes do not love their neighbor as themselves. Many other Christians think that they cannot love their neighbor as themselves unless they sometimes do not love God with *all* their heart, *all* their soul, or *all* their mind. A hermeneutic of imagination helps us understand that both assumptions are logically flawed and untenable. Since the double command to love God and love our neighbor as ourselves is the express purpose and goal of the Bible, there is no competition between love for God on the one hand and love for our neighbor on the other. And this prevents us from interpreting texts that promote the love of God in ways that diminish care for our neighbor. And conversely, it prevents us from interpreting texts that promote care for our neighbor in ways that undermine our loving submission to God's will.

A hermeneutic of imagination helps us to remember several things: We cannot love our neighbor as ourselves unless we also love God; we cannot love God with all our heart, soul, and mind unless we also love our neighbor as ourselves; we cannot love God or neighbor unless we also love ourselves; and ultimately, we cannot love ourselves unless we love *God and our neighbor* with all our heart, all our soul, and all our mind.

Ellen Charry puts it similarly: "Self-love is the happy life because it is the way of obedience, quite apart from simply enjoying objects of desire."[34] Pursuing the moral life *is* self-love. "God, and only God, can heal love by retargeting and empowering us to love rightly and well."[35] Here, finally, is a love triangle in which everybody wins, a love triangle where each loves all without diminishing any.

The Bible exists to generate love—love of God, neighbor, and self—as James Andrews puts it in his commentary on Augustine's *On Christian Doctrine*:

> The church, in need of instruction in how to love God and neighbor, turns attentively to scripture to hear the will of God spoken through the historical words of the prophets and apostles, turns to hear so as to act in accordance with what is heard.[36]

34. Ellen T. Charry, *God and the Art of Happiness* (Eerdmans, 2010), 161.
35. Charry, *God and the Art of Happiness*, 158.
36. James A. Andrews, *Hermeneutics and the Church: In Dialogue with Augustine* (University of Notre Dame Press, 2012), 218.

How is it then that the written record of the Word of God has acquired such a reputation for generating hatred, love's opposite? It is because the church, the community of those who recognize the Bible as Scripture, consists of flawed human beings. We tend to read it in ways that justify who we are and how we behave. And yet, "because the church is sinful, ever in need of God's gracious guidance, scripture exists: 'it is—or ought to be—a knife at the church's heart.'"[37] And a hermeneutic of imagination encourages us to let Scripture do its transformative work, to let it do what it is meant to do:

> That is the *telos* of scripture: the reestablishment of fellowship between God and humanity, fellowship between humans and their neighbors, in other words, the creation of the double love of God and neighbor, the restoration of fellowship sundered by sin. Such a *telos* requires an understanding of the reader as one who lacks this double love and who needs to be shown how to love appropriately.[38]

The Bible has always generated love for God, others, and self, and a hermeneutic of imagination helps us rediscover this. As we read with this in mind, we cannot but be inspired to love ourselves through the recognition of how loved we are by him who most deserves to be loved.[39] We cannot but respond with love for the God who first loved us, and to respond with love for all and everything around us, because everything and everyone around us are equally loved by God. We are liberated to love ourselves properly, as we were meant to, not at the expense of others but because we love who we have become through loving others. In the final analysis, then, loving others as ourselves enables us to "love kindness" (Mic. 6:8), to love how we love others, and to love ourselves as we love them.

A hermeneutic of imagination informs not only our beliefs but also our actions. Orthodoxy and orthopraxy belong together.

> Because of scripture's role in the economy of salvation, one must supplement the rule of faith with the rule of love. In line with its *telos*, reading scripture is ultimately about living in the here and now on the way to proper fellowship with God *and with one another*. The *regula fidei* establishes the overarching

37. Andrews, *Hermeneutics and the Church*, 218, quoting John Webster, *Word and Church: Essays in Christian Dogmatics*, 2nd rev. ed. (Bloomsbury T&T Clark, 2016), 46.

38. Andrews, *Hermeneutics and the Church*, 219.

39. "To speak about God therefore means to speak of what God does for me, that he loves me, a sinner. If saying yes to what he does for me means that I say yes to his love for me in my letting-him-do-this, then to love God means, in an existential sense, to let-oneself-be-loved-by-him." Hannelore Jauss, *Der liebebedürftige Gott und die gottbedürftige Liebe des Menschen: Ursprung und Funktion der Rede von der Liebe des Menschen zu Gott als alttestamtentlicher Beitrag zur Gotteslehre*, Beiträge zum Verstehen der Bibel 25 (Lit Verlag, 2014), 550 (our translation).

> narrative of scripture, the specific things one finds there about God and his creation. But again, the Christian faith is about more than intellectual assent. At its most basic level, there are always two aspects to faith—understanding and relationship. For that reason, scriptural interpretation operates with a second rule, the *regula dilectionis*, understanding how a passage connects to love, the primary driving force of the Christian life. That is, the rule of love, like the rule of faith, norms the reading of scripture.[40]

If our reading of the Bible only informs what we believe and fails to shape how we feel and behave, we have not understood what God's Word wants to teach us: "So anyone who thinks that he has understood the divine scriptures or any part of them, but cannot by his understanding build up this double love of God and neighbour, has not yet succeeded in understanding them."[41] Comments Andrews: "It is not enough, therefore, simply to read scripture theologically in light of the rule of faith; one must also read it in light of the rule of love."[42] How a hermeneutic of imagination motivates love for neighbor in public life we will explore below in chapter 8.

Conclusion

Modern readers who fail to read Scripture with imagination regularly miss the transformative power of the emotions that biblical texts reflect and evoke. Not all negative emotions are bad emotions.

While we have not had time to explore this fully, a hermeneutic of imagination will help prevent the evocation of unintended emotions. Such emotions are stirred up inadvertently, often through simple misunderstandings due to cultural differences. Since these unintended emotions also lead to misinterpretations, they unnecessarily alienate modern readers. Imaginative reading will not ignore or suppress such emotions, nor will it explain them away in simplistic fashion. Rather, it will use them as prompts for intentional engagement and deep reflection.

Readers tend to assume that the Bible aims to evoke only "positive" emotions in its readers, such as compassion or love. In line with our observations about the combination of divine love and anger, however, a hermeneutic of imagination helps us to discover that the Bible frequently aims to evoke *righteous anger* in readers, usually against perpetrators who victimize other

40. Andrews, *Hermeneutics and the Church*, 223.

41. Augustine, *On Christian Doctrine* 1.36.40, in Augustine, *On Christian Teaching*, trans. Roger P. H. Green (Oxford University Press, 2008), 27.

42. Andrews, *Hermeneutics and the Church*, 224.

human beings. Imaginative reading reveals that the Bible aims to promote compassion for and solidarity with the *victims* who appear in its texts, and the flip side of this support for victims is the evocation of revulsion toward the perpetrators.

Bible readers, like their God, are meant to develop righteous anger, leading to a desire to go beyond caring for the victims and to hold perpetrators accountable for their crimes. This kind of righteous anger is designed to motivate readers of the Bible to be actively involved in issues related to social justice by tending to the needs of the victims and defending them against their oppressors—taking on the wicked and opposing their exploitative schemes *before* they can harm others.

CHAPTER FIVE

A Hermeneutic of Imagination Draws Attention to the Humorous Dimensions of Scripture

It is important to recognize humor when we read biblical texts. If we miss it where it is present, we will misinterpret the Bible. And traditional methods of reading have frequently missed humorous aspects in Scripture.[1] Building on our initial comments in chapter 2, we begin with a case study on Micah 6:6–8 to demonstrate the importance of imagination for identifying and accurately interpreting humor in the Bible—missing the humor in this passage has devastating consequences. As we shall see, a hermeneutic of imagination helps us see humor where other reading methods have failed. Accurate detection and interpretation rely on subject-specific knowledge in the field of humor studies to inform our imagination. Following the case study we will therefore cover the universality of humor and briefly explore traditional and modern theories of humor. We will demonstrate how insights from the field of humor studies informed our imaginative reading of Micah 6:6–8, insights that are transferable to other humorous texts in the Bible.

1. See, e.g., Yehuda Thomas Radday, "On Missing the Humour in the Bible: An Introduction," in *On Humour and the Comic in the Hebrew Bible*, ed. Yehuda Thomas Radday and Athalya Brenner-Idan, Journal for the Study of the Old Testament Supplement 92 (Almond Press, 1990), 21–38.

Devout Piety or Scatological Sarcasm? A Case Study on Micah 6:6–8

We are picking up from two brief observations earlier in chapter 2. There, we first used this passage to illustrate how imagination can help us see problematic details in Scripture as opportunities for deeper exploration leading to new insights. We also used it to illustrate that intentional ambiguity, even and especially when it is less obvious and thus more difficult to detect, invites imaginative engagement and promises immense reward. Now we dive deeper into the passage to demonstrate that reading passages like this and many others in Scripture demand an imaginative approach that is attuned to the dynamics of humor in literary texts.

To recap, Micah 6:6–7 records an inquiry to the prophet Micah, quoted here from the traditional translation of the NRSV: "With what shall I come before the Lord, and bow myself before God on high? Shall I come before him with burnt offerings, with calves a year old? Will the Lord be pleased with thousands of rams, with ten thousands of rivers of oil? Shall I give my firstborn for my transgression, the fruit of my body for the sin of my soul?"

We noted that interpreters tend to take these questions at face value—as a sincere inquiry by a "concerned citizen" who is convicted by the prophet's words in 6:1–5 and who now seeks to repent. They are taken as expressions of sincere and pious devotion. We noted that, consequently, most interpreters feel compelled to make this offer to sacrifice one's firstborn child sound more acceptable than it is.[2] Here we look at a few examples in more depth, also paying attention to the wider context.

Micah 6:1–8 is typically subdivided into two parts, a "covenant lawsuit" in verses 1–5 and a "Torah liturgy" in verses 6–8.[3] The first part is a tirade in which the Lord addresses his people through the words of the prophet, accusing them of having broken their covenant with God. The second part is presented in a question-answer form, and "the question-answer section is the people's response to the suit brought against them. Verse 8 is the prophet's response to the people's questions."[4] Ralph Smith's interpretation is representative:

> If vv 6–8 are related to vv 1–5, they supply Israel's response to the implied charge against her. She had displeased Yahweh but she claims ignorance. She asks God what he wants. What must she bring with her when she comes into

2. Francis I. Andersen and David Noel Freedman, *Micah: A New Translation with Introduction and Commentary*, 1st ed., The Anchor Bible 24E (Doubleday, 2000), 523–24; and Ralph L. Smith, *Micah–Malachi*, Word Biblical Commentary 32 (Word, 1984), 50–51.

3. Smith, *Micah–Malachi*, 50.

4. Smith, *Micah–Malachi*, 50.

> his presence that will make her acceptable? This question represents one of the two basic ideas about religion. How can man approach God? One answer is: with sacrifice, things, good works.[5]

In Smith's view, the items the inquirer lists as possible offerings to God are presented sincerely:

> The questions about sacrifice are comprehensive. Burnt offerings *represented* total dedication. Calves a year old *represented* the most desirable kind of sacrificial animal. Thousands of rams and ten thousand rivers of oil *represented* lavish sacrifice. One's first-born *represents* one's most valuable possession.[6]

Smith assumes that the language is not entirely literal, as the repeated verb *represented* or *represents* (four times) indicates. Smith implicitly hints that the *quantities* of the various provisions may be hyperbolic. Nonetheless, the burnt offerings are real offerings, the calves are real calves, the rams are real rams, the oil is real oil, and the firstborn is a real child.

Francis Andersen and David Noel Freedman, by comparison and contrast, go one step further. For them, the proposed items in the list of offerings are "the typical oblations of the regular cult,"[7] including the firstborn, as the following comment demonstrates: "It would seem that all such remedies, including the sacrifice of a child, *were serious options for everyone*, king and citizen alike, at that time."[8]

They even consider the stated amounts and values of the offerings as earnest propositions: "the quantities are rich, extravagant, as is fitting."[9] The list of offerings and their quantities is taken to have been proposed sincerely, as a remark on verse 6 reveals: "Here is the voice of one concerned citizen, prepared to take the most drastic measures."[10] So earnest is this concerned citizen's proposal to sacrifice their own child to God that Andersen and Freedman take pains to make it appear more reasonable and more acceptable than it is: "Far from indicating cruelty or callousness of parent towards the child, the action gained poignancy and efficacy precisely from the fact that the child was treasured; it was the person's most treasured possession."[11] Moreover, Andersen and Freedman attempt to justify

5. Smith, *Micah–Malachi*, 51.
6. Smith, *Micah–Malachi*, 51 (emphasis added).
7. Andersen and Freedman, *Micah*, 523.
8. Andersen and Freedman, *Micah*, 524 (emphasis added).
9. Andersen and Freedman, *Micah*, 523.
10. Andersen and Freedman, *Micah*, 524.
11. Andersen and Freedman, *Micah*, 524.

their concerned citizen's proposal to sacrifice their child with theological arguments:

> Recognizing that in Israel all sacrifice was not only representative, but in some sense substitutionary, then, the closer the affinity between the sacrificer and the sacrifice, the more valuable and efficacious the sacrifice. If the truly ultimate sacrifice is one's self, then the offering of the firstborn son is legally, biologically, and relationally the closest we can come to self-sacrifice.[12]

Andersen and Freedman's "concerned citizen," then, is not only serious and sincere; his intention to sacrifice his own firstborn son also makes him a *model* citizen—from Andersen and Freedman's theological perspective, at least.

So, does the Bible suggest that child sacrifice is an acceptable way for approaching God? Smith, Andersen, and Freedman, representative of many, seem to think so. In fact, there is a broad consensus that it was at the time. Heath Dewrell's monograph *Child Sacrifice in Ancient Israel*, the most comprehensive study on the subject to date, also demonstrates this.[13] He introduces verses 6–7 with the comment that "the Israelites themselves reply, asking what they must do to get Yahweh to act in the present."[14] Dewrell considers the supplicant's assumption that Yahweh might be pleased with the sacrifice of one's child as "striking," but he also takes it as sincere: "Micah implies that his listeners believed that Yahweh could potentially be persuaded to act by the sacrifice of a firstborn child." He then continues:

> There is no indication in the text of Mic 6:1–8 that firstborn sacrifice was understood as qualitatively different from the sacrifice of calves, ram, or oil. Indeed, the logic of the oracle seems to proceed from sacrifices that would have been perceived as acceptable (burnt offerings of calves) to those that would have been viewed as even more effective (thousands of rams and myriads of oil), finally culminating in the most precious of all possible sacrifices—the offering of a firstborn child. The rhetoric of the oracle demands that Yahweh be understood as viewing such a sacrifice as not only pleasing but as even more pleasing than untold quantities of other, less precious offerings. *The sacrifice*

12. Andersen and Freedman, *Micah*, 524.

13. Heath D. Dewrell, *Child Sacrifice in Ancient Israel*, Explorations in Ancient Near Eastern Civilizations 5 (Eisenbrauns, 2017). The discussion of Mic. 6:1–8 appears on pp. 99–108.

14. Dewrell, *Child Sacrifice in Ancient Israel*, 100. In a footnote to his translation of the text of verse 7, he states: "נפשי, originally and most literally 'my throat,' parallel to בטני 'my belly,' earlier in the line. Unfortunately, the pun does not translate well into English" (Dewrell, *Child Sacrifice in Ancient Israel*, 100n24). As we shall see, this was a missed opportunity. Dewrell neglects the function of the pun. Once its humorous purpose is uncovered, the pun does, in fact, translate very well.

> *of one's firstborn child is depicted as extraordinary, but there is no indication that the oracle is presenting the sacrifice as in any way intrinsically unsuitable.* Thus, the context of the oracle implies that all of the offerings are extremely valuable and, at least in theory, acceptable, even if current circumstances had caused Yahweh to reject *all* sacrifices as ineffective.[15]

In other words, Dewrell interprets the passage to reflect the legitimacy of child sacrifice in the Bible. He concludes his discussion of the passage by identifying the proposed sacrifice of the inquirer's firstborn child as a mode of child sacrifice under desperate circumstances,[16] similar to King Mesha sacrificing his son to avert defeat in a war against a coalition of Israelites, Judeans, and Moabites in 2 Kings 3: "The sacrifices of both Mesha and Micah . . . are offered in situations of distress requiring extraordinary divine intervention,"[17] as sacrifices of last resort "during desperate circumstances."[18]

This brief review of standard treatments of the Micah passage illustrates the devastating consequences that can arise when interpreters miss the humor in biblical texts. This high-stakes example reveals two dangerous consequences that emerge from traditional interpretations. On the one hand, scholars like Dewrell conclude that child sacrifice is explicitly legitimized in the Bible. The consequence here is that the Bible's credibility as a reliable and authoritative guide in religious practice is undermined. On the other hand, scholars like Andersen and Freedman, while aiming to defend biblical credibility, perforce make child sacrifice in the Bible sound more acceptable than it is. This tends to promote attitudes and behaviors that prioritize religious practice at the expense of children's well-being, even though modern parents do not sacrifice their children in a literal sense. The consequence here is that the Bible becomes a means to legitimate abusive behavior toward the vulnerable. The first consequence creates a theological problem regarding the Bible's credibility. The second consequence creates an ethical problem regarding the Bible's capacity to serve as a reliable guide for human behavior.

15. Dewrell, *Child Sacrifice in Ancient Israel*, 102–3 (emphasis added).

16. Dewrell, *Child Sacrifice in Ancient Israel*, 107–8.

17. Dewrell, *Child Sacrifice in Ancient Israel*, 107. We do not have space to explore the Meshah episode at the level it deserves. Suffice it to say that, in contrast with Dewrell, we explain the efficacy of his sacrifice not with recourse to Israelite beliefs in its legitimacy but rather against the background of occult foreign practices that—effective though they were due to demonic influence—were prohibited in Israel. For a sustained argument on the potential efficacy of such practices, see Esther E. Acolatse, *Powers, Principalities, and the Spirit: Biblical Realism in Africa and the West* (Eerdmans, 2018).

18. Dewrell, *Child Sacrifice in Ancient Israel*, 108.

In the face of this, a more imaginative engagement with biblical texts that reckons with and competently identifies the humor in passages like Micah 6:6–7 makes an invaluable contribution to the Bible's theological credibility and ethical veracity.

Earlier in chapter 2, we noted that ambiguity in Micah 6:6–7 is far from obvious, and this is why traditional interpretations have missed it as well as its humorous function. Interpreters have seen only the obvious, superficial meaning of the passage. Its deliberate sarcasm with its blasphemous defiance has escaped their attention because it is so unexpected in a sacred religious text like the Bible. Here only an imagination that enables us to step into the shoes of the offended audience at the receiving end of the prophetic invective (see chap. 4) together with careful observation of what is said and how it is said (see chaps. 1–3) can help us to identify the humorous sarcasm in this series of questions. The passage demands intense imaginative engagement, yet the interpretive investment offers rich returns.

Our imaginative reading identifies three aspects in Micah 6:1–8 that expose the blasphemous sarcasm in verses 6–7. We will begin with an analysis of the interlocutors in verses 1–7, especially looking at how the speaker and the addressee are presented. Then we will consider the list of proposed sacrifices, with special attention to their value, their respective quantities, and the sequence in which they appear. Third and finally, we will explore the humorously sarcastic quality of the ambiguous expression פְּרִי בִטְנִי חַטַּאת נַפְשִׁי (lit. "the fruit of my belly [for] the sin of my throat").

A Comparison Between the Dynamic of Interlocutors in Micah 6:1–5 and 6:6–7

Even though in Micah 6:1–5 God speaks to the people of Jerusalem through the prophet Micah, the prophet reports the divine message in direct speech. Consequently, here God refers to himself using the first-person singular and addresses his people in the second person by means of imperatives and second-person pronoun suffixes. This creates the impression of an intensely immediate, personal, and intimate connection between speaker and audience that sets up a contrast with what follows.

In Micah 6:6–7, the speaker (a representative of the people) responds to the divine speech without speaking to God directly. Rather, he *speaks to* the prophet and only *talks about* God in the third person.[19] What is more, the

19. Andersen and Freedman have already noticed this, even though they misconstrue its significance: "The use of third-person pronouns ('he') rather than direct address ('thou') suggests a certain distance between the speaker and Yahweh. The language could imply an actual absence

petitioner's vocabulary in reference to God is sparse and creates distance. For example, the description of the Lord as "an exalted God" may not reflect deference. Rather, once we read with imagination, it is not difficult to conjure up the phrase being performed in an overstated tone expressive of sarcastically hyperbolical exaggeration, a mock concession of divine superiority that the speaker resents and ultimately rejects. In comparison with God's intensely personal appeal, the human response lacks personal touch and directness. It is studiously formal and indirect and uses formulations that create distance. In conclusion, the speaker uses language that betrays his sense of alienation from his deity. As we shall see, this contrast feeds into the humorous quality of verses 6–7.

The Value, Quantity, and Sequence of Proposed Sacrifices in Micah 6:6–7

In response to the divine challenge from the prophet's mouth, an individual retorts with a sequence of four questions in which he apparently requests confirmation regarding the suitability of six items for the purpose of appeasing divine wrath triggered by his sin (חַטַּאת נַפְשִׁי, "the sin of my soul [lit. 'throat']," v. 7). However, the series of proposed sacrifices does not list items that belong to the same category or progress smoothly from less to more valuable to express the speaker's desperation and sincerity, as traditional interpretations assume.[20] Rather, the reference to "burnt offerings" is specified as several "one-year-old calves."[21] This already is a lavish offering,[22] but perhaps

---

of Yahweh in the perception of the speaker. To whom, in that case, would such questions be addressed? Are they purely rhetorical, as the person asks himself what they might do? Does the speaker expect the prophet to arbitrate? . . . So it is possible that this oblique language is the protocol of social distance, of servility, in which an inferior avoids second-person pronouns, and even first-person forms, casting the whole into third person. Here, however, the 'I' is prominent" (Andersen and Freedman, *Micah*, 524). Andersen and Freedman correctly note the unusual quality of the speaker's use of language, the "certain distance" between the speaker and his God, but their explanation fails to account for it. There is no deference here; the prominent use of first-person verbs and pronouns in the speaker's questions contradicts this, a prominence that Andersen and Freedman note but cannot explain.

20. Note, e.g., Dewrell's comment, quoted above: "The logic of the oracle seems to proceed from sacrifices that would have been perceived as *acceptable* (burnt offerings of calves) to those that would have been viewed as *even more effective* (thousands of rams and myriads of oil), finally culminating in *the most precious of all* possible sacrifices—the offering of a firstborn child." Dewrell, *Child Sacrifice in Ancient Israel*, 102 (emphasis added).

21. Frank Moore Cross, "A Phoenician Inscription from Idalion: Some Old and New Texts Relating to Child Sacrifice," in *Scripture and Other Artifacts: Essays in Honor of Philip J. King*, ed. M. D. Coogan, J. C. Exum, and L. E. Stager (Westminster John Knox, 1994), 99, cited approvingly by Andersen and Freedman, *Micah*, 523.

22. "Calves a year old represented the most desirable kind of sacrificial animal." Smith, *Micah–Malachi*, 51.

an understandable one if the speaker were both well-to-do and plagued by an intense sense of guilt and sincere remorse over his sins.

The items in the next question, however, are less valuable. Rams are less valuable than calves, and oil is less valuable than rams. Despite this, however, the value of these offerings is artificially inflated through their unrealistic quantities, "*thousands* of rams" (בְּאַלְפֵי אֵילִים) and "*ten thousands of rivers* of oil" (בְּרִבְבוֹת נַחֲלֵי־שָׁמֶן, v. 7). So many rams all at once are practically inconceivable as an offering brought by an individual, unless that individual were the king of a prosperous country.[23] Similarly, "rivers of oil" (נַחֲלֵי־שָׁמֶן) refers to a quantity of oil that is unpractical, even fantastical, in and of itself, and that is before we take into consideration that the speaker is inquiring whether "*tens* of thousands" (רִבְבוֹת) of these would be enough. One might argue that the large number is meant simply to indicate a very large quantity,[24] and this is how it is typically understood, but this does not explain how such a large number of *rivers* of oil could possibly be presented by an individual or even an entire community. While the items are less valuable, their quantities are intentionally exaggerated, fantastical, and thus blatantly unrealistic. As we shall see, this combination is a deliberate technique to create sarcasm through partial incongruence paired with extreme exaggeration.

The value of the next item in the list, now in conspicuous contrast as a singular item, nonetheless far surpasses the value of all the others—בְּכוֹרִי, "my firstborn." The speaker inquires whether his firstborn child would be sufficient to appease God's wrath. Is he serious? We think not, despite the scholarly consensus.[25] Rather, flinging the offer to sacrifice his firstborn child in the prophet's face, he intends it as an acerbic insult to God, for it sarcastically

23. According to 1 Kings 8, King Solomon offered so many sacrifices in the form of sheep and cattle during the procession of the ark of the covenant to the newly built temple that they could not be counted (vv. 4–5); and after the temple's dedication, he offered 22,000 cattle and 120,000 sheep over a fifteen-day period (vv. 63–64).

24. Ludwig Koehler, Walter Baumgartner, and Johann Jakob Stamm, *The Hebrew and Aramaic Lexicon of the Old Testament*, trans. M. E. J. Richardson (Brill, 2001), 2:1175.

25. Child sacrifice was practiced in the ancient Near East, including Israel and Judah. (A particularly disturbing example is the sacrifice of Jephthah's daughter in Judg. 11.) In fact, Israel's God famously claimed all firstborn children in Israel as his own, to be redeemed through the substitutionary slaughter of an animal or a cash payment. Heath Dewrell explains: "In most cases, firstborn children are to be 'redeemed' via the offering of a sheep (e.g., Exod 34:19–20) or a cash payment to the priests (e.g., Num 18:15–16). But in at least one case no form of redemption is mentioned (Exod 22:28–29), possibly indicating that firstborn children were sacrificed in some Yahwistic circles" (Dewrell, "Child Sacrifice in Ancient Israel," *Ancient Near East Today* 5, no. 12 [December 2017], http://www.asor.org/anetoday/2017/12/child-sacrifice-ancient-israel). However, reading the relevant texts with imagination, we disagree with Dewrell's speculation that the lack of a form of redemption in Exod. 22:28–29 may indicate biblical legitimization of child sacrifice. Rather, the strong tradition of children supposed to be redeemed elsewhere in

combines what appears to be the ultimate sacrifice with a practice that is explicitly prohibited according to the biblical witness. The offer of the "firstborn" is insincere, and the next phrase, "the fruit of my belly for the sin of my throat," provides further evidence in favor of this conclusion.

The Ambiguous Quality and Humorous Function of the Phrase "the Fruit of My Belly for the Sin of My Throat" in Micah 6:7

The next phrase, considered superfluous or simply ornamental by most interpreters and thus rarely commented on,[26] exposes the real intention behind the speaker's mention of his firstborn.

The phrase tends to be translated in somewhat interpretive fashion, as in the NRSV's and the NIV's "the fruit of my body for the sin of my soul." Translations like this aim to be more readable by decoding—or so the translators think—two popular metaphors commonly considered "dead" and thus in need of paraphrase to unearth what they "really" mean.[27] (For a critique of such "decoding" of figurative language, see chap. 3 above. For a critique of such translation techniques, see chap. 6 below.) The two expressions in question are the words **בִּטְנִי**, "my belly," and **נַפְשִׁי**, "my throat." Unimaginative translations like the above, common as they are, effectively remove ambiguity and consequently obscure two powerful wordplays that make the statement such a clever, albeit offensive, insult in the original, which literally reads "the fruit of my *belly* for the sin of my *throat*" (the two metaphors, which also function as wordplays, are italicized).[28]

Scripture suggests that this practice is implied here too: Absence of evidence (in Exod. 22:28–29) is not evidence of absence.

26. If it is at all discussed it is typically presented as a simple paraphrase. Sometimes it is seen as emphatic, but there is no reflection on the purpose and function of such emphasis.

27. The Wycliffe Bible has "the fruit of my *womb* for the sin of my soul," taking the reference to the belly to be a metonymy for the female reproductive organ. Most translations shy away from this option because the speaker is presumably male. The Good News Bible's interpretive translation goes even further: "my firstborn child to pay for my sins."

28. For detailed discussions of both terms that reveal their metaphoric potential, see Silvia Schroer and Thomas Staubli, *Body Symbolism in the Bible* (Liturgical Press, 2001), 56–67, 68–82. Elsewhere in the Old Testament, the phrase "the fruit of my belly" does indeed refer to the corporate womb of Israel, as for example in Deut. 28:18: "Cursed shall be the fruit of your womb (אָרוּר פְּרִי־בִטְנְךָ), the fruit of your ground, the increase of your cattle and the issue of your flock." Here the nation of Israel is addressed as a single male who, nonetheless, has a "belly" that figuratively represents the wombs of all Israelite women. In this meaning of the phrase, the representative Israelite speaker in Mic. 6:6–7 ostensibly references various passages where God has promised to bless Israel in the past, such as Deut. 28:4: "Blessed shall be the fruit of your womb (פְּרִי־בִטְנְךָ), the fruit of your ground, and the fruit of your livestock, both the increase of your cattle and the issue of your flock." See also Deut. 7:13 and 28:11. Similarly,

But what is so funny yet offensive, even blasphemous, about this apparently innocuous expression? Answer: it contains two amphibologies (phrases that have two or more intended meanings), so it only looks innocent when in reality it has second meanings that form a slur that is only slightly disguised in the Hebrew.

A literal translation reveals alternative meaning potential: "the fruit of my belly for the sin of my throat." The expression "sin of my throat" can also refer to the speaker's consumption of unclean food. This hypothesis gains momentum through a similar formulation in Proverbs 18:20: "From the fruit of a man's mouth (מִפְּרִי פִי־אִישׁ) his belly is filled (תִּשְׂבַּע בִּטְנוֹ); the yield of the lips brings fullness (תְּבוּאַת שְׂפָתָיו יִשְׂבָּע)" (AT). Here the fruit of the mouth metaphorically refers to food that fills the stomach, which suggests a common structural metaphor for both expressions. Once this double entendre has been discovered, then, it is only a small step to a reinterpretation of the expression "the fruit of my belly." The "fruit" of the belly refers not only to children but also to excrement, waste matter discharged from the bowels after the unclean food has been digested. This may appear far-fetched initially, but reluctance to take this interpretive move has more to do with reader expectations and the offensive nature of the wordplay than with the text.

Interim Conclusion: Sarcasm in Micah 6

In this case study, we began with a brief review of standard treatments of the Micah passage that miss its humorous dimension to illustrate the devastating consequences that can arise when interpreters miss the humor in biblical texts. This high-stakes example reveals two dangerous consequences, related to but distinct from each other, that emerge from traditional, unimaginative interpretations. First, this misinterpretation creates an ethical problem. Those who trust the Bible as a reliable guide in matters related to religious practice are misled to believe that—at least here—it encourages or at least condones child sacrifice. While it is extremely unlikely that anybody would ever take the idea of child sacrifice literally, this is nonetheless problematic because even a symbolic or figurative understanding may encourage religious behavior where vulnerable members of a family or faith community may be maltreated in more subtle ways. The next challenge arises naturally from this. Second, failure to detect the humor creates a theological problem. For those who question, doubt, or at least wonder about the authoritative role of the Bible, its apparent encouragement of child sacrifice undermines Scripture's credibility.

---

the word נפש regularly functions as a synecdoche, a special kind of metaphor, for the whole person of a human being, hence the popular translation as "soul."

We then engaged in an imaginative reading of the passage with special attention to its humorous capacity. This part opened with a comparison between the interlocutors in verses 1–5 and those in 6–7, and we noted that—despite the confrontational tone—there is an intimate relationality between God and his audience in verses 1–5 that shifts conspicuously to a studious distancing between the speaker and his God in the response of verses 6–7 that signals it may not be as conciliatory as traditional interpretations suggest.

Then we considered the escalation of values and quantities in the sequence of proposed sacrifices and discovered a progressive escalation in which the series reached unrealistic, hyperbolical dimensions that signal the communication may not be as sincere as traditional interpretations suggest.

Finally, we imaginatively explored the ambiguous quality and humorous function of the words "the fruit of my belly for the sin of my throat" in Micah 6:7 and uncovered that they contain two amphibologies: (1) the phrase "the sin of my throat" is a metaphor not only for sin in general but also for *the consumption of unclean food*, and (2) the phrase "the fruit of my belly" is not only a metaphor for a child but also a reference to *excrement*, and thus an only thinly veiled, intentional insult to the prophet and his God.

In conclusion, we discovered an instance where a speaker in the Bible responds to prophetic invective with sarcastic humor that is meant to relieve the speaker's tension by insulting the prophet and his God. This resolved two important problems that arise from traditional, nonimaginative readings that miss or ignore the humorous potential of biblical texts. The false impression that Scripture seems to encourage or at least condone child sacrifice is avoided, and the Bible's credibility as a text inspired by God that provides reliable and trustworthy guidance for religious practice is upheld. Imagination draws attention to the humorous dimensions of Scripture and thus prevents misreading of humorous biblical texts that may undermine the Bible's ethical value and theological credibility.

In the remainder of this chapter, we will argue for the universality of humor and briefly explore traditional and modern theories of humor to demonstrate the importance of insights from the field of humor studies to build interpretive skill that enables imaginative readings of humorous biblical texts.

Humor Is Universal

Objections to the identification of humor in historically, culturally, and linguistically remote texts like the Bible are often made on the basis that humor is so culturally specific that modern interpreters can never be sure whether their identifications of specific texts as humorous concur with reality. However, even though "the type of humor expressed and/or appreciated may vary considerably across cultures," writes Annarita Guidi, "humor per se is universal."[29] Consequently, humor can be communicated and understood across diverse historical and cultural horizons and across diverse languages, even when such humor is expressed in culturally specific ways.

A good example to illustrate this dynamic is punning, one of the most popular forms of verbal humor. The actual puns that can be produced in a given language depend on the phonemic structure of that language alone, but punning as such can be and is produced in all of them.[30]

Since humor is "a universal aspect of human experience, occurring in all cultures and virtually all individuals throughout the world,"[31] and since human languages can be translated into one another, humor can, at least in principle, be understood across cultures and historical circumstances. Guidi has shown that punning, as the best-studied cross-cultural humoristic mechanism, is a "humor universal" that "can thus be seen as evidence of the fact that speakers share a cross-linguistic knowledge . . . and exploit it for humorous purposes."[32]

Traditional Theories of Humor Help Us Recognize Humor in the Text

There are three widely accepted traditional theories about humor: the superiority theory, the relief (or release) theory, and the incongruity theory. These are sometimes discussed in the literature as if they were in competition, but in reality they are complementary, describing the dynamics of different kinds of humorous manifestations. These theories arose mainly from the fields of philosophy and classical rhetoric, and they often include ethical appraisals.[33] Our descriptions of the theories begin with an explanation of how each envisages the production and perception of humor. A distinctive feature of our imaginative approach to the interpretation of humor is our exploration of *why* the dynamics of superiority, release, and incongruity prompt the experience of amusement in those who perceive the humor, and what positive effects this experience has on readers of the Bible.

29. Annarita Guidi, "Humor Universals," in *The Routledge Handbook of Language and Humor*, ed. Salvatore Attardo (Routledge, 2017), 19.

30. Cf. J. Morton, "Anthropology," in *Encyclopedia of Humor Studies*, ed. Salvatore Attardo (Sage, 2014), 46–47, quoted in Guidi, "Humor Universals," 17.

31. Guidi, "Humor Universals," 18.

32. Guidi, "Humor Universals," 28.

33. Cristina Larking-Galiñanes, "An Overview of Humor Theory," in *The Routledge Handbook of Language and Humor*, ed. Salvatore Attardo (Routledge, 2017).

Superiority theory explores how feeling superior to others or making others appear inferior to us makes us feel better about ourselves and can cause amusement and make us laugh at them. In this kind of humor, the hearer or reader is encouraged to imagine themselves as superior to the target—the butt of the joke.[34] This kind of humor makes us feel better in the face of real enemies or circumstances that may have intimidated us. Laughing about others has the capacity to make us feel more confident and to energize us to face our real challenges with courage. In our case study on humor in Micah 6:6–7, the speaker attempts to reverse the power dynamics between himself and his disobedient community on the one side, and God and his prophet on the other.

Relief theory, sometimes also called release theory, explores how the release of tension causes amusement and laughter. Here in particular the focus is on the physiological and psychological benefits of laughter through release of tension, as well as relief from a sense of inferiority caused by stressors such as guilt, shame, embarrassment, fear, anxiety, and so on.[35] In this kind of humor, the audience is invited to laugh and thereby imagine that the stress or strain they have been experiencing is much less serious or threatening than it initially appeared. Again, the real cause for amusement is the experience of feeling better about oneself. In our case study on humor in Micah 6:6–7, the speaker achieves release from guilt and the accompanying dread of divine judgment by encouraging himself and the audience to imagine that the prophet's accusations are unfounded and that, consequently, any fear of divine judgment is unnecessary. The release of tension makes the audience feel better in the face of stress factors that otherwise have impaired their sense of worth and well-being. Laughing at what until now had worried or embarrassed them helps them to feel stronger and more in control of whatever may stand in the way of their wellness.

Incongruity theory focuses on *cognitive* status and explores how the experience of incongruity—which makes us feel curious about how the cognitive dissonance might be resolved—is overcome. This kind of humor causes the audience to imagine a scenario incongruous with reality. Cognitive dissonance can make us feel intellectually inadequate or inferior. Consequently,

34. Common mechanisms to produce such amusement are ridicule and derision. Here in particular, questions of social and moral appropriateness arise. Larking-Galiñanes, "Overview of Humor Theory," 4. Two forms of humor generated by superiority are socially and morally more acceptable. The first is when speakers put themselves down through self-effacing or self-deprecating remarks, which are often (but not always) of a more benign nature but still achieve the desired effect. The second is when the audience consists of members who are or perceive themselves to be less powerful or influential than the group whose originally perceived superiority is undermined by a sort of humor that reverses the power dynamics.

35. Larking-Galiñanes, "Overview of Humor Theory," 5.

the resolution of cognitive dissonance leads to a release of tension, and the often surprisingly trivial remedy causes relief and amusement, often leading to laughter. Lighthearted intellectual riddles create a sense of incongruity whose artificially constructed nature is exposed through simple resolutions. We feel affirmed because we realize that our intellectual limitations were not as grave as we feared. The resolution of incongruity makes us feel superior in comparison to our former selves, causing us to laugh at our own gullibility—at having fallen for the cognitive setup that created the apparent incongruity when, all along, there was none. The typically trivial nature of the resolution, for example through punning, creates a sense of playfulness that adds to the amusement. If these examples of incomprehensibility can be resolved, then others we are facing or might face in the future can be overcome as well. In our case study on humor in Micah 6:6–7, we noticed that the amount and value of proposed offerings were incongruously large, causing us to suspect sarcasm, which dissolved cognitive dissonance created by child sacrifice apparently being condoned in this biblical text.

In sum, a hermeneutic of imagination empowers us to identify humorous passages in Scripture and to interpret such humor wisely, as in the case of Micah 6:6–7. And the traditional theories of humor help us to appreciate its beneficial impact upon Christian faith and practice. Modern theories of humor add further value to our interpretation of humor.

Modern Theories of Humor and the Imagination

The two most important theories of humor to emerge in the last four decades come from the field of linguistics: the semantic-script theory of humor, first presented by Victor Raskin in 1985,[36] and the general theory of verbal humor, proposed by Salvatore Attardo and Raskin in 1991, building on Raskin's original work.[37] In addition, relevance theory and the phenomenon of "hidden transcripts" in situations of power imbalance between speakers or authors and their audiences play an important role in our understanding of humor. In what follows, we hope to fill a gap in the academic literature on humor and imagination. Until now, work on imagination has paid little to no attention to its crucial function in the production and perception of humor. Conversely,

36. Victor Raskin, *Semantic Mechanisms of Humor* (Reidel, 1985).

37. Salvatore Attardo and Victor Raskin, "Script Theory Revis(it)ed: Joke Similarity and Joke Representation Model," *Humor: International Journal of Humor Research* 4, no. 3 (1991): 293–347. For a detailed discussion of both linguistic theories, see Salvatore Attardo, "The General Theory of Verbal Humor," in *The Routledge Handbook of Language and Humor*, ed. Salvatore Attardo (Routledge, 2017), 126–42.

academic work on humor has paid next to no attention to the importance of imagination in the production and perception of humor.

The Semantic-Script Theory of Humor

According to Raskin's hypothesis, two conditions are necessary and sufficient for a text to be funny: (1) the text is compatible, fully or in part, with two different scripts; (2) the two scripts with which the text is compatible are opposite in a manner that creates the humorous effect.[38]

"Scripts" in this sense are "intuitively clear entities: they are important elements of our knowledge of the world that consists of a large number of routines on how we do and see things. It is our knowledge of scripts that allows us . . . to understand."[39] A script in this sense is "a dynamic, structured set of information about the world."[40] More recently, the main aspect of Raskin's theory has been paraphrased as "opposing and overlapping frames," with "frames" replacing Raskin's original term "scripts" because that term may imply "something static or universal" rather than "the *relationships* of knowledge that are implied by the speaker and dynamically inferred" by the audience.[41]

While ambiguity is a necessary condition for humor to occur, it is not sufficient on its own. It must be accompanied by a certain incompatibility between the two possible meanings. All ambiguous texts are compatible with two (or more) scripts, but not every ambiguous text is funny.[42]

When both conditions are met, however, humor arises because the humorous text purposefully suggests an *initial* meaning based on what appears to be the more obvious script. It is here that the essential role of the imagination for the production and perception of humor comes into view. The following quotation illustrates this:

> The hearer consciously and unconsciously draws on knowledge, memories, and observations of similar interactions to build what Raskin calls *a Text World Representation, which may be compared to a scene unfolding in the hearer's*

38. Raskin, *Semantic Mechanisms of Humor*, 99.

39. Salvatore Attardo and Victor Raskin, "Linguistics and Humor Theory," in *The Routledge Handbook of Language and Humor*, ed. Salvatore Attardo (Routledge, 2017), 53.

40. Peter S. Perry, "And Now for Something Completely Different: An Introduction to Humor and Biblical Performance," in *Biblical Humor and Performance: Audience Experiences That Make Meaning*, ed. Peter S. Perry, Biblical Performance Criticism 20 (Cascade Books, 2023), 10.

41. Perry, "Something Completely Different," 10–11, citing Seana Coulson, *Semantic Leaps: Frame-Shifting and Conceptual Blending in Meaning Construction* (Cambridge University Press, 2001); and Francisco Yus, *Humour and Relevance*, Topics in Humor Research 4 (Benjamins, 2016).

42. Raskin, *Semantic Mechanisms of Humor*, 100.

mind, perhaps complete with details of senses such as sight and sound filled in dynamically by the hearer.[43]

The italicized words echo in remarkable detail some of the key aspects of imagination discussed above in chapter 1 and in our conclusion to chapter 3. Raskin's text world representations, the key components for the perception of humor, cannot be created without using our imagination.

As the humorous text continues, however, a second—originally less obvious—script is activated. The shift from one script or frame to the other happens via a punch line or similar prompt that "triggers the switch from the one script to the other by making the hearer backtrack and realize that a different interpretation was possible from the very beginning."[44] It is this *forced reinterpretation* that makes the communication funny,[45] and here, too, imagination is key for the production and perception of humor, even though the importance of the imagination for the detection of the two scripts' (or frames') incompatibility has not received the attention it deserves in the academic literature.[46] In our case study of Micah 6:6–7, for example, it was the counterfactually fantastical value of the sequence of proposed offerings that prepared for the frame-switch from apparently sincere devotion to sarcastic defiance.

In the written record of a humorous encounter like our case study on Micah 6:6–7, not all of the contextual information that had been available to the interlocutors may be available to its readers. Even so, however, readers will naturally and effortlessly visualize situations in which the recorded exchange took place, and their comprehension of the scene and the significance of the various parts of the verbal exchange will depend strongly on this imagined context, as we discussed in our case study.[47] In other words, reduced contex-

43. Perry, "Something Completely Different," 10 (emphasis added).

44. Attardo and Raskin, "Script Theory Revis(it)ed," 308.

45. Raskin explains how humorous texts succeed in purposefully misleading hearers at the initial stage. In a given communicative event, "the speaker and hearer find themselves in a particular situation and they are jointly aware of its many features. This linguistic and extralinguistic contextual information is taken into account when the sentence is uttered and comprehended *and it becomes part of the intended meaning*." Raskin, *Semantic Mechanisms of Humor*, 63 (emphasis added).

46. Important scholarly work on the difference between how something appears and how it really is has been documented in Paige E. Davis, "Imaginary Friends: How Imaginary Minds Mimic Real Life," in *The Cambridge Handbook of the Imagination*, ed. Anna Abraham (Cambridge University Press, 2020), 373–89. An important next step will be to apply the insights gained from this line of inquiry to the production and perception of humor through frame-switching.

47. Even in those rare cases where contextual information is insufficient to determine meaning-in-context, Raskin observes, "the hearer supplies it from his previous experience." Raskin, *Semantic Mechanisms of Humor*, 63.

tual information prompts imaginative simulation of contextual information that makes the utterance comprehensible, similar to the process of amodal completion described above in chapter 1.[48]

Raskin's semantic theory of ambiguity describes what we prefer to call a *dynamic of automatic disambiguation*. This dynamic is foundational for the production and perception of humor, for it describes the first building block in the mechanics of humor production. Speakers or authors who want to say something funny draw on this dynamic of automatic disambiguation and consciously mislead their audience's imagination at the initial stage of the humorous communication.

Raskin explains the general contours of the semantic theory that undergirds his semantic-script theory of humor,[49] as well as the theory itself,[50] and we agree with his account. His exploration of the semantic mechanisms of humor provides "a unifying theoretical and formal basis for various intuitions people share about humor as well as a conceptually simple and intuitively appealing explanation of the human ability to produce and understand jokes."[51] What is more, it helps "formulate the necessary and sufficient conditions for a text to be funny,"[52] and we hope to have demonstrated that imagination is an additional ingredient that is necessary for the production and perception of less obvious humor.

Even so, more recent reflection on relevance-theoretic aspects of humor not only confirms the value of the semantic-script theory of humor but also provides a more comprehensive and elegant justification.

Relevance-Theoretic Aspects of Humor

Relevance theory is a cognitive pragmatics theory that aims to identify "underlying mechanisms, rooted in human psychology, which explain how

48. Raskin describes the process of interpretation in cases of ambiguity. Audiences tend to reconstruct only one of several possible meanings in ambiguous statements, because very often "only one in which the sentence can be used is obvious to the speaker: it is either the real context in which the sentence occurs or the imaginary context which comes to his mind most easily" (Raskin, *Semantic Mechanisms of Humor*, 63). In other words, then, in unintentionally ambiguous communication, the speaker will not make the effort to eliminate the ambiguity because he or she knows full well which meaning is intended, and naturally assumes that the hearer will know this too. Conversely, therefore, "usually only one meaning of a potentially ambiguous sentence is perceived by the hearer—for exactly the same reasons. Normally the *speaker's obvious context* coincides with the *hearer's obvious context*" (63–64).

49. Raskin, *Semantic Mechanisms of Humor*, 59–98.

50. Raskin, *Semantic Mechanisms of Humor*, 99–147.

51. Raskin, *Semantic Mechanisms of Humor*, 147.

52. Raskin, *Semantic Mechanisms of Humor*, 147.

humans communicate with one another."[53] It explores the inferences that hearers or readers need to undertake to make sense of speakers' or writers' utterances, inferences that therefore tend to be encoded into such utterances in more or less predictable and thus perceivable ways. Or, to put it in slightly different terms, the theory proposes that hearers or readers can "identify the speaker's communicative intentions (his/her intended interpretation of the utterance) based on what the speaker has coded verbally (i.e., spoken, written, typed) or nonverbally" in the utterance,[54] and the human capacity for imagination is crucial for achieving this feat.[55] Five correlated relevance-theoretic principles explain the successful interpretation of humorous texts.[56]

First, cognitive economy based on relevance. The necessity of economic *cognitive processing* leads to the development of the principles of communicative and cognitive relevance.[57] The *cognitive principle of relevance* explains how human brains can process successfully the huge amounts of information input we encounter in typical communicative events.[58] It is our capacity for imagination that enables us to do this.

Second, communicative economy based on relevance. The need for economic *communication* encourages speakers to say much less than what they mean. There is "a substantial gap between what the speaker says and what the speaker intends to communicate."[59] Vice versa, this principle also prompts interlocutors to interpret much more than what they hear. In relevance-theoretic terms, this is possible through *inference*.[60] Economic efficiency is an extraordi-

53. D. Sperber and D. Wilson, *Relevance: Communication and Cognition* (Blackwell, 1986), 32, quoted in Francisco Yus, "Relevance-Theoretic Treatments of Humor," in *The Routledge Handbook of Language and Humor*, ed. Salvatore Attardo (Routledge, 2017), 189.

54. Yus, "Relevance-Theoretic Treatments of Humor," 189.

55. Relevance theory addresses "the predictions of relevance that speakers make when choosing an utterance or text for transferring their thoughts to other people" (Yus, "Relevance-Theoretic Treatments of Humor," 189). In other words, the theory assumes that communicators typically aim to render their utterances as transparent as possible. And for this reason, they tend to make economic choices as to what words to include in their communications, with the goal of guiding their interlocutors into making the correct inferences, which make the communication successful.

56. We present them in an order different from Yus's and add our own modifications based on cognitive science and the study of human imagination to show how they are connected.

57. Cf. Max Jones and Sam Wilkinson, "From Prediction to Imagination," in *The Cambridge Handbook of the Imagination*, ed. Anna Abraham (Cambridge University Press, 2020), 96.

58. "We have an evolved psychological capacity to focus our attention on what might be relevant, and dismiss what is bound to demand excessive effort in exchange for little reward" (Yus, "Relevance-Theoretic Treatments of Humor," 189). This ability to sift out what is relevant from what is not prevents us from being overwhelmed by the inevitable inclusion of other data in the numerous communications we constantly receive.

59. Yus, "Relevance-Theoretic Treatments of Humor," 190.

60. Yus, "Relevance-Theoretic Treatments of Humor," 190.

nary cognitive achievement possible through our imaginative capacity to "fill the gap," through amodal completion and other, often-synesthetic imaginative cognitive processes.[61]

We can now appreciate the foundational role of the *communicative principle of relevance* for the production and perception of humor. Its explanatory power makes it an indispensable tool to produce communicative utterances and their successful interpretations, including humorous ones. The communicative principle of relevance claims that "every utterance conveys a presumption of its eventual relevance."[62]

Third, cognitive and communicative economy and the principles of cognitive and communicative relevance. The cognitive principle of relevance at first looks like it is contradicting its communicative counterpart. However, it is a necessary *complement* to the communicative principle. The two principles of relevance *in combination* ensure cognitive economy by encouraging us to be as economical as possible and as thorough as necessary in our interpretive efforts.[63] The human mind is amazing, and imagination is at the heart of it.

Finding the right balance between efficiency and accuracy ensures that the communicative intent is achieved with *cognitive economy*. This is particularly

61. Jones and Wilkinson, "From Prediction to Imagination." On amodal completion, see Bence Nanay, "Perception and Imagination: Amodal Perception as Mental Imagery," *Philosophical Studies* 150 (2010); and Amy Kind, "Philosophical Perspectives on Imagination in the Western Tradition," in *The Cambridge Handbook of the Imagination*, ed. Anna Abraham (Cambridge University Press, 2020), 70. As Yus rightly claims, "Utterances always underdetermine (i.e., are less informative than) the eventual interpretation that is obtained from them" (Yus, "Relevance-Theoretic Treatments of Humor," 190). Speakers and authors achieve this through *implicature*, encoding just enough information to prompt readers or hearers to make the *imaginative inferences* to interpret humorous utterances in just the intended ways.

62. Yus, "Relevance-Theoretic Treatments of Humor," 189. In reality, this is of course not always the case, since human communicators rarely communicate flawlessly. Nonetheless, humans tend to have working theories on the basis of which they proceed, and this is one of them. The claim that "every utterance conveys a presumption of its eventual relevance" explains not only why communicators tend to underdetermine their communicative utterances but also why they can afford to do so, all the while fulfilling the principle of communicative economy. The need for communicative economy reduces communicative utterances to their essential components, the smallest number of parts that will still ensure effective communication. It also motivates the interlocutor to use all available information in that underdetermined text, because it is the most efficient method to reach an effective interpretation, one that makes sense of *all* that is there and at the same time, through inferences, enables the interlocutor to discern *more* than is there.

63. Yus proposes that the communicative principle of relevance is a subcategory of the cognitive principle of relevance (Yus, "Relevance-Theoretic Treatments of Humor," 189). As I have shown, however, it may be better to see both principles of relevance as subprinciples of the principle of cognitive economy.

important for humorous utterances.[64] It is our capacity for imagination that enables us to follow this principle and make the necessary inferences.

Fourth, automatic cognitive ranking based on relevance. The brain's capacity to rank alternative possible interpretations according to relevance is also motivated by the drives for economic cognition and economic communication.[65] Above we already mentioned that communicative utterances tend to be underdetermined and hence ambiguous. If the human brain had to weigh all possible interpretive mutations of communicative utterances all the time, the necessary cognitive energy would simply be too high. For this reason, the human brain has developed the capacity to "assess candidate interpretations for the same input in a specific context and rank them in terms of relevance."[66] And since the brain does this automatically, at an unconscious level,[67] effective communication is achieved effortlessly.

Humorous utterances tend to be even more underdetermined than others. In this regard, they are similar to poetry in that they are highly ambiguous and so have an even higher number of possible interpretations than other communicative utterances.[68]

Consequently, an application of relevance theory to humorous utterances explains how the drives for cognitive and communicative economy with their associated principles of cognitive and communicative relevance combine with the human brain's capacity for automatic cognitive ranking to guide the composition and perception of utterances as funny. Humorous effects, such as amusement and entertainment, are achieved in predictable patterns and thus almost effortlessly because of our ability to imagine more

64. Since they tend to be short on informative input, much may appear irrelevant for cognitive processing. The *economic* side of the drive for *cognitive economy* threatens to stimulate the *cognitive principle of relevance* to kick in. This would cause lack of interest and lead to quick, superficial readings, resulting in shallow, even erroneous interpretations. At this point, the *cognitive* part of the drive for cognitive economy causes the *communicative principle of relevance* to kick in and stimulate a more thorough engagement with the communication, resulting in imaginative inferences that make it meaningful not in terms of its informative quantity but in terms of its entertainment value.

65. As we shall see shortly, this supports the idea of hierarchically organized "knowledge resources," the most important refinement that the general theory of verbal humor adds to the semantic-script theory of humor.

66. Yus, "Relevance-Theoretic Treatments of Humor," 190.

67. Yus, "Relevance-Theoretic Treatments of Humor," 190.

68. Yus explains: "We just cannot be aware of all the possible interpretations of an utterance and then opt for one; instead, we automatically opt for the most relevant one without even noticing that alternative interpretations were also possible. This is frequently exploited in humorous communication, in which hearers are often led to select an initially relevant interpretation. This choice turns out to be inadequate and has to be replaced with an initially more unlikely but eventually correct interpretation." Yus, "Relevance-Theoretic Treatments of Humor," 190.

than we see or hear, as we discovered in our exploration of imagination in chapter 1.

Fifth, predictability of interpretations based on relevance. Relevance theory helps to explain how the human brain processes information effectively. This contributes to cognitive science in general, not least by offering a coherent account for how humans can correctly and with relatively little effort choose between competing interpretations. Conversely, the interpretive decision based on relevance conditioned by the drives for cognitive and communicative economy also makes such interpretive choices predictable. Since interlocutors subconsciously "search for the most relevant and effort-relieving information," the speaker or writer can imagine and predict, "can hold more or less precise expectations about which inferential strategies and steps the hearer is going to perform or go through."[69]

As we observed in our discussion of the traditional theories of humor above, it is the often *surprising* quality and the often *trivial* nature of the additional information that prompt the perception of the interpretive incongruity's resolution as funny. In our case study on Micah 6:6–7, it is the apparently redundant phrase "the fruit of my belly [for] the sin of my throat" that turns out to be most relevant for triggering the perception of the speaker's utterance as humorously sarcastic rather than devotedly pious. Again, it is the human capacity for imagination that undergirds these relevance-theoretic principles.

Relevance-theoretic aspects of humor offer an elegant explanation for how humor is produced and understood that improves Raskin's original explanation. Relevance theory also fits well with the most important refinement that the general theory of verbal humor contributes to the semantic-script theory—the postulate of hierarchically organized knowledge resources, which we explore next.

The General Theory of Verbal Humor

Hierarchically organized "knowledge resources" constitute the most important refinement that the general theory of verbal humor (GTVH) has contributed to the semantic-script theory of humor. We will briefly explain

69. Yus, "Relevance-Theoretic Treatments of Humor," 190. In other words, speakers or writers can *imaginatively predict and thus control* what inferences their interlocutors will make. They can manipulate the interpretive choices of their interlocutors and force them into an initial, erroneous interpretation. This manipulative scheme sets their interlocutors up through the intentional inclusion and combination of *some* relevant information, while other information that would have forced the correct interpretation is temporarily withheld. Once that extra information is released, however, the original interpretation is exposed as false and the new interpretation is forced upon the interlocutor.

what they are and how they contribute to the production and appreciation of humor. Their existence adds further weight to the relevance-theoretic insights discussed in the previous section, since knowledge resources explain how cognitive economy can be achieved by the human brain.

The theory postulates six hierarchically organized knowledge resources. In descending order of importance, these are (1) the script opposition knowledge resource, (2) the logical mechanism knowledge resource, (3) the situation knowledge resource, (4) the target knowledge resource, (5) the narrative strategy knowledge resource, and (6) the language knowledge resource.[70] The degree of similarity between humorous utterances reflects the hierarchy of the knowledge resources, so that if two humorous utterances differ only in language, they are very similar, whereas if they differ in script opposition, they are very different.[71]

First, the script opposition knowledge resource. Attardo and Raskin demonstrate that "the number of [script] oppositions is finite and limited."[72] "At the most abstract level," they explain, "the joke opposes the *real* to the *unreal*, that is, factual reality to an imagined one." Again, imagination plays a crucial role in this process.[73]

In the analysis of potentially humorous texts, it is important first to identify the text-specific instantiation of the script opposition, before it is sorted into one of the higher-level, abstract, more general opposition categories.[74]

Below, we will apply the script opposition knowledge resource to power-charged communications in which humor is used to enable the expression of the hidden transcripts of the powerless in public and thus to facilitate the

70. Attardo, "General Theory of Verbal Humor," 127–28.

71. Attardo, "General Theory of Verbal Humor," 128.

72. Attardo and Raskin, "Script Theory Revis(it)ed," 308.

73. There are various levels of abstraction or generality to these script oppositions. At a lower or intermediate level of abstractions is the contrast between *actual versus nonactual*, *normal versus abnormal*, and *possible versus impossible*. At the lowest level of abstraction, such oppositions can appear in a range of oppositions that are typical subcases of a *good versus bad opposition*, such as *life versus death*, *sex versus no sex*, *money versus no money*, or *high versus low*. Attardo and Raskin, "Script Theory Revis(it)ed," 308. Of course, many more examples of oppositions exist in humor, but they can all be seen as examples that fit into these categories.

74. Attardo explains: "Summing up, each humorous text will instantiate one very abstract Script Opposition in a very concrete text-specific opposition, which will generally require at least one of the scripts in the opposition to be explicitly stated in the text and the other to be directly or at least easily retrievable inferentially/abductively from the text. There may be any number of intermediate scripts, increasingly abstract, bridging the distance between the scripts occurring in the text and the very abstract oppositions identified by Raskin (1985)" (Attardo, "General Theory of Verbal Humor," 133–34). This distinction is helpful because it facilitates the *detection* of humor, even in cultures and languages that are different from those of the interpreter.

declaration of truth to power. This will also explain the deployment of humor rather than explicit rebellion in our case study on Micah 6:6–7.

Second, the logical mechanism knowledge resource. This knowledge resource is "the part of the GTVH that accounts for the resolution of the incongruity (script opposition and overlap)."[75] Importantly, it usually is partial, playful, and nonserious (see above on the typically trivial nature of the resolution of incongruity). It is "the attempt by the text to explain away the incongruity by justifying it."[76] Imaginative reading uses these insights to explain apparent incongruities in the biblical text, deliberate textual incongruities and ambiguities that are resolved playfully and humorously but with didactic intent, as in our case study on Micah 6:6–7.

Third, the situation knowledge resource. This knowledge resource "is essentially the overall macroscript that describes the background" in which the events of a humorous utterance take place.[77] It is important to distinguish the technical use of the term "situation" and its description as a "macroscript" in the GTVH from the context in which the humorous utterance is *performed*. There is a difference between the "situation," the background in which *the events of the humorous utterance take place*, and the real-life context in which the speaker utters it. "The GTVH is a theory of competence, so it logically could not encompass contextual factors, which are by definition part of performance."[78]

Biblical texts regularly activate stereotypical situations and their macroscripts to cause amusement. They frequently report the contexts in which humor is performed. For this reason, the identification of humorous utterances and their interpretation requires that readers engage imaginatively with the texts and infer from the literary context which situation and macroscript are implied in the potentially humorous utterances or events recorded in the literary context, as we did in our case study on Micah 6:6–7. This includes imaginative visualizations of the performance of the potentially humorous text, including the role of those who perform it as well as the implied audience attending the performance. For this reason, we will offer below a proposal toward a "performance knowledge resource."

Fourth, the target knowledge resource. This knowledge resource is relevant only for *aggressive* humorous utterances, for example jokes that have a target,

75. Attardo, "General Theory of Verbal Humor," 133.

76. Attardo, "General Theory of Verbal Humor," 133. Cf. the comments above on how the resolution of cognitive incongruity causes us to laugh at our own gullibility at having fallen for the cognitive setup that created the apparent incongruity when, all along, there was none.

77. Attardo, "General Theory of Verbal Humor," 131.

78. Attardo, "General Theory of Verbal Humor," 131.

usually a human person or their activities. Such human activities may include institutions, practices, beliefs, and so on. They are the "butt" of the joke. In some texts, the presumed targets of potentially humorous utterances are explicitly mentioned. Sometimes the readers themselves may be the target. In our case study on Micah 6:6–7, the prophet and his God were the target, an unexpected and counterintuitive target that has consequently been difficult to detect by later readers of the text.

Fifth, the narrative strategy knowledge resource.[79] Narrative strategy as knowledge resource describes the indispensable components of humorous utterances, including the component that signals that the utterance is meant to be humorous. The distribution of these components in the narrative sequence is also of interest, and in particular the relative position of the so-called punch line or jab, which signals, in its own way, the utterance's humorous quality. The position of the punch line is important because "the absence of a punch line in final position is the defining difference between jokes and anecdotes."[80] In our case study on Micah 6:6–7, we discovered that the phrase "the fruit of my belly [for] the sin of my throat," in final position, was the punch line that triggered the perception of humor and enabled the resolution of cognitive dissonance initiated through the list of proposed offerings in verse 6.

There are two especially popular narrative strategies that are typical of humorous utterances: (1) question-answer formats, which indicate riddles or pseudoriddles; and (2) sequences or lists, such as "a three-step sequence," popular in humorous utterances "because it is the smallest number of repetitions necessary to set a pattern of expectations and breaking it."[81] The need to establish a pattern in order to enable its violation is very likely the reason why three-part sequences are both the most frequent and the funniest.[82] In our case study on Micah 6:6–7, we encountered both of these narrative strategies, but it was our imaginative approach that helped us to discover their humorous function.[83]

79. Attardo now admits that using the term "narrative" in the designation narrative strategy was a misnomer because it may give the false impression that this knowledge resource is concerned with narratology. Cf. Attardo, "General Theory of Verbal Humor," 130.

80. Attardo, "General Theory of Verbal Humor," 130, citing Elliott Oring, "Between Jokes and Tales: On the Nature of Punch Lines," *Humor: International Journal of Humor Research* 2, no. 4 (1989).

81. Attardo, "General Theory of Verbal Humor," 130.

82. Attardo, "General Theory of Verbal Humor," 130.

83. Additional aspects of narrative strategy relevant to the analysis of humorous utterances introduced by Attardo include (1) the distinction between jab and punch lines ("a jab line and a punch line differ in their placement within the text: a punch line occurs at the end of the text, whereas a jab line occurs anywhere else"; they also "differ in terms of their functions: jab lines are not disruptive of the development of the main interpretation of the text, whereas punch

Our imaginative approach to reading biblical texts suggests surprisingly many potentially humorous biblical texts, including longer ones. And they exhibit a variety of textual strategies that fall under Attardo's narrative strategy knowledge resource.

Sixth, the language knowledge resource. The language knowledge resource includes "a full phonological, morphological, syntactic and lexical description of the text" as well as "statistical information about how frequently various kinds of expressions occur at each linguistic level (i.e., phonemes and clusters of phonemes, as well as the frequency of occurrence of morphemes, phrases, etc.)."[84] A careful analysis of phonological features is essential because of the popularity and prominence of punning for the production of humorous effects,[85] and awareness of frequency levels will enable the distinction between accidental occurrences and intentional usage to add humorous effect. Of equal interest are syntactic ambiguities,[86] and we would add grammatical ambiguities to this list. Reading with imagination promotes careful observation with the assumption that all aspects of biblical texts are potentially meaningful. This includes linguistic ambiguities and anomalies, such as the intentional breaking of conventions, very much like what we encountered in our case study on Micah 6:6–7.

Humor and Performance

The final item in this list of knowledge resources is offered as a heuristic exercise, an initial foray into how potentially humorous utterances may have been *performed* in ways that made them humorous. We hope to make a modest contribution toward a theory of humor performance.[87]

On the level of the performance of humorous utterances, relevance-theoretic analyses can be of immense value. Here the work of Elisa Gironzetti on prosodic and multimodal markers of humor is instructive.[88] A multimodal

---

lines often force a reinterpretation of said interpretation"); (2) the distribution of the humor along the textual vector; and (3) the typology of humorous texts based on (a) the presence or absence of a narrative disruption and (b) the presence of a humorous central complication. Finally, the way longer narratives are used to produce humorous effects in the otherwise turn-based flow of normal conversations also belongs to the narrative strategy knowledge resource. So far, little work has been done on this. Attardo, "General Theory of Verbal Humor," 130.

84. Attardo, "General Theory of Verbal Humor," 128.

85. Attardo, "General Theory of Verbal Humor," 129.

86. Attardo, "General Theory of Verbal Humor," 129.

87. See also the essays collected in Peter S. Perry, ed., *Biblical Humor and Performance: Audience Experiences That Make Meaning*, Biblical Performance Criticism 20 (Cascade Books, 2023).

88. Elisa Gironzetti, "Prosodic and Multimodal Markers of Humor," in *The Routledge Handbook of Language and Humor*, ed. Salvatore Attardo (Routledge, 2017), 408–11.

approach to the analysis of the performance of humorous utterances pays attention to auditory modulation of the voice (intonation, pitch, speed, emphasis, pause, etc.); nonlinguistic markers of humor such as laughter, smiling, and eye movements; as well as the impact of other forms of body language in human interactions. The *written* records of potentially humorous utterances in the biblical texts rarely mention such multimodal markers. Nonetheless, more subtle linguistic markers appear more frequently than has been recognized until now, and they invite imaginative engagement, including the reconstruction of the multimodal nonlinguistic markers we have just mentioned.[89]

An imaginative reading approach will pay special attention to textual clues that imply or suggest multimodal markers of emotion as well as multimodal markers of humor, as for example in our case study on Micah 6:6–7, which would benefit from a reconstruction of the speaker's nonverbal markers of humor. Such textual traces invite readers to make inferences about the performance of reported speech as it occurs in the texts, and this offers promising avenues for the identification of humor in the Bible.

Imaginative reading of the Bible will help us detect more texts that may be humorous than we previously could because it encourages us to pay special attention to textual clues that prompt the inference of nonlinguistic markers in the *performance* of texts, especially where reported speech occurs, as in Micah 6:6–7. This will fire readers' imaginations to expect more humorous utterances in the Bible, and it will help us to detect textual markers that indicate the humorous potential of utterances. One especially important aspect in the performance of humor is the distribution of power between the actors in texts. To this we now turn.

Imagination Helps Us See Disguised Humor in the Biblical Text

Humor can also act as a factor of release in situations of domination and subordination. In this part of the chapter, we will consider a social scientific approach to the analysis of the power relations between dominant and subordinate groups developed in James Scott's study *Domination and the Arts of Resistance: Hidden Transcripts*, published in 1990.

The role of hidden transcripts in Scott's analysis of power relations has explanatory power for the role of script oppositions in Raskin and Attardo's

89. Cf. especially David Rhoads, "Performance Criticism: An Emerging Methodology in Second Testament Studies—Part I," *Biblical Theology Bulletin* 36 (2006); and David Rhoads, foreword to *Biblical Humor and Performance: Audience Experiences That Make Meaning*, ed. Peter S. Perry, Biblical Performance Criticism 20 (Cascade Books, 2023), as well as the essays throughout that volume.

theory of humor, and vice versa. The dynamics of power imbalance directly affect the performance of humor, and humor is one of the main vehicles for the negotiation of power imbalance. In what follows we seek to make an original contribution to the field of humor studies by integrating script opposition in humor theory with performance criticism in the analysis of public and hidden transcripts in the theory of social relations.

Scott discovered the existence of "hidden transcripts" in his effort "to understand the politics of resistance by poor Malay peasants to changes in rice production that systematically worked to their disadvantage." Scott observed that the peasants tended to avoid "irrevocable acts of public defiance." Instead, they preferred "to make use of disguise, deception, and indirection" to resist in clandestine fashion, "while maintaining an outward impression, in power-laden situations, of willing, even enthusiastic consent," a dynamic that would have misled "anyone who regarded the calm surface of political life . . . as evidence of harmony between classes."[90] The same dynamic, we believe, was also at work in Micah 6:6–7, as our review of the history of its interpretation suggests.

The existence of "hidden transcripts" and their counterpart, "public transcripts," helps to explain what is going on in such circumstances of imbalanced power relations.[91] Even so, "the necessity of 'acting a mask' in the presence of power produces, almost by the strain of its inauthenticity, countervailing pressure that cannot be contained indefinitely."[92] The suppression of the powerless creates a counterpressure of resistance below the surface of compliance. Occasionally, and increasingly over time, the hidden transcript presses to the surface.[93] Scott explores this under the heading of political disguise.[94] Often, of course, a public performance of the hidden transcript demands such a heavy disguise that the disguise threatens to all but eliminate the pleasure of its performance.[95]

90. James C. Scott, *Domination and the Arts of Resistance: Hidden Transcripts* (Yale University Press, 1990), 17.

91. "If subordinate discourse in the presence of the dominant is a public transcript, I shall use the term *hidden transcript* to characterize discourse that takes place 'offstage,' beyond direct observation by powerholders. The hidden transcript is this derivative in the sense that it consists of those offstage speeches, gestures, and practices that confirm, contradict, or inflect what appears in the public transcript. . . . The hidden transcript is produced for a different audience and under different constraints of power than the public transcript. By assessing the discrepancy between the hidden transcript and the public transcript, we may begin to judge the impact of domination on public discourse." Scott, *Domination and the Arts of Resistance*, 4–5.

92. Scott, *Domination and the Arts of Resistance*, 9.

93. Scott, *Domination and the Arts of Resistance*, 14.

94. Scott, *Domination and the Arts of Resistance*, 136–82.

95. Even so, however, "while it is surely less satisfying than an open declaration of the hidden transcript it nevertheless achieves something the backstage can never match. It carves out a

Here the role of humor comes into play, for it allows the hidden transcript to take to the stage. While it remains true that "nearly all public action by subordinate groups is pervaded by disguise,"[96] humor permits this disguise to wear its heart on its sleeve. Humor increases the margin of error in the probing of limits. The cloak of humor allows the contours of the hidden transcript to be so thinly veiled inside the public transcript that, for those in the know, it is in fact on full display. Those who perform it and those who witness it are rewarded with the satisfaction of getting away with an oblique expression of the hidden transcript in the public domain.[97] It is humor that makes this possible, for the coexistence of two competing scripts in the humorous expression, one compliant and the other defiant, masks seditious meanings because the opposing script offers concealment. And the thinner the veil, the greater the satisfaction, as in our case study on Micah 6:6–7. The same dynamic, we are convinced, is also at work in the book of Ecclesiastes and in the proverbs of Agur in Proverbs 30.[98] Potentially humorous expressions are so popular because they are especially effective. They succeed and are appreciated because they "dare to preserve as much as possible of the rhetorical force of the hidden transcript while skirting danger."[99]

And for this reason, their identification requires imagination, as in Micah 6:6–7, the book of Ecclesiastes, and the proverbs of Agur, to name but a few biblical examples. It "requires a more nuanced and literary reading simply because the hidden transcript has had to costume itself and speak more warily,"[100] and this is of course where imagination comes into its own to help us identify hidden humor in the biblical texts. Reading the Bible with imagination facilitates the integration of the semantic-script theory of humor with the dynamics of power. In turn, this facilitates the identification and interpretation of ambiguous meanings in the biblical texts that would otherwise remain hidden.

---

public, if provisional, space for the autonomic cultural expression of dissent. If it is disguised, it is at least not hidden; it is spoken to power. This is no small achievement of voice under domination." Scott, *Domination and the Arts of Resistance*, 166.

96. Scott, *Domination and the Arts of Resistance*, 182.

97. Cf. Scott, *Domination and the Arts of Resistance*, 153.

98. See Knut M. Heim, *Ecclesiastes*, Tyndale Old Testament Commentaries 18 (InterVarsity, 2019); Knut M. Heim, "Humor and Performance in Ecclesiastes 7:23–8:1," in *Biblical Humor and Performance*, ed. Peter S. Perry, Biblical Performance Criticism (Cascade Books, 2023); and Knut M. Heim, "Of Leeches, Lizards, and Lions: The Humorous Function of Animal Talk in Proverbs 30," in *Human Interaction with the Natural World in Wisdom Literature and Beyond: Essays in Honour of Tova L. Forti*, ed. Mordechai Cogan, Katharine J. Dell, and David Glatt-Gilad, The Library of Hebrew Bible/Old Testament Studies 720 (Bloomsbury T&T Clark, 2023).

99. Scott, *Domination and the Arts of Resistance*, 165.

100. Scott, *Domination and the Arts of Resistance*, 165.

The importance of this for reading the Bible cannot be underestimated. Just as social science in general tends to be "focused resolutely on the official or formal relations between the powerful and the weak," so readers of the Bible typically encounter mainly what happens according to the *public* transcripts, both in encounters between the powerful and the powerless and in encounters between God and his people. It is an imaginative approach to reading that helps us to see through the disguise.[101]

Conclusion

In this chapter, we focused on Micah 6:6–7 as a case study for humor, examining how humorous elements can significantly influence textual interpretation. We closely analyzed this passage to understand how humor shapes meaning, providing insight into both its rhetorical function and its reception by an ancient audience. The methodologies recapped below can help us find humor all over the Bible. We can find it in well-known humorous passages in books such as Jonah, as well as in less obvious yet even more startling locations such as Psalm 23 explored at the end of this work, or even in more startling locations such as the hidden humor in Psalm 58. Missing humor or ignoring it on the basis of theological assumptions can lead to problematic outcomes.

Modern humor theories make valuable contributions to the detection and interpretation of humorous materials in the Bible. The semantic-script theory of humor illustrates that biblical humor often relies on two overlapping but conflicting frames of meaning, where an initial, seemingly straightforward interpretation is later subverted by an unexpected or exaggerated twist. We

101. The objection may be raised that, surely, God does not need to pretend, and therefore the public transcript of God and the hidden transcript of God are identical. Consequently, it may appear that there is *no hidden transcript* with God. However, the Bible is peppered with texts that are critical of the powerful, such as royalty and other members of the elite. And it is the powerful who will be among the first and most important readers of the compositions produced by the human authors of the Bible. This explains why, apart from many of the prophetic texts, critique of major figures, including King David and King Solomon, is so muted in many of the biblical narratives. On the surface, they follow the public transcript, which mandates deference and respect. The hidden transcript of social and religious critique, meanwhile, is visible only in subtle hints and allusions, in careful turns of phrase and implied emotions. Sanction is relegated to underdetermined language because frequently the human authors of Scripture have no choice but to express their dissent—even dissent sanctioned and inspired by God—in clandestine forms that conform with the *public* transcript. This is one of the main reasons why—with the partial exception of the prophetic literature and narrative literature about prophets—the critique of the powerful tends to be so muted and understated in the Bible. And this is why we need imagination to identify not only clandestine humor in the Bible but also the hidden transcript beneath the public transcript in texts about powerful human figures in the Bible.

illustrated this with the example in Micah 6:6–7, where the apparent piety of the speaker collapses under the weight of absurdly hyperbolic offerings, revealing sarcasm rather than sincerity. Recognizing these opposing scripts is essential for correctly identifying humor in biblical texts.

The relevance-theoretic aspects of humor show us that humor in the Bible operates within the same cognitive economy that governs all communication. We use our imagination to create and understand humor in every area of life, and so did the biblical authors. All audiences, including the audience of the biblical authors, naturally seek the most relevant interpretation with the least effort in both verbal and written interactions. Humor exploits this tendency by first leading the audience toward an expected meaning before shifting to highlight incongruity. The extravagant sacrifices in Micah 6:6–7 are humorous because, while they initially appear reasonable, they become increasingly implausible, inviting the audience to use their imagination, reassess their understanding, and recognize the speaker's mockery.

The general theory of verbal humor shows us that biblical humor relies on hierarchically structured knowledge resources, where we explored six layers and how they interact to create humorous effects. In Micah 6, the punch line of the passage is not a joke in the modern sense but a rhetorical climax understood through an imaginative interaction with the text. Recognizing how these structural elements function prevents misunderstandings that could otherwise justify problematic theological conclusions.

Humor in performance reminds us that biblical humor was not originally words on a page but something performed audibly with intonation, timing, and nonverbal cues that amplified its meaning. As we use traditional methods to evaluate the text, we must remember to imagine them as the performances that they were. Our imaginative reconstruction of Micah 6:6–7 allowed us to fully grasp the humor of the text.

The intersection of imagination and humor in the biblical text helps us uncover how those in subordinate positions subtly challenged authority. A lively imagination paired with genuine humility are required to identify these examples because biblical humor is often veiled, operating in the hidden transcripts that allow the critique of power to be presented under the cover of ambiguity. Micah 6:6–7 is an example of how such veiled humor can be more readily seen when read with imagination.

CHAPTER SIX

A Hermeneutic of Imagination Informs Our Translation Theory and Practice

While academic study of biblical passages usually begins with a careful translation of the text from the original biblical languages, we have deferred the topic until now because chapters 1–5 have demonstrated the need for the original and fostered a desire for it.

And yet, translate we must. The biblical languages are "dead" languages in the sense that there are no native speakers alive today. They are *acquired* languages, even for top Bible scholars. Academics tend to work with their own translations and with standard Bible translations that are considered most conducive to academic study, such as the NRSV and the NRSVue in English. Even when they work from the original languages, then, they tend to begin their work by producing modern equivalents in their own native language, be that German, English, Spanish, French, Korean, Chinese, Wolof, Swahili, or Yoruba. Such translations are a necessary and inescapable part of the process. Inadvertently, however, they encourage thinking in one's own language rather than the original language of the text, and this inhibits imaginative engagement.

In chapters 1–5, we explored why we need imagination to properly understand the literary and rhetorical features of Scripture, including its quirks, oddities, and foreign elements. In this chapter, we demonstrate that to date we have often been prevented from employing our imagination because of our translations, and we argue that a hermeneutic of imagination calls for and benefits from imaginative translations.

We propose that translations best suited to a hermeneutic of imagination will therefore reflect—as much as possible—the vocabulary, grammar, syntax, word order, and other particularities of the source text in the target language. We need a translation theory and practice that preserves the imaginative features of Scripture and accurately reflects its unique characteristics—including those that may strike the translator as unusual, idiosyncratic, superfluous, potentially humorous, and even odd or obscure. The resulting translation should *not* sound natural in the target language but should sound artificial and foreign, reminding us that we are reading a text translated from a different language that has reached us from a different time and place. This will help academic students of Scripture to think as much as possible in terms of the text's original language rather than their own. The benefits are phenomenal, as we shall see.

Is there such a thing as a "best" Bible translation? Many people think so and passionately advocate for their favorite. However, the question cannot be answered in absolute fashion. There is no one translation to rule them all. Here we draw on the widely accepted skopos theory of translation first proposed by Katharina Reiss and Hans Vermeer.[1] The quality of a translation needs to be measured by how well it meets its specific purpose. Andy Cheung explains:

> This approach, translating according to audience needs, relativises translation and accords with what translation studies researchers call "skopos theory," the idea that the form of a translation should be shaped by its intended purpose among a target audience. Under skopos theory, any translation type, be it foreignising or domesticating, idiomatic or literal, gender neutral or otherwise, is potentially viable according to the particular needs of the translation's readers. It is purpose driven translation: give the customers what they want, in other words.[2]

The skopos theory of translation helps us appreciate that any translation type—whether foreignizing or domesticating, idiomatic or literal—can be a valid translation. Therefore, the purpose of this chapter is not to develop a "better" translation theory that aims to produce the "best" translation in an

1. Katharina Reiss and Hans J. Vermeer, *Towards a General Theory of Translational Action: Skopos Theory Explained*, trans. Christiane Nord (Routledge, 2014).

2. Andy Cheung, "Foreignising Bible Translation: Retaining Foreign Origins When Rendering Scripture," *Tyndale Bulletin* 63, no. 2 (2012): 258.

absolute sense. Rather, we aim to present the case for a theory and associated practices that are more suited for the purpose (*skopos*) of reading Scripture with imagination. Which translation techniques and practices promote perception of and appreciation for Scripture's imaginative nature? To answer this question, we expose why modern translations obscure the imaginative nature of Scripture and then develop the contours of an imaginative theory of Bible translation.

The following discussion focuses on translations of the Bible into English, but the principles underlying the different versions apply to all modern languages.

Modern Translations Obscure the Imaginative Nature of Scripture

Modern Bible translations in general tend to obscure the imaginative nature of Scripture, as we shall see below. So-called domesticating translations do this in a very distinctive way.

Why Domesticating Translations Inhibit Imaginative Engagement

In the second half of the twentieth century, Bible translation theorists argued that domesticating translations of the Bible, which adhere to the principle of dynamic equivalence, are best. Eugene Nida, a prominent advocate for dynamic equivalence, explains:

> The principle of dynamic equivalence implies that *the quality of a translation is in proportion to the reader's unawareness that he is reading a translation at all.* This principle means, furthermore, that the translation should stimulate in the new reader essentially the same reaction to the text as the original author wished to produce in his first and immediate readers. The application of this principle of dynamic equivalence *leads to far greater faithfulness* in translating, since accuracy in translation cannot be *reckoned* merely in terms of corresponding words but *on the basis of what the new readers actually understand.*[3]

The quote highlights that in Nida's understanding dynamic equivalence theory prioritizes understandability above all else. This is also evident in the introductions of two prominent English Bible translations that follow the theory: the Good News Bible (GNB) and the Contemporary English Version (CEV).

3. Eugene A. Nida, *Good News for Everyone: How to Use the Good News Bible (Today's English Version)* (Word, 1977), 13 (emphasis added).

According to the Good News Bible's foreword, it "seeks to state clearly and accurately the meaning of the original texts in words and forms that are widely accepted by people who use English as a means of communication." It attempts to "set forth the Biblical content and message in standard, everyday, natural form of English" and aims to "give today's readers maximum understanding of the content."

The GNB's preface explains the basic principles the translators followed: While admitting that "at times the original meaning cannot be precisely known," they aimed for "ascertaining as accurately as possible the meaning of the original" and then sought to "express that meaning in a manner and form easily understood by the readers," trying to "avoid words and forms not in current or widespread use."

The preface further explains: "Every effort has been made to use language that is natural, clear, simple and unambiguous." And consequently, "there has been no attempt to reproduce in English the parts of speech, sentence structure, word order, and grammatical devices of the original languages." The GNB has achieved the goal of understandability to an exemplary degree.

The Contemporary English Version is similar but takes the implementation of dynamic equivalence one step further. Its introduction claims that the CEV aims to follow not the *form* of the King James Version but its *spirit*. "That the Scripture may be understood even by ordinary people was a primary goal of the translators of the *King James Version*," the translators explain. They then quote Martin Luther to the effect that to ascertain the kind of language to be used when translating the Bible, "we must inquire about this of the mother in the home, the children on the street, the common man in the marketplace. We must be guided by their language, the way they speak, and do our translating accordingly." Based on statistics that indicate that "almost half of U.S. adults have very limited reading and writing skills," the translators then explain that "a contemporary translation must be a text that an inexperienced reader can *read aloud* without stumbling, that someone unfamiliar with traditional biblical terminology *can hear without misunderstanding*, and that everyone can *listen to with enjoyment* because the style is lucid and lyrical."

The result, therefore, is "an English text that is enjoyable and easily understood . . . , regardless of . . . religious or educational background." This is indeed a worthy goal for an accessible Bible translation, and the CEV has achieved it. However, the achievements of the GNB and the CEV come at a price.

Above we noticed how proponents have argued that translations based on the principle of dynamic equivalence are the most accurate. Nida made this clear: "The application of this principle of dynamic equivalence leads to far greater faithfulness in translating, since accuracy" should be assessed "on the basis of what the new readers actually understand."[4] Are these claims justified? We think not. For domesticating translations are based on fundamental misunderstandings, and they obscure the fact that the biblical texts were not written with communicative ease in mind.

The main idea of dynamic equivalence is that a modern Bible translation should have the same effect on its readers today as the original would have had on its original readers. This is in fact a very good principle, one that our imaginative reading approach affirms unreservedly. From the perspective of a hermeneutic of imagination, however, the dynamic equivalence theory has three fundamental flaws.

The first flaw is the supposition that biblical writers wanted to be as obvious and clear as possible in everything they said. We have shown in chapters 1–5, especially our chapter on the role of figurative language, that this is simply not the case.

The second flaw is that the claim that "the quality of a translation is in proportion to the reader's unawareness that he is reading a translation at all" is unsustainable.[5] As we shall see below, the ethics and aesthetics of translation suggest that a modern equivalent that is "conspicuous as a translation of a foreign writing"—wearing its origins from a different time and place on its sleeves—has immense value given the remote roots of the Bible's original languages and cultures.[6]

The third flaw is the principle that even readers with little or no education or religious background should be able to understand the Bible without instruction and effort. This assumption is not only mistaken but also far-fetched, given the Bible's nature and origin. Where did the idea come from? It developed from a popular misunderstanding of the Reformation doctrine of the clarity or perspicuity of Scripture.

In the next several paragraphs, we will take a short detour and briefly consider the role that the doctrine played in the history of the Reformation to explore how this misunderstanding arose.

The two most prominent Bible translations of the Reformation were Luther's translation into German (the *Lutherbibel*) and the so-called King James Bible or King James Version, produced by a translation committee commissioned and authorized by King James, the Protestant ruler of England, to provide a version of the Bible in English. As the original introductions to the

4. Nida, *Good News for Everyone*, 13.
5. Nida, *Good News for Everyone*, 13.
6. Cheung, "Foreignising Bible Translation," 273.

Lutherbibel and the King James Version demonstrate, both translations aimed at what we now call dynamic equivalence. They wanted their translations to be as accessible to contemporary readers as the original texts had been to their intended audiences.

Importantly, however, both Luther and the committee responsible for the KJV also applied the principle of formal equivalence in their work. This principle encapsulates the idea that *the way we know through the language that we use to think* is essential for human understanding. We have already explored this important insight above, in our discussion of the role of figurative language in a hermeneutic of imagination.

By contrast, the Bible translation specialists who developed the theory of dynamic equivalence *in its modern form* misunderstood Luther and the KJV translation committee's emphasis on dynamic equivalence to mean that *even people with little or no religious or educational background should be able to understand the Bible effortlessly, without need for interpretation.*

How did this misunderstanding arise? The doctrine of *claritas Scriptura* was a polemical tool to challenge one of the rules for the reading of Scripture in the Roman Catholic Church, namely, that the only acceptable Bible translation was the Vulgate, which had been translated into the Latin vernacular by Jerome in the fourth century and remains the standard Bible translation for the Roman Catholic Church to the present day. Modern translations were discouraged on the basis that untrained laypeople would be unable to understand the true meaning and were likely to become confused by or even misunderstand the Word of God.[7]

In response, the Reformation doctrine stipulates that the Bible is "clear" in its meaning, at least regarding the main tenets of the Reformation understanding of the gospel. In later times, however, this stipulation was applied more widely to include *all contents* of the Bible and *all readers* of the Bible. Ultimately, the doctrine of the clarity of Scripture also began to entail that the Bible was written not for experts with special knowledge and interpretive skills but for the common people.

Having explored the origin of this popular misunderstanding, we now return to the main two arguments that refute its veracity.

First, most members of ancient populations were illiterate. The biblical authors knew that they were not writing for the common man or woman,

7. As a by-product of this argument, regulation did of course ensure that the official church hierarchy retained firm control over the interpretation and thus the accepted meaning of Scripture. This was one of the motivations for the Reformers' insistence that the Bible belonged in the hands of the common people, to enable them to determine for themselves what the Bible said about various controversial issues of the day.

for the common men and women of their day could not read what they wrote. In fact, numerous texts in the Bible itself imply or explicitly state that biblical texts need interpretation and explanation. We will mention just three examples among many: (1) The words of the Ethiopian eunuch in Acts 8:26–40. When Philip heard him reading the prophet Isaiah, he asked him, "Do you understand what you are reading?" To which the Ethiopian replied, "How can I, unless someone *guides me*?" (ὁδηγήσει, lit. "shows me the way," Acts 8:30–31). (2) The comment in 2 Peter 3:15–16. "Paul wrote to you according to the wisdom given him, speaking of this as he does in all his letters. There are some things in them hard to understand, which the ignorant and unstable twist." (3) The priest Ezra. He is described as "a scribe skilled in the law of Moses" (Ezra 7:6), as a man who "had set his heart to study the law of the Lord and to do it, and to teach the statutes and ordinances in Israel," and as "the scribe, a scholar of the text of the commandments of the Lord and his statutes for Israel" (Ezra 7:10, 11). These descriptions characterize him as a highly trained expert with specialist knowledge in the interpretation of an artifact, the biblical law of Moses. And in the book of Nehemiah, we learn that Ezra's public reading of Scripture needed interpretation: "The Levites . . . helped the people to understand the law, while the people remained in their places. So they read from the book, from the law of God, with interpretation. They gave the sense, so that the people understood the reading." And as a result, "the people went their way . . . to make great rejoicing, because they had understood the words that were declared to them" (Neh. 8:7–8, 12).

Second, the biblical texts were written to a particular people in a particular place and time. The Bible may have been written *for* us (Rom. 15:4), but it certainly was not written *to* us. "The Bible is not a Western Book. To be sure, it has generated ideas and attitudes that can be found everywhere in Western cultural and religious history. But the plain fact is that it was written by, for, and about people in the ancient Mediterranean world whose culture, worldview, social patterns, and daily expectations differed sharply from those of the modern West."[8]

In conclusion, then, we must reject Nida's claim that Bible translations that follow the principle of dynamic equivalence—as he and others at the end of the twentieth century understood it—are more faithful than others for basing their evaluation of accuracy on what readers actually understand. Skopos theory supports the idea that translations like the GNB and

8. Richard L. Rohrbaugh, *The New Testament in Cross-Cultural Perspective* (Cascade Books, 2007), ix, quoted in Cheung, "Foreignising Bible Translation," 263.

the CEV have a place for certain audiences, but claims to their superiority are misguided. And from the perspective of a hermeneutic of imagination, the principle of dynamic equivalence must be applied differently and more astutely.

Why Modern Translations in General Inhibit Imaginative Engagement

The following paragraphs relate to modern English translations in general, including but not restricted to domesticating translations. We draw on David Bentley Hart's reflections in the introduction to his own translation of the New Testament. His critiques of current Bible translations into English highlight how modern translations inhibit imaginative engagement with Scripture.[9] The key problem is that modern translations tend to obscure the linguistic profile that is unique to each specific biblical text as well as the texts' varied literary qualities, which often retain a persuasive rhetoric even if the Greek is not reflective of a literary masterpiece.

Dissatisfied with existing translations that "obscured aspects of the original texts which I thought extremely important," Hart claims that "all the existing standard English translations render a great many of the concepts and presuppositions upon which the books of the New Testament are built largely impenetrable," adding that "most of them effectively hide (sometimes forcibly) things of absolutely vital significance for understanding how the texts' authors thought."[10]

In his opinion, dynamic equivalence theory encourages translators "to make the line between translation and interpretation perilously hazy."[11] Compare this with the quotation from Nida, above: "The quality of a translation is in proportion to the reader's unawareness that he is reading a translation at all."[12]

Hart also reflects on the circumstance that most modern translations are the product of translation committees. "The inevitable consequence of this is that many of the most important decisions are negotiated accommodations, achieved by general agreement, and favoring only those solutions that

9. David Bentley Hart, *The New Testament: A Translation* (Yale University Press, 2017). His approach by and large reflects what we consider an imaginative translation, and while some of his comments are specific to the New Testament, they also apply to the Old Testament. We have resisted the impulse to systematize Hart's comments because his raw and somewhat disorganized presentation adds to the compelling force of his points.

10. Hart, *The New Testament*, xiv.

11. Hart, *The New Testament*, xiv.

12. Nida, *Good News for Everyone*, 13.

prove the least offensive to everyone involved."[13] The end result is a "process of natural selection" that almost automatically excludes "the most straightforwardly literal" renderings.[14] "All such renderings," he concludes, "become ineluctably mired in the anodyne blandness and imprecision of 'diplomatic' accord."[15] We concur: Modern translation theories that prioritize readability tend to eliminate or at least reduce the need for imagination in reading the Bible, often when it is most needed.

Hart also is critical of how theological commitments can influence modern translations: "Even the most conscientious translations tend, at certain crucial junctures, to use language determined as much by theological and dogmatic tradition as by the 'plain' meaning of the words on the page."[16]

Other problems with modern translations arise from the sheer weight of traditional renderings: "Where difficult words or syntactical uncertainties or grammatical obscurities appear in the Greek, the solutions favored by earlier translators are generally carried over by their successors, even where there may be more plausible or more interesting alternatives."[17]

In the final analysis, Hart concludes, "those who cannot read the original Greek are deprived of any way to see in the text of scripture a vast number of those verbal connections, conceptual ambiguities, and semantic oddities that are, in a very real sense, inseparable from its essence."[18]

In conclusion, modern translations do indeed obscure the imaginative nature of Scripture. Understandability comes at the expense of the Bible's literary profile and quality. The drive for communicative efficiency obscures most of the Bible's imaginative quirks and features—elements that the original authors and editors used to invite imaginative engagement.

Toward an Imaginative Theory of Bible Translation

In the final part of this chapter, we will explore how a hermeneutic of imagination contributes to a modern theory of Bible translation that showcases the Bible's imaginative qualities. We begin with a case study on David Bentley Hart's translation of the New Testament, continue with exploring the recent trend toward foreignizing translations in secular translation theories, and conclude with the contours of an imaginative translation of the Bible.

13. Hart, *The New Testament*, xiv.
14. Hart, *The New Testament*, xiv.
15. Hart, *The New Testament*, xv.
16. Hart, *The New Testament*, xv.
17. Hart, *The New Testament*, xvi.
18. Hart, *The New Testament*, xvi.

Case Study: David Bentley Hart's New Testament—an Imaginative Translation

Building on Hart's critiques of current Bible translations above, we explore Hart's reflections on his own translation, which exhibits important characteristics of an imaginative translation of the New Testament. His work forms a solid platform for how a hermeneutic of imagination can influence future translations of the Bible.

Hart describes the motivation for his own translation effort in the following terms: "The prospect of writing a version that would be by my lights as scrupulously faithful as I could make it, that would not merely reiterate conventional readings of the text, and that would allow me to call attention to features of the Greek original usually invisible in English version proved irresistible."[19] What he aims for, then, is a "reconstructive" translation that will "help awaken readers to mysteries and uncertainties and surprises in the New Testament documents that often lie wholly hidden from view beneath layers of received hermeneutical and theological tradition,"[20] in other words a translation that makes "the familiar strange, novel, and perhaps newly compelling."[21]

This is how Hart describes the style of his translation. He prefers formal to dynamic equivalence, with an "almost pitilessly literal translation" that aims to "make the original text as visible as possible." For example, he does not "fill in syntactical lacunae," "rectify grammatical lapses," or "draw a veil of delicacy over jarring words or images."[22] Even "where the Greek of the original is maladroit, broken, or impenetrable, so is the English of my translation; where an author has written bad Greek . . . I have written bad English."[23] He aimed "to preserve uncertainties that I did not want to presume to dispel" and tried to capture the "concise, urgent, precipitous quality" of texts, including "fragmentary formulations."[24]

This also includes "sudden shifts of tense," a feature not only of the New Testament's Greek but also of the Old Testament's Hebrew and Aramaic, which, in Hart's view, is "somewhat enchanting." Hart captures the performative quality of these shifts in tense: "It has something of the immediacy of a person standing among friends and relating a story, perhaps a little

19. Hart, *The New Testament*, xvi.
20. Hart, *The New Testament*, xvi–xvii.
21. Hart, *The New Testament*, xvii.
22. Hart, *The New Testament*, xvii.
23. Hart, *The New Testament*, xviii.
24. Hart, *The New Testament*, xviii.

breathlessly, lapsing naturally into the present tense at critical moments, then withdrawing into the past again."[25]

Words that have acquired theological overtones with time are usually translated by their literal meanings in English (precisely to achieve dynamic equivalence, which Hart elsewhere disavows!) to make the reader aware that they were once ordinary words with ordinary meanings: "My aim is simply to make the modern English reader 'hear' the words of the text as words with common meanings, as early Greek-speaking Christians would have done."[26]

Hart also renders "particular words throughout the text by the same English 'equivalent' whenever possible" to preserve "an obvious bit of wordplay [that otherwise] would be lost" or "where words with the same root are used in what seems like a more than accidental association."[27]

The foreignizing dimension of Hart's approach can be seen in the following comment: "Part of the task of illuminating the original text for Anglophone readers raised on the standard translations is . . . to give them a sense of the strangeness of the text: the novelty, the impenetrability, the frequently unfinished quality of the prose and of the theology." At times this may result in translations that reflect "the more unfamiliar or more baffling interpretation of a difficult passage," which in Hart's view may frequently be the more accurate construal.[28]

Even so, the larger aim remains "rendering the entire text into modern English as gracefully as possible without sacrificing the literal meaning of the original."[29] Yet he maintains that "in the long twilight struggle between felicity and fidelity, the latter should always win out in the end."[30]

In evaluation of Hart's translation, a particularly important literary achievement relevant for a hermeneutic of imagination is that his "mulish stubbornness regarding the idiosyncrasies of the text" allowed the voices of the different texts to retain their authentic distinctives, their unique linguistic profiles. By contrast, traditional translations, "in evening out the oddities of the text, tend to flatten the various voices of the writers into a single clean, commodious style (usually the translator's own)."[31] Hart's ideas are eminently conducive for a hermeneutic of imagination. In the final part of this chapter,

25. Hart, *The New Testament*, xviii, xix.
26. Hart, *The New Testament*, xix.
27. Hart, *The New Testament*, xx.
28. Hart, *The New Testament*, xx.
29. Hart, *The New Testament*, xxi. "Meaning" may not be the right term here.
30. Hart, *The New Testament*, xxi.
31. Hart, *The New Testament*, xxiii.

we will present our own vision for a translation of the Old Testament Hebrew and Aramaic that promotes an imaginative reading of the Bible.

Foreignizing Translations Showcase the Bible's Imaginative Nature

We will now explore how a recent trend in translation theory, the preference for "foreignizing" translations, impacts a Bible translation theory and associated practices inspired by a hermeneutic of imagination. Translation theorist Lawrence Venuti argues on ethical grounds that translations should be written, read, and evaluated with greater respect for linguistic and cultural differences.[32] The case for foreignizing translations of the Bible "whereby the foreign origins of the source text are made conspicuous in the translation" has also been made by Andy Cheung:[33]

> The Bible is a natural participant in foreignizing translation because it already contains much material with foreign origins. . . . Indeed, the *original* readers of the Bible found cultural elements difficult to understand, as in the case of Boaz and the sandal-removing ritual which necessitated in-text explanation in Ruth 4:7. The Bible itself is unashamedly foreign in many aspects.[34]

Consequently, Cheung claims, "any translation, any interpretation, any reading of these texts must deal with the historical distance that exists between the world and life referred to in these writings and the world and life of the modern interpreter."[35]

Cheung demonstrates the advantages of foreignizing Bible translations with compelling examples of anachronisms, biblical imagery and terminology, metaphor, neologisms, and transliteration. His examples illustrate the importance of foreignizing translation for a hermeneutic of imagination. We will demonstrate this with his discussion of the translation of metaphors. He concedes that the avoidance of metaphor aids "ease of understanding" but emphasizes that retaining metaphors in literal fashion has the advantage of "seasoning target texts with foreign flavour."[36] He notes that "the retention of metaphor, idiom, and biblical imagery, can be a powerful means by which Bible readers are educated about the original culture of the Old and New Testament."[37]

32. Lawrence Venuti, *The Scandals of Translation: Towards an Ethics of Difference* (Taylor & Francis, 1998).

33. Cheung, "Foreignising Bible Translation," 257, with reference to Lawrence Venuti, *The Translator's Invisibility: A History of Translation*, 2nd ed. (Routledge, 2008).

34. Cheung, "Foreignising Bible Translation," 259 (emphasis added).

35. Cheung, "Foreignising Bible Translation," 259–60.

36. Cheung, "Foreignising Bible Translation," 265.

37. Cheung, "Foreignising Bible Translation," 273.

He then evaluates a discussion of metaphors by Nida and Jan de Waard, proponents of domesticating Bible translations. They note that "the expression 'circumcision of the heart' (Rom. 2:29) is rarely understood *unless people have been specifically instructed* as to the figurative significance of circumcision" to support their suggestion to replace the metaphoric expression with an interpretive paraphrase.[38] Their example reveals two problems.

The first amounts to an extreme form of individualism. Since "De Waard and Nida are pessimistic about the likelihood of readers being taught about circumcision,"[39] they assume *a highly individualistic scenario* where readers engage with the Bible on their own rather than within a community of fellow believers. This reflects neither the reality of most Bible readers anywhere—ever—nor what the authors envisaged when they wrote the texts that eventually became part of the Bible.

The second amounts to a patronizing attitude toward readers of the Bible. Cheung illustrates this with an anecdote told by Marshall Broomhall describing the tensions between Western translators and their Chinese counterparts in early collaborations on Chinese Bible translation:

> For the first time all, or nearly all, of the figures of speech contained in the original Greek appeared in the Mandarin version. "To be clothed upon with a house," or "to put on a man," are fairly bold figures. In previous translations the temptations had been to paraphrase such expressions or give a marginal reading but during the work of this committee one of the Chinese scholars broke in: *"Do you suppose that we Chinese cannot understand and appreciate metaphors? Our books are full of them, and new ones are welcome."*[40]

It is not difficult to work out why Chinese Bible scholars, as early as the first half of the twentieth century, found the simplifications imposed on biblical texts by the removal of figurative language from earlier translations into Mandarin so offensive. It revealed to them the patronizing attitude toward Chinese readers that had guided those earlier Western translators.

One wonders whether it is similarly individualistic and condescending attitudes that prompted Bible translation theorists of the second half of the twentieth century to prefer domesticating and simplifying translations for the general reading public everywhere, including populations where Christianity

38. Jan de Waard and Eugene Nida, *From One Language to Another: Functional Equivalence in Bible Translating* (Nelson, 1986), 38, quoted in Cheung, "Foreignising Bible Translation," 267 (emphasis added).

39. Cheung, "Foreignising Bible Translation," 267.

40. Marshall Broomhall, *The Bible in China* (The British and Foreign Bible Society, 1934), 93, quoted in Cheung, "Foreignising Bible Translation," 267 (emphasis added).

has had an established religious and cultural presence for centuries. Consequently, there is a real and present danger that more sophisticated modern readers, in China and elsewhere, experience Bible versions based on dynamic equivalence as childish and simplistic.[41]

Cheung concedes that from the perspective of skopos theory, "a multitude of 'correct' translation possibilities emerge, each depending on target user function," and we agree. Even so, however, translations that enable "a target text to be made conspicuous as a translation of a foreign writing"—translations that are "unashamedly alien, even brazen," about their origins from different times and places—carry "particular advantages given the remote roots of the Bible's original language and culture."[42]

In sum, we conclude, also on ethical grounds, that a hermeneutic of imagination favors a translation that emphasizes the Bible's origin from a different time and place, and from a different culture and language. The question that arises next is this: How should a foreignizing translation reflect its foreign origins? By way of conclusion, the following paragraphs include our answer to this question.

A Hermeneutic of Imagination Inspires the Contours of an Imaginative Bible Translation

As we have seen, for the sake of readability modern translations into English and other modern languages frequently smooth over details in the original Hebrew, Aramaic, or Greek that appear unusual. Yet, it is precisely these quirks and other unusual features in the original that are purposefully employed by the authors to fire our imagination.[43] Modern translations that iron out the oddities in Scripture conceal those aspects of the text that promote more accurate interpretations through the stimulation of our imagination. With apologies to Alonso Schökel, therefore, we propose the following principle for modern Bible translations that aim to evoke the same effect in their modern readers as the originals did in their first readers: What has been *written* with imagination must be *translated* with imagination.

While here is not the place to develop a full theory of Bible translation that puts this principle into practice, we want to emphasize that, in contrast with

41. Cheung, "Foreignising Bible Translation," 272.

42. Cheung, "Foreignising Bible Translation," 273.

43. To illustrate this, we draw on a discussion of such unusual features in J. Richard Middleton, *Abraham's Silence: The Binding of Isaac, the Suffering of Job, and How to Talk Back to God* (Baker Academic, 2021). In our view, Middleton's is the most imaginative and insightful interpretation of the so-called binding of Isaac in Gen. 22 available today. He notes no less than four unusual features in the original that are obscured by the CEV.

how the principle of dynamic equivalence has been implemented in many modern translations, imaginative translations need to preserve and perhaps even highlight unusual features present in the original. They need to be *foreignizing* and *problematizing* translations in the sense that they preserve the biblical texts' origins in different languages, times, and places and consciously reflect what might be considered quirks and oddities in the original. They need to draw readers' attention to these features rather than obscure them because the original intended audiences would have experienced many if not all of them as unusual too. A truly dynamic translation that evokes—as far as possible—the same response in modern readers as the original aimed to evoke in ancient readers and hearers is therefore a semantically, grammatically, and syntactically expressive translation that reflects the feel of the original Hebrew, Aramaic, or Greek of the biblical texts.[44]

It needs to be quite literal rather than idiomatic. The disadvantage of idiomatic renderings is that they already interpret the text, thus narrowing down the various options for understanding it. The problem here is a tendency that is not easy to eliminate completely, but one that imaginative translations seek to avoid as much as is humanly possible—*the tendency to encode the translator's interpretation into the translation*. By contrast, imaginative translations allow readers to experience for themselves the multivalent quality of the biblical texts by exposing their imaginative form and content. This invites readers into imaginative engagements with the texts that do justice to their imaginative qualities.

An imaginative translation will preserve figurative language and ambiguity, for example by reproducing words, phrases, and entire sentences and passages that are deliberately underdetermined. An imaginative translation reflects openness to different meanings through grammatically, syntactically, and semantically expressive, even *problematizing* formulations so that readers in the target language may experience how a contemporary native speaker may have experienced the original text when first hearing or reading it.

This includes the opportunity to observe not only the poetic artistry of the originals but also their potential for oral performance: "Careful translation alerts us to . . . underlying oral factors and elicits aspects of performance that might otherwise go unnoticed: repetition; wordplay; implied gestures; expectation of audience reception and involvement; use of ready-mades, pauses, and silences that intend to engage audiences."[45] Since the majority of the biblical

44. Knut M. Heim, *Ecclesiastes*, Tyndale Old Testament Commentaries 18 (InterVarsity, 2019), 17.

45. Jeanette Mathews, *Prophets as Performers: Biblical Performance Criticism and Israel's Prophets* (Wipf & Stock, 2020), 4.

books' first generation of intended readers was illiterate and thus depended on others reading the texts to them, and since those who were able to read and had access to the text were reading them out loud, it is plausible, even likely, that most biblical texts were written with an ear toward their public, audible performance right from the start. Much can be gained from this kind of expressive translation:

> What do we gain if we consider the biblical texts as scripts for performance? Imagination becomes a key aspect to inquiry as I consider aspects such as the tone of delivery, the inclusion of a gesture, the intention behind a word that is now lost in translation.[46]

The aim of an imaginative translation is therefore to reflect such performance-oriented aspects of the original, to reflect as much as possible the specific character of the original, including all the imaginative components that went into its composition. The aim of an imaginative translation is not to render the biblical texts into smooth English. Instead, if something sounds unusual, quirky, vague, funny, or strange in the original, an imaginative translation will render it to sound equally unusual, quirky, vague, funny, or strange in its modern translation.

46. Mathews, *Prophets as Performers*, 5.

CHAPTER SEVEN

A Hermeneutic of Imagination Inspires Us to Conduct Our Academic Study of Scripture Theologically and to Undertake Our Theological Study Academically

The aim of this chapter is to demonstrate that academic study of the Bible can fruitfully be combined with reading it as Scripture, and that our imaginative approach is a really good way to accomplish this feat.

The Bible is the most-studied human artifact, period. It has been studied intensely for thousands of years, including by people with the brightest minds of their times. Therefore, if someone were to come up with an interpretation of a biblical text that is *radically* different from previous interpretations, the likelihood of the new understanding being wrong is high. Does this undermine the project of a hermeneutic of imagination?

We do not think so. Imaginative readings of the Bible regularly produce new interpretations that are worth considering, in the academy and in the church. Perhaps not all of them will pass the test of time, but we are quite confident that many will. Reading with imagination will at times produce genuinely new interpretations, but rarely will these be so radically different that their validity can be ruled out without further consideration.

Having said that, because imaginative readings regularly produce fresh insights and new interpretations, or because they resurrect interpretations of the past that have more recently been abandoned, forgotten, or neglected, it is essential that imaginative readings of the Bible draw on the wisdom of other scholars, both past and present. But are theological and academic studies of the Bible even compatible? We will argue below that the academic study of the Bible can fruitfully be combined with reading it as Scripture. We will show not only that an imaginative approach is a good way to combine the academic and theological study of Scripture but also that this type of reading is not in conflict with other academic or theological methodological approaches.

A Hermeneutic of Imagination Offers an Intellectually Compelling Model for the Integration of Theological and Academic Study of the Bible

Theological interpretation of the Bible, as opposed to purely academic approaches that intentionally exclude religious beliefs and set aside theological concerns, has made something of a revival in recent times, beginning with Brevard Childs's canonical approach[1] and continuing with various theological approaches proposed by a range of academics from a variety of backgrounds.[2]

In the first half of the twenty-first century, a review of the history of the interpretation of the Bible from a postmodern and postliberal perspective reveals that the ways in which the Bible has increasingly been studied in Western academic contexts have treated it as an academic artifact and considered it, by and large, as set apart from its origins in the Jewish and Christian faith communities of synagogue and church.

Michael Legaspi's careful and nuanced study of these developments, with special focus on German orientalist and Old Testament scholar Johann David Michaelis (1717–91) as a representative exponent of these trends, has demonstrated persuasively that, with the waning of scriptural authority in the West during Michaelis's lifetime, the prevailing context of religious strife,[3]

1. See, e.g., Brevard S. Childs, *Biblical Theology in Crisis* (Westminster, 1970); B. S. Childs, *The Book of Exodus: A Critical, Theological Commentary*, Old Testament Library (Westminster, 1974); B. S. Childs, *Introduction to the Old Testament as Scripture* (SCM, 1979); B. S. Childs, *Biblical Theology of the Old and New Testaments: Theological Reflection on the Christian Bible* (SCM, 1992); and B. S. Childs, *Isaiah: A Commentary*, Old Testament Library (Westminster John Knox, 2001).

2. Cf., e.g., Craig G. Bartholomew and Heath A. Thomas, eds., *A Manifesto for Theological Interpretation* (Baker Academic, 2016); and R. R. Reno, *The End of Interpretation: Reclaiming the Priority of Ecclesial Exegesis* (Baker Academic, 2022).

3. The Thirty Years' War, fought from 1618 to 1648 along confessional lines between states that had remained Roman Catholic and states that had turned to Protestantism, cost the lives of approximately 30 percent of the European population. See "Dreißigjähriger Krieg," *Brockhaus Enzyklopädie*, vol. 5 (Brockhaus, 1996–1999), 671.

and the overall skepticism of the age, academics began in response to seek a new approach to the Bible. They started to approach it as an object of inquiry whose interpretation could be managed by the deployment of critical tools and methods alone.[4] The following quotation captures Legaspi's overall argument:

> Biblical scholars at the Enlightenment university were employees of the state charged with creating a way of studying the Bible that would allow it to nourish a common life [based] on new principles. They set aside the scriptural Bible, bound as it was to the confessional identities that had torn Europe apart. In a decisive moment, Michaelis lent his talents and energies to the creation of a new academic Bible keyed to the unifying power of the postconfessional state. In doing so, he showed that academic criticism could not only generate new interpretive frameworks, it could also provide the study of a textualized Bible with a hospitable *place*—the philosophical faculty of the university—and a useful *purpose*—the reinforcement of religious irenicism.[5]

If Legaspi is correct—and he has made a strong argument that needs to be taken seriously in the academy and in the church—this means that the academic study of the Bible as practiced in the discipline of biblical studies, to which our own project aims to contribute, is a secular enterprise sponsored by secular institutions with secular interests. Consequently, a purely academic study of the Bible bypasses the purpose for which it was originally written and compiled. (What this purpose is we will explore shortly.) Purely academic study of the Bible leads to the "death of Scripture," as the provocative title of Legaspi's study claims.

Consequently, Legaspi believes that efforts to combine academic and theological interpretation of the Bible are futile. In his conclusions, he makes a stunning claim to this effect. Although he elaborates on this in one and the same paragraph, we will break it into three parts for clarity's sake. In the first part, he advocates for a strict separation:

> I believe that the scriptural Bible and the academic Bible are fundamentally different creations oriented toward rival interpretive communities. Though in some way homologous, they can and should function independently if each is to retain its integrity. While it is true that the scriptural reader and the academic interpreter can offer information and insights that the other finds useful or interesting, they remain, in the end, loyal to separate authorities.[6]

4. Michael C. Legaspi, *The Death of Scripture and the Rise of Biblical Studies*, Oxford Studies in Historical Theology (Oxford University Press, 2011).

5. Legaspi, *Death of Scripture*, 168. Here and in subsequent quotations, Legaspi employs the term "scriptural" for what we call "theological."

6. Legaspi, *Death of Scripture*, 169.

In the second part, he concedes that academic study of the Bible can be "useful":

> I grant the moral seriousness of the modern critical project, and, to a modest degree, the social and political utility of the academic Bible. I also grant the intellectual value of academic criticism. A rational, irenic study of the Bible supported by state resources and disciplined by academic standards cultivated across a range of fields has produced, in a relatively short time, an astonishing amount of useful information.[7]

In the third part, however, he dismisses academic study of the Bible for its failure to provide intellectually compelling interpretations that explain what the Bible aims to accomplish in its readers:

> It has become clear, though, that academic criticism in its contemporary form cannot offer a coherent, intellectually compelling account of what this information is actually *for*.[8]

We agree with some of Legaspi's claims and disagree with others. We agree that the hegemony of a purely academic study of the Bible needs to be challenged. However, we disagree with his conclusion that theological and academic study of the Bible "can and should function independently if each is to retain its integrity."

In support of our disagreement, we point to the middle section of the quotation. Here Legaspi lists some of the achievements of academic biblical study. These achievements are not just "useful"; they make *essential contributions* also to those readers who read the Bible as Scripture. First, the contribution of academic biblical studies to the social and political welfare of modern societies is more significant than Legaspi admits, as we will demonstrate shortly. Second, a purely theological study of the Bible has often promoted partisan, narrow-minded, and divisive interpretations and applications of biblical content, in the past and in the present. And sometimes these have led to severe social and political consequences. For this reason, we are convinced that an "irenic study of the Bible supported by state resources" should continue to play an essential role in holding faith communities accountable to genuinely biblical standards and virtues, even as this accountability comes from secular sources. These can be demonstrated through a reading of Scripture that is "disciplined by academic

7. Legaspi, *Death of Scripture*, 169.
8. Legaspi, *Death of Scripture*, 169.

standards cultivated across a range of fields," in ways that religious readers will find hard to refute at worst, and positively inspiring at best. Third, the immense intellectual contributions of academic study over a short time are extremely valuable for reading the Bible as Scripture. In conclusion, we are convinced that academic study of the Bible can fruitfully be combined with reading it as Scripture, and our imaginative approach is a really good way to make it happen.

Legaspi believes this cannot be done, as the following quotation demonstrates:

> There is value in the social and moral by-products of academic criticism, in things like tolerance, reasonableness, and self-awareness. The problem is that these rather thin, pale virtues seem only thinner and paler when compared to the classic virtues associated with the scriptural Bible: instead of bland tolerance, *love* that sacrifices itself; instead of an agreeable reasonability, *hope* that opens the mind to goodness and greatness that it has not yet fully imagined; and instead of critical self-awareness *faith* that inspires and animates the human heart. Academic criticism tempers belief, while scriptural reading edifies and directs it. In this sense, they work at cross-purposes.[9]

We agree with Legaspi's positive evaluation of the classic biblical virtues—faith, hope, and love—at the expense of the bland merits of tolerance, agreeable reasonability, and self-awareness. We are inspired by just how much the classical biblical virtues outshine the secular ones.

However, Legaspi espouses an idealized abstraction when he states that reading the Bible as Scripture automatically produces these virtues. The opposite is often the case. Our work as public ministers in the church and our work in faith-based seminaries has exposed us to how often Christian faith communities in the real world fail to practice them. In the real world, faith-based readers and communities often lack the basic virtues of tolerance, reasonableness, and self-awareness that can be the seedbeds for cultivating the more excellent virtues of faith, hope, and love.

Consequently, a hermeneutic of imagination reminds us that academic study of the Bible can make many valuable and essential contributions to reading the Bible as Scripture. It inspires us to use academic methods for all they are worth, in ways that allow theological and academic study to benefit each other. We agree with Legaspi that *purely* theological reading is incompatible with *purely* academic study. But a hermeneutic of imagination encourages us to practice our theological reading with more academic rigor,

9. Legaspi, *Death of Scripture*, 169.

and it encourages us to practice our academic study with more spiritual vigor. As a result, both the academy and the church will benefit.

Consequently, a hermeneutic of imagination inspires and enriches academic analysis of the Bible. As we will discuss in the conclusion, God "makes himself known and present to people through sacred Scripture."[10] If this is true, then academics, too, can encounter God's presence and experience his transforming power. In turn, their academic work will mediate God's presence and transformative power more effectively to those who read Scripture to inform their Christian faith and practice.[11]

A Hermeneutic of Imagination Harnesses the Academic Study of the Bible for Its Theological Interpretation

We will explore the wisdom in the academic work of other scholars under three main headings, organized by the popular metaphor of the world behind the text, the world within the text, and the world in front of the text, as for example proposed by W. Randolph Tate:

> In present scholarship, there are three different groups of theories regarding the locus and actualization of meaning: author-centered (with attention directed to the world behind the text), text-centered (with the focus on the world within the text, or the textual world), and reader-centered (where the spotlight is trained upon the world in front of the text, or the reader's world).[12]

A hermeneutic of imagination not only can coexist with standard academic methods but also can enhance the various standard methods within the discipline of biblical studies. As will be clear by now, however, we do not think that a *purely* academic deployment of these methods can exploit their potential to its full extent. Consequently, our discussion will regularly include reflections on how each method can be used imaginatively, in line with the overall argument of this volume. We are advocating for an "imaginative application of different critical approaches and theoretical frameworks,"[13] to put

10. William M. Wright IV and Francis Martin, *Encountering the Living God in Scripture: Theological and Philosophical Principles for Interpretation* (Baker Academic, 2019), 1.

11. Cf. Wright and Martin, *Encountering the Living God in Scripture*, 6.

12. W. Randolph Tate, *Biblical Interpretation: An Integrated Approach*, 3rd ed. (Baker Academic, 2013), 2.

13. Holly Morse and Katherine E. Southwood, introduction to *Psalms and the Use of the Critical Imagination: Essays in Honour of Professor Susan Gillingham*, ed. Holly Morse and Katherine E. Southwood, The Library of Hebrew Bible/Old Testament Studies 710 (T&T Clark, 2022), 1.

it in the memorable words of Holly Morse and Katherine Southwood in their Festschrift for Susan Gillingham. While Morse and Southwood emphasized reception history, however, we focus on reading with imagination in general.

Before we begin, two caveats are in order. First, we will survey many of the standard academic methods for studying the Bible, but there are many more; they, too, can be applied imaginatively to enhance our reading of the Bible. Second, our survey of the different methods is just that, a survey. Of necessity, our discussion will highlight their most important characteristics and discuss these with special attention to how they can be integrated into a hermeneutic of imagination. For more comprehensive surveys of these and other methods, we refer our readers to standard handbooks on the methods of biblical study.[14]

With these caveats in mind, we begin with methods that focus on the world *behind* the text. These include archaeology, textual criticism, and form, source, and redaction criticism. Next, we will look at the world *within* the text, and here we will focus on rhetorical criticism, literary criticism, and intertextuality. Finally, we will look at the world *in front of* the text, where we will engage with feminist and womanist criticism; ideological criticism; and reception history and the history of interpretation.

The Value of a Hermeneutic of Imagination for Study of the World Behind the Text

Archaeology. Archaeology makes important contributions to biblical studies in general and to imaginative readings of the Bible in particular. The study of archaeology has been defined as

> partly the discovery of the treasures of the past, partly the meticulous work of the scientific analyst, partly the exercise of the creative imagination. . . . But it is also the painstaking task of interpretation so that we come to understand what these things mean for the human story.[15]

While archaeology is not a "handmaid" to biblical scholarship,[16] it nonetheless illuminates the general cultural background, direct biblical connections,

14. Representative examples include William P. Brown, *A Handbook to Old Testament Exegesis* (Westminster John Knox, 2017); and J. W. Rogerson and Judith M. Lieu, eds., *The Oxford Handbook of Biblical Studies* (Oxford: Oxford University Press, 2006).

15. C. Renfrew and P. Barn, *Archaeology: Theories, Methods and Practice* (Thames & Hudson, 1996), 11, quoted in John R. Bartlett, "Archaeology," in *The Oxford Handbook of Biblical Studies*, ed. J. W. Rogerson and Judith M. Lieu (Oxford University Press, 2006), 567.

16. Bartlett, "Archaeology," 572.

and new evidence regarding the historicity of the biblical accounts, and it frequently provides information that is crucial for a hermeneutic of imagination because it helps us fill in gaps that we perceive in the texts because the original authors did not feel the need to include information that was readily available to their original readers.[17]

Nonetheless, archaeology also has its limitations. First, no matter how detailed the evidence, that evidence is not as objective as one might think, because it, too, needs interpretation. Second, archaeological evidence always has gaps, and so the picture remains incomplete.[18]

Textual criticism. The Old Testament in modern Bibles is based almost entirely on two manuscripts from the tenth and eleventh centuries CE. These are the Aleppo Codex and the Codex Leningradensis. While the Greek New Testament is based on a critical reconstruction based on careful assessment of the best available evidence collated from thousands of textual witnesses, the modern critical editions of the Hebrew Bible / Old Testament are of the "diplomatic" type, often called the Masoretic Text (MT).

The task of textual criticism is "to examine the text's reliability from the perspective of its transmission history since it has been painstakingly copied—by hand—many times over since the composition of the texts in the seventh to second centuries [BCE] (and perhaps a little earlier) until the earliest manuscripts in the Middle Ages that have survived into the present."[19]

Textual criticism "aims at the recovering or reconstruction of the original wording of a given literary work by evaluating the text as attested in several, diverging manuscripts."[20] The standard work on the textual criticism of the Hebrew Bible, from a technical and scholarly perspective, is Emanuel Tov's *Textual Criticism of the Hebrew Bible*.[21] One of the more accessible volumes suitable for students is Paul Wegner's *A Student's Guide to Textual Criticism of the Bible*.[22]

Textual criticism is an indispensable tool for reading the Bible with imagination, as it helps readers to evaluate parts of the biblical texts that appear strange, incomplete, or erroneous against the work of specialists who have evaluated the evidence. Frequently, imaginative reading will lead to fresh solutions that confirm the original nature of textual characteristics that

17. Bartlett, "Archaeology," 572–74.

18. Bartlett, "Archaeology," 574.

19. Arie van der Kooij, "Textual Criticism," in *The Oxford Handbook of Biblical Studies*, ed. J. W. Rogerson and Judith M. Lieu (Oxford University Press, 2006), 579.

20. Van der Kooij, "Textual Criticism," 582.

21. Emanuel Tov, *Textual Criticism of the Hebrew Bible*, 2nd rev. ed. (Fortress, 2001).

22. Paul D. Wegner, *A Student's Guide to Textual Criticism of the Bible: Its History, Methods and Results* (IVP Academic, 2006).

beforehand appeared problematic, as for example in the case of Ecclesiastes 7:27, where the gender of the otherwise male persona of Qoheleth (see Eccles. 1:2 and 12:8) suddenly switches to a female voice, indicating that the surrounding, apparently misogynist verses 26 and 28 have been performed in the high-pitched voice of a woman to achieve a humorous effect. (For detailed discussion of the passage, see my [Knut Heim's] commentaries on Ecclesiastes and especially my performance-oriented study on Eccles. 7:23–8:2.)[23] On occasion, imaginative reading of the Bible will provide fresh support for an alternative textual witness that departs from the standard texts in the Aleppo Codex or Codex Leningradensis.

In our work, many conjectural emendations proposed in the *Biblia Hebraica Stuttgartensia* have supported imaginative engagement with texts that are grammatically, syntactically, or semantically problematic. The editors of the various books frequently present so-called conjectural emendations—that is, alternative readings without support from textual witnesses. The goal of these conjectural emendations is to "restore" adherence to various "rules" of the Hebrew language. For the beginning student, these conjectural emendations can be extremely helpful to prompt imaginative engagement. For our part, we have found that they tend to support our own sense that there is something odd happening in the text, and we are encouraged to continue with an imaginative exploration of why the text seems unusual. More often than not, of course, the textual oddity is not an error of the author or subsequent scribes but an artistic feature of the text that prompts imaginative reading.

A similar dynamic presents itself when the versions offer a variety of translations. Traditionally, these have been interpreted as indirect evidence that those translations may have worked from different *Vorlagen*—that is, from Hebrew manuscripts that were different from each other—even when there are no textual witnesses to this effect. By contrast, our imaginative approach to textual criticism encourages us to ask why the ancient translators arrived at translations that encoded different *interpretations* of the original Hebrew. More often than not, the source texts themselves are intentionally ambiguous, inviting imaginative engagement, and the fruit of the translators' imaginative engagement results in the divergent translations.

Form, source, and redaction criticism. These methods aim to be "scientific" explorations of the prehistory of biblical texts, reconstructing how they have

23. Cf. Knut M. Heim, "Humor and Performance in Ecclesiastes 7:23–8:1," in *Biblical Humor and Performance*, ed. Peter S. Perry, Biblical Performance Criticism (Cascade Books, 2023); Heim, *Ecclesiastes*; and Knut M. Heim, *Ecclesiastes*, Zondervan Exegetical Commentary on the Old Testament (Zondervan Academic, 2025).

reached their present shape.[24] Underlying the methodologies of form, source, and redaction criticism is the conviction that "the illumination of the literary genesis of the final form of a text is . . . an integral part of its elucidation and understanding."[25] The three methods, while distinct, nonetheless build on one another.

Form criticism aims to understand why a given literary unit has been given the specific form it has, in distinction to the forms that other, similar language units have that belong to the same genre or text type.[26]

The aim of *source criticism* is to identify stages of development in the composition of a text's final form, with a special interest in the text's earliest part, to which other parts have successively been added.[27]

The aim of *redaction criticism* is to identify the interests that motivated those who combined the various earlier parts of texts—as identified through form and source criticism—in the precise ways in which they can now be found in the text's final form, and thus discern the intended purpose of the whole, as distinct from the intended purposes of its various earlier parts before their combination.[28]

A hermeneutic of imagination focuses our attention on the biblical texts as we now have them, not on their reconstructed earlier parts for their own sake. Nonetheless, explorations into the literary genesis of a text can be extremely helpful, if they are used to illuminate it in its final form. The *questions raised* in these textual approaches can be immensely helpful—even if the answers are not always convincing since of necessity they remain speculative.

This is readily acknowledged by Reinhard Müller and Juha Pakkala, the authors of an important recent study of editorial techniques in the Bible that aims to refine the traditional methods of literary criticism:

> As one of the goals of this book is to investigate the methodological basis of literary criticism,[29] an important section of each analysis is a hypothetical discussion on whether the documented editorial change could have been detected without the older or more original version being preserved. It is clear

24. Johannes P. Floss, "Form, Source, and Redaction Criticism," in *The Oxford Handbook of Biblical Studies*, ed. J. W. Rogerson and Judith M. Lieu (Oxford University Press, 2006), 591.

25. Cf. Floss, "Form, Source, and Redaction Criticism," 593.

26. Cf. Floss, "Form, Source, and Redaction Criticism," 593–603.

27. Cf. Floss, "Form, Source, and Redaction Criticism," 603–7, esp. 606.

28. Cf. Floss, "Form, Source, and Redaction Criticism," 608–11.

29. The English translator of Müller and Pakkala employs the term "literary criticism" as a direct translation of the German term "Literarkritik," the technical term in German-language scholarship for the methods of form, source, and redaction criticism. This is quite different from the typical English-language usage of the term "literary criticism," which describes the exploration of the world within the text, which we explore below.

> that some subjectivity is inherent in discussing such hypothetical cases, yet we will lay the arguments on the table for any criticism, and in any case we will pursue a critical evaluation.[30]

Humility is the key, as Müller and Pakkala emphasize in the conclusions to their study:

> We have emphasized the uncertainties involved in the results of literary criticism. Any results and reconstructions should be seen as abstractions of a complicated development and as approximations towards still poorly known ancient realities. That omissions, replacements, and transpositions occasionally took place highlights the unfeasibility of fully reconstructing what happened to the texts.[31]

A refined literary criticism as proposed by Müller and Pakkala can be immensely informative for reading the Bible with imagination, especially when practitioners come clean about its provisional nature:

> When we acknowledge its limitations, literary criticism has a better chance of convincing biblical scholarship at large. To put it differently, an uncompromising focus on exact redactional reconstructions may do harm to the method and obstruct its reception by other scholars. Die-hard redaction-critical reconstructions based on single sentences or even words can hardly convince.[32]

Consequently, a hermeneutic of imagination can benefit enormously from insights into how the real-life faith convictions and faith-based attitudes and behaviors of the actual people who wrote the texts and for whom the texts were written may have changed over time. It helps us to put ourselves into the shoes of the original biblical writers and readers:

> Allowing the hypothetical and abstract nature of reconstructions, literary criticism has the potential to regain its central role in biblical studies, for it provides significant information about various aspects of early Judaism, such as general development of concepts, practices, and societal circumstances, which would otherwise be lost.[33]

So if *imaginative* form criticism helps us to identify the typical forms of similar language units of the same genre or text type, if it helps us to observe

30. Reinhard Müller and Juha Pakkala, *Editorial Techniques in the Hebrew Bible: Toward a Refined Literary Criticism*, Resources for Biblical Study 97 (SBL Press, 2022), 30.
31. Müller and Pakkala, *Editorial Techniques in the Hebrew Bible*, 547.
32. Müller and Pakkala, *Editorial Techniques in the Hebrew Bible*, 547.
33. Müller and Pakkala, *Editorial Techniques in the Hebrew Bible*, 547.

how a specific text unit is different from its type, and if it helps us to explore why its authors may have given it that particular shape and even departed from the expected, then the results become immensely informative for imaginative engagement with the biblical texts.

Similarly, *imaginative* source criticism will proceed with a humility that is commensurate with its hypothetical nature, since reconstructions of the earliest parts of a biblical text must inevitably remain speculative. Even so, imaginative reflection on why later parts may have been added in the reconstructed stages of development in the composition of the text's final form, and how such reconstructed hypothetical additions have enriched the biblical text as we now have it, can be immensely fruitful.

Our reading of the Bible also benefits greatly from *imaginative* redaction criticism. Again, humility given the speculative nature of this work is the starting point. Then an exploration of what may have motivated those who combined the earlier parts of a text and shaped them into a coherent whole to give the resulting composite its final form can help us to discern the intended purpose of the whole, as distinct from the intended purposes of its various earlier parts before their combination. Our imaginative hermeneutic thus inspires redaction-critical work that is similar, in many respects, to the canonical approach in the work of Childs and others.[34]

The Value of a Hermeneutic of Imagination for Study of the World Within the Text

Rhetorical criticism. Rhetorical criticism studies how the rhetorical techniques employed in biblical texts affect their readers, how they "seek to convince their readers or change their readers' perspectives."[35] Rhetorical criticism of the Hebrew Bible / Old Testament became popular in biblical studies with James Muilenberg's 1968 presidential address to the Society of Biblical Literature, in which he urged Bible scholars to analyze biblical texts as "works of art" through "a close reading" that pays attention to "stylistic features and elements of literary aesthetics."[36] In many ways, it remains questionable whether rhetorical criticism is an actual method in the traditional sense. Perhaps it is more a set of guidelines.[37]

34. Cf., e.g., Childs, *Book of Exodus*; Childs, *Introduction to the Old Testament as Scripture*; Childs, *Biblical Theology of the Old and New Testaments*; and Childs, *Isaiah*.

35. Margaret M. Mitchell, "Rhetorical and New Literary Criticism," in *The Oxford Handbook of Biblical Studies*, ed. J. W. Rogerson and Judith M. Lieu (Oxford University Press, 2006), 617.

36. Mitchell, "Rhetorical and New Literary Criticism," 618, citing James Muilenberg, "Form Criticism and Beyond," *Journal of Biblical Literature* 88 (1969).

37. Mitchell, "Rhetorical and New Literary Criticism," 619.

Since rhetoric is "the art of influencing individuals and groups to believe, act, feel, and value in particular ways," it is reasonable to assume "that ancient Jewish and Christian writers generally wrote with those ends in mind and shaped their literary works accordingly," and to read those works "as dynamic interventions in the lives of social groups."[38]

A hermeneutic of imagination draws enthusiastically on rhetorical criticism because both are interested in the artistic quality of the biblical texts and how that artistry is employed to influence the Bible's readers. Like rhetorical criticism, a hermeneutic of imagination "regards a text as a vehicle of persuasion, designed to change the world by changing what people believe, value, and desire to do."[39] And, following Elisabeth Schüssler Fiorenza's lead, rhetorical criticism practiced imaginatively will take the public, political, and ethical responsibilities of biblical scholarship seriously.[40] Since interpretation itself is rhetorical and ideologically committed, we will pay special attention to the power dynamics not only in the biblical texts themselves but also in the interpretive work that we and others do and in the lives of the various audiences for whom we and others interpret Scripture.[41] Consequently, to practice rhetorical criticism imaginatively, we will have to be critically self-aware and apply our interpretive work ethically, with a keen eye on the Bible's supreme goal—to inspire love for God, self, and neighbor—which we discussed at the end of chapter 4.

Literary criticism. A hermeneutic of imagination elevates literary criticism to a level of prominence in the academic study of Scripture. There is a natural affinity, since literary criticism understands the biblical texts as literature, as works of art that, in their final form, are unified pieces of art and deserve "a close reading of precise details of the text," which in turn "appreciates especially the *dynamism of the world inside the text*."[42] Reading the Bible as literature means "paying careful attention to things that matter to its internal life, such as its plot, characters, internal tensions, and poetic and metaphorical forms."[43] Reading with imagination helps us to treat the Bible as we would treat other works of great literary caliber. Understanding and appreciating any great work of art, literary or otherwise, requires the use of our imagination, and the Bible is no exception.

38. Greg Carey, "Rhetorical Criticism," in *The New Cambridge Companion to Biblical Interpretation*, ed. Ian Boxall and Bradley C. Gregory, Cambridge Companions to Religion (Cambridge University Press, 2023), 91.

39. Carey, "Rhetorical Criticism," 108.

40. Cf. Carey, "Rhetorical Criticism," 102–3.

41. Carey, "Rhetorical Criticism," 109.

42. Mitchell, "Rhetorical and New Literary Criticism," 626.

43. Mitchell, "Rhetorical and New Literary Criticism," 627.

Intertextuality. Intertextuality concerns the study of all features that bring a given text into an open or hidden relationship with other texts. It is very productive for a hermeneutic of imagination, because "wherever there is a community of readers who hearken to earlier texts as powerful and evocative voices with a claim to be heard in the present, intertextual writing and reading will take place."[44] It lies at the very heart of a hermeneutic of imagination, for the writer "is a reader of texts . . . before s/he is a creator of texts," and a text is available only through the process of reading; what the reader perceives when he or she reads a text is due to the cross-fertilization of what he or she reads by all the texts that the reader has read or known before.[45]

Biblical texts persistently and imaginatively use earlier material from the Bible to draw on the *cultural force* that those earlier texts bring with them as part of the canon of the Old and New Testaments. This evokes a *social energy* that reinforces the newer texts that quote or allude to the older ones.[46] In other words, they draw on the imaginations of readers who recognize the allusions or quotations. The allusions to or quotations from earlier biblical texts carry their original contexts with them, for those contexts are imaginatively present in the memory of the writers who use them and in the memory of the readers who recognize them.[47]

Most theories of intertextuality emphasize the reader's role at the expense of the author's.[48] By contrast, *imaginative* engagement with the intertextual dimensions of biblical texts values both equally. Reading the Bible with imagination draws naturally on literary readings of the Bible. There is much overlap in every way.

The Value of a Hermeneutic of Imagination for Study of the World in Front of the Text

Work concerned with the world in front of the text includes feminist and womanist criticism, ideological criticism, and reception history and the history of interpretation.

44. Richard B. Hays, *Echoes of Scripture in Paul* (Yale University Press, 1989), 15, quoted in Knut M. Heim, "The Perfect King of Psalm 72—an 'Intertextual' Inquiry," in *The Lord's Anointed: Interpretations of Old Testament Messianic Texts*, ed. P. E. Satterthwaite, Richard S. Hess, and Gordon J. Wenham (Eerdmans, 1995), 231.

45. J. Still and M. Worton, eds., *Intertextuality: Theories and Practices* (Manchester University Press, 1990), 1–2, quoted in Heim, "Perfect King of Psalm 72," 232.

46. Heim, "Perfect King of Psalm 72," 232–33.

47. Heim, "Perfect King of Psalm 72," 233.

48. Heim, "Perfect King of Psalm 72," 234.

Feminist and womanist criticism. Following Dorothee Sölle, Marie-Theres Wacker defines *feminism* as "the emergence of women from a state of submission for which they themselves were responsible or which others had attributed to them."[49] She adds that "feminist exegesis is correspondingly a scientific engagement with the Bible with the intention of contributing to the emancipation, liberation, and empowering of women."[50]

Importantly, feminist engagement with the Bible in this sense is both a method and a hermeneutical approach. It is "not simply a *method* of biblical interpretation in the sense of a particular technique for analysing texts, but a *critical hermeneutic* of engagement with the Bible and in this sense feminist *criticism*."[51] As a consequence, feminist and womanist engagements with the Bible both complement and critique existing methods of biblical scholarship. The following paragraph describes various related approaches to the Bible from the perspectives of women from different backgrounds and with a variety of interests. Since traditional feminism has focused mainly on the concerns of "white, West, Christian, hetero-sexual middle-class women,"[52] newer approaches focus on broader concerns of women with a wider range of perspectives:

> There is "Womanist" biblical criticism as practiced by black American women; there is the approach of "mujeristas," the women of Central and Latin America, as well as the Bible readings of Asian "women theologians" or the approach of African women. Christian feminist engagement with the Bible has other procedures and thematic concerns compared with a Jewish feminist engagement with the Bible; and criticism of society, politics, and the economy is not carried out with the same sharpness by all of these. Lesbian and queer (gender-confusing) exegetical approaches bring in yet other perspectives.[53]

There are important *hermeneutical* questions related to reading the Bible with imagination from the full breadth of women's concerns and interests:

> For women who understand themselves as believing Christians and wish to relate themselves to Christian tradition, the Bible presents a particular challenge. On the one hand it is regarded as Holy Scripture, which remains normative for the teaching and practice of the churches. On the other hand, in the history of

49. Marie-Theres Wacker, "Feminist Criticism and Related Aspects," in *The Oxford Handbook of Biblical Studies*, ed. J. W. Rogerson and Judith M. Lieu (Oxford University Press, 2006), 634.

50. Wacker, "Feminist Criticism and Related Aspects," 634.

51. Wacker, "Feminist Criticism and Related Aspects," 634.

52. Wacker, "Feminist Criticism and Related Aspects," 634.

53. Wacker, "Feminist Criticism and Related Aspects," 634–35.

> Christianity women have always suffered from particular gender-specific limitations, indeed discriminations, which have been based upon this Holy Scripture.[54]

Reading the Bible with imagination exposes traditional practices, which co-opted the Bible as an instrument of oppression against women, as sinful and wrong. Imaginative reading of the Bible empowers the Christian church to accept that the origins of the biblical texts within a historical patriarchal framework have conditioned the presentation of scriptural content from male perspectives. Imaginative theological reflection enables the recovery of gender-neutral interpretations of biblical content. Reading the Bible with imagination prioritizes the concerns of women in reading the Bible against the grain of male-oriented reading traditions and liberates the Bible from its patriarchal background.

The *methodological* questions related to a hermeneutic of imagination from the full breadth of women's concerns and interests have implications for all the scholarly methods related to biblical interpretation. Imaginative reading of the Bible exposes the extent to which biblical texts are so ingrained in their historical circumstances that attitudes recorded in them impair the essential equality of all humans.[55] Reading the Bible with imagination thus enthusiastically agrees with Irmtraud Fischer's approach of "gender justice" in biblical interpretation.[56] Drawing on Fischer's exegesis of gender justice, a hermeneutic of imagination has two important advantages that promote gender justice in biblical interpretation.

First, a hermeneutic of imagination demonstrates how unexamined and preconceived norms have influenced traditional biblical interpretation in ways that have perpetuated gender injustice by creating the impression that such injustice was promoted in the biblical texts themselves. This exposes the fact that the maltreatment of women in the Christian tradition was caused not by the biblical texts themselves but by unexamined prejudices of male readers who mistook the realities of gender inequality in the ancient world of the Bible as *prescriptive* rather than *descriptive*.

Second, a hermeneutic of imagination can thus help to liberate us from gender prejudices, both ancient and modern, that until now have impaired our interpretations. It enables a reading of the biblical texts with genuine

54. Wacker, "Feminist Criticism and Related Aspects," 635.

55. Cf. Wacker, "Feminist Criticism and Related Aspects," 643–46.

56. Irmtraud Fischer, *Women Who Wrestled with God: Biblical Stories of Israel's Beginnings* (Liturgical Press, 2000); Irmtraud Fischer, *Rut*, Herders Theologischer Kommentar zum Alten Testament (Herder, 2001); and Irmtraud Fischer, *Gotteskünderinnen: Zu einer geschlechterfairen Deutung des Phänomens der Prophetie und der Prophetinnen in der Hebräischen Bibel* (Kohlhammer, 2002), cited in Wacker, "Feminist Criticism and Related Aspects," 646.

concern for the well-being of all. Consequently, a hermeneutic of imagination actively seeks to correct gender injustice and promotes the restoration of gender fairness and equality.

Ideological criticism. There are two spheres of interest in ideological criticism: reflection on ideological influences in the production of the biblical texts themselves and reflection on the sociological situatedness of the interpreters of the Bible.[57]

Ideological criticism is not a value-neutral perspective. It arose from the Marxist tradition, and for this reason alone it is suspect to many Christian readers. Some of their reservations are justified, because ideological criticism has been used to undermine not only the ideological positions of interpreters of the Bible but also the validity of the Bible itself. The term has been used in political discourse as one of abuse, for example by dubbing the interpretation of someone with whom one disagrees as "ideological," and thus doctrinaire or narrow.[58]

Christopher Rowland explains that, in the Marxist tradition, "the ideological concerns the ways in which language and meaning are used . . . to legitimate the prevailing, usually unequal power relations in society."[59] Understood in this way, ideology "functions in the interests of the wielders of power . . . who have an interest in maintaining things as they are and the interpretation of the world as it is, thereby enabling the economic interests of those with most wealth and influence to continue to wield that influence."[60]

There is a significant overlap between ideological criticism and reading the Bible with peripheral vision, which we explore in chapter 8. Reading the Bible with imagination enthusiastically combines ideological criticism with the study of the Bible's reception history. The study of how the conscious or unconscious ideological commitments of interpreters have influenced their understanding of the Bible during different periods of history helps us to learn from past mistakes.[61] Imaginative reading appreciates the important contribution of ideological criticism because it relativizes the point of view of dominant readings of the past, which more often than not have been skewed

57. Christopher Rowland, "Social, Political, and Ideological Criticism," in *The Oxford Handbook of Biblical Studies*, ed. J. W. Rogerson and Judith M. Lieu (Oxford University Press, 2006), 656. Rowland's chapter focuses on ideological criticism, but he includes the terms "social" and "political" in the title to draw attention to the importance of social context and power relations.

58. Rowland, "Social, Political, and Ideological Criticism," 657.

59. Rowland, "Social, Political, and Ideological Criticism," 657, citing David McClellan, *Marxism and Religion: A Description and Assessment of the Marxist Critique of Christianity* (Macmillan, 1987).

60. Rowland, "Social, Political, and Ideological Criticism," 657.

61. Rowland, "Social, Political, and Ideological Criticism," 656.

through the unexplored assumptions of dominant groups of readers, who tend to assume that how they read and interpret the biblical texts is both "normal" and "objective"—and thus normative—when in reality it is not.

Ideological criticism done imaginatively promotes awareness of the readers' own approaches as well as awareness of the approaches of others through history, including the constraints and biases that each interpreter's approach imposes upon the way they interpret the Bible.[62]

As a direct and intended side effect, this also has the important advantage of promoting openness to the value that the interpretations of others contribute to the interpretive enterprise. They provide a constructive check on the exclusive validity of one's own interpretation that can improve one's understanding of the Bible and thus stimulate fresh thinking that further improves the quality of one's interpretive results.[63]

Reception history and the history of interpretation. Important texts have afterlives, and this has powerful implications for a hermeneutic of imagination. Already within the Bible, later texts not only *allude to* or *quote* earlier biblical material, a phenomenon that we explored above under the name intertextuality, but also *interpret* and *respond to* earlier biblical texts because later biblical writers and their intended readers value them as powerful and evocative voices that continue to communicate to them the words of God in written form, even long after the lifetime of the original authors and the first generation of readers.

Consequently, inner-biblical interpretation takes place,[64] and so there is a significant overlap with intertextuality. However, when the response to earlier biblical texts moves beyond interpretation to *reinterpretation* and *adaptation*, as for example in the afterlife of the dynastic promise to David in 2 Samuel 7—in Psalm 89 and elsewhere—we speak of a *reception history*, the history of the effects that this text has had over time.

A reception history of 2 Samuel 7 thus traces the *history of interpretation* that responds to the theological significance of the original promise by transforming it over time into a covenant, the Davidic covenant with all its enduring theological and practical implications for Jewish messianism and Christianity.[65]

62. Rowland, "Social, Political, and Ideological Criticism," 656.

63. Rowland, "Social, Political, and Ideological Criticism," 657.

64. Michael Fishbane, *Biblical Interpretation in Ancient Israel* (Oxford University Press, 1985).

65. See, e.g., Knut M. Heim, "The (God-)Forsaken King of Psalm 89: A Historical and Intertextual Enquiry," in *King and Messiah in Israel and the Ancient Near East*, Journal for the Study of the Old Testament Supplement Series (Sheffield Academic, 1998).

The histories of interpretation of biblical texts reveal their meaning potential by exploring what they have meant to readers through time. The reception histories of biblical texts are similar, but they explore how readers have *used* and *applied* their interpretations of those texts, for example in art or real-life scenarios.

As a result, the histories of the interpretation of biblical texts and their reception histories are in themselves powerful examples of readings of the Bible through time, and they can both inspire our own readings with imagination and, where appropriate, function as correctives. Earlier readings, by way of comparison, can help us to evaluate the quality of our own imaginative interpretations and vice versa, as a reception history of the book of Jonah illustrates.

Case Study: The Reception History of the Book of Jonah and an Imaginative Reading of the Book as Humorous

As we discussed in our chapter on the role of humor in reading the biblical texts with imagination, not everything that has been written on the meaning of biblical texts is characterized by wisdom. Sometimes correct observations, such as the identification of humor in the book of Jonah, have been *used* unimaginatively to arrive at interpretations and applications that evidently lack wisdom because they are anti-Jewish and thus antibiblical and anti-Christian. In the words of Yvonne Sherwood, the book has been "closed down" by reading it in "bad taste" because it has habitually paired Jonah with Jewishness.[66] Sherwood documents, in thirty-nine pages, what she calls "the mainstream" of interpretations of the book of Jonah.[67] Her exploration of the reception history of the book of Jonah includes no less than sixteen pages of documentation and analysis of anti-Jewish statements in twentieth-century critical Christian commentaries.[68] Here is an excerpt from her findings:

> Adjectives that characterize Jonah as the recalcitrant, lazy pupil slide into adjectives that conjure up the spectre of the Enlightenment/Lutheran legacy of Jonah the Jew. Jonah is "self-centered, lazy, hypocritical and altogether inferior to the wonderful pagans around him"; he is *revêche et têtu* ("cantankerous and bad-tempered"), *Engherzig* [*sic*] (narrow-minded), "mulish,"

66. Yvonne Sherwood, *A Biblical Text and Its Afterlives: The Survival of Jonah in Western Culture* (Cambridge University Press, 2000), 2.

67. Sherwood, *A Biblical Text and Its Afterlives*, 48–87.

68. Sherwood, *A Biblical Text and Its Afterlives*, 59–74.

> "good-for-nothing," "sinister," "petty," "ludicrous," a "bigot" who is eyeless with hate.[69]

Shockingly, this is just a miniature excerpt from page after page documenting similar interpretations. The following comments from Sherwood expose the cause:

> Seeping through the strangely diverse designations of Jonah as lazy pupil, bungling peasant, bigot, and clown, bleeding beneath the professional, polite, critical veneer, are clearly barely metaphorized and deflected anti-Semitic designations. Jonah's "bloodthirsty hope," poison-filled psyche, eyeless hatred, and religious monstrosity evoke a familiar welter of medieval mythologies: the Jew as murderer, monster, the dehumanized Other, "eyeless" hence faceless, convicted of blood-lust and the blood-libel.[70]

Sherwood demonstrates that interpretations of the book of Jonah as humorous also follow this pattern of anti-Jewish prejudice:

> Jonah the clown makes his appearance in the mid-1960s when the text, now redrafted as satire, is performed on the scholarly comedy circuit (is this an attempt to mitigate the violence, I wonder, to dilute the polemical force with a touch of comedy?). Turning on what they call the "harsh light of satire," Wolff and Good put on a bit of a theological slapstick in which Jonah, bungling xenophobe, trips over the truth of Romans 3.29 to the appreciative hoots and cheers of the audience (thus, as Linda Nochlin observes, in a different context, "once more irony puts Jewish figures in their place"). "How the narrator laughs at the Hebrew who takes great pains to flee from his God, and in the process, and against his will, brings non-Israelites to believe in this God," chuckles Wolff, while Good, having promised a price on the "absurdity of God," in fact revels in the absurdity of Jonah.[71]

Humor at the expense of Jonah can be even more overtly anti-Jewish, as the following observations demonstrate:

> In 1981, a slicker comedian takes the mike, milking the text's puns, playing the pauses just right: "The fish," pronounces Holbert, pausing, looking round the

69. Sherwood, *A Biblical Text and Its Afterlives*, 64–65, with references to the sources where these statements appear.

70. Sherwood, *A Biblical Text and Its Afterlives*, 66.

71. Sherwood, *A Biblical Text and Its Afterlives*, 75, quoting Hans Walter Wolff, *Jonah and Obadiah*, trans. Margaret Kohl, Hermeneia (Augsburg, 1986), 109; and Edwin M. Good, "Jonah: The Absurdity of God," in *Irony in the Old Testament* (SPCK, 1965), 55.

> smoke-filled room, "who is literally sick of the prophet's false piety" (pausing again, lips twitching, waiting)—"throws up." The laughter and groans that circulate from the critical one-liner promptly dissipate, however, when the figure of Jonah the Zionist takes the stage, and the book shifts from satire to political manifesto.[72]

The implications that arise from Sherwood's reception history of the book of Jonah are highlighted in Amy Erickson's landmark commentary on the book:

> As Yvonne Sherwood points out, when modern commentators read Jonah as a comedy, they tend to do so at the expense of Jonah: he is funny (read: pathetic), while the non-Israelites (proto-gentiles) are noble and faithful; he is petulant, narrow-minded, disobedient, and xenophobic, while God is merciful, forgiving, and loving to all people. In these readings, the humor is binary and aimed exclusively at the (Jewish) other.[73]

If we want to appreciate the humor in the book appropriately, Erickson concludes, we need "to take seriously that the humor in these texts is likely to spare no one,"[74] because "each of the characters is capable of making the audience laugh at themselves and at the others with whom they are in relationship."[75]

Our case study demonstrates just how important the history of the interpretation of biblical texts is. The reception history of the Bible is essential for a hermeneutic of imagination, as Sherwood and Erickson have demonstrated regarding the book of Jonah. Any reading that identifies humor in the book, as our imaginative reading does, needs to appreciate it is a playful humor that holds up a mirror to *all* religious readers—Jewish, Christian, or Muslim. There is a little Jonah in all of us.

Conclusion

In this chapter, we surveyed many of the standard academic methods for studying the Bible. We explored how they can be applied imaginatively to enhance our reading of the Bible. Our discussion focused on their most important

72. Sherwood, *A Biblical Text and Its Afterlives*, 75. Sherwood imagines Holbert as a comedian in the smoke-filled backroom of a bar. The quotation, which in the original reads "the big fish throws up," is from John C. Holbert, "Deliverance Belongs to YHWH! Satire in the Book of Jonah," *Journal for the Study of the Old Testament* 21 (1981): 74.

73. Amy Erickson, *Jonah: Introduction and Commentary*, Illuminations (Eerdmans, 2021), 49.

74. Erickson, *Jonah*, 49.

75. Erickson, *Jonah*, 49–50.

characteristics, paying special attention to how they can be integrated into a hermeneutic of imagination. What we discovered is that a hermeneutic of imagination enriches academic study and that academic methods are indispensable for a hermeneutic of imagination. Academic methods imaginatively employed are essential for reading the Bible.

Why does all this matter? As we have shown, a hermeneutic of imagination helps us to explore more clearly and more accurately the worlds behind, within, and in front of the text. Archaeology is used not simply to validate or disprove the claims of Scripture but as a way for the reader to enter imaginatively into the world of the text. Additionally, we have shown that reading with imagination works in combination with the various critical disciplines to enhance their usefulness, not to replace them or render them obsolete.

Study of the world within the text and a hermeneutic of imagination naturally go together. We demonstrated that the disciplines of rhetorical and literary criticism as well as intertextuality require us to use our imagination to enter the world of the text, and they also require us to understand our own culture and position in history as well as the depth of our desire to be transformed by the text.

Finally, we discovered that a hermeneutic of imagination enhances varying contextual and ideological criticisms. Not only does it help us to imagine ourselves within the worlds of the biblical texts, but it also empowers us to bring our own contexts and identities with us in ways that are more authentic. This motivates us to interact constructively with scholars who approach the biblical texts from contexts and with attitudes and perspectives that are different from our own. A hermeneutic of imagination inspires us to learn from others, and even more so when they disagree with us. It empowers us to read with the interests of others in mind—an important perspective that we explore in the following chapter.

CHAPTER EIGHT

A Hermeneutic of Imagination Expands Our Vision So We Embody the Moral Imagination of Scripture

A hermeneutic of imagination harnesses the moral imagination of the Old and New Testaments and puts it to work.[1] As imaginative readers of the Bible, we contend for justice with confidence and hope. Why? Because the texts of the Old Testament "understand justice as being possible in this world because they accept that the cosmos is justly ordered under the rule of a just God,"[2] and reading these texts imaginatively focuses our attention on the important role of social justice in the Bible.

We will first introduce a new perspective for a hermeneutic of imagination, the idea of reading Scripture with peripheral vision. This approach encourages us to read the Bible with the interests of others in mind, with a special concern and affection for the vulnerable. It encourages us to interpret and apply the Bible for the benefit of others. Second, we will explore hermeneutical implications that arise from reading the Bible with imagination. Third, we will explore the relationship between the Old and New Testaments and demonstrate that the Old Testament is at least as important for Christian faith and practice as the New Testament. Fourth, we will provide further support for this claim with an excursus on the unique ethical contributions that the

1. Cf. Walter J. Houston, *Contending for Justice: Ideologies and Theologies of Social Justice in the Old Testament*, The Library of Hebrew Bible/Old Testament Studies 428 (T&T Clark, 2006), 228.

2. Houston, *Contending for Justice*, 229.

Old Testament has made to human flourishing. Fifth, we will demonstrate that God's righteousness and justice promote the role of social justice in a hermeneutic of imagination. Sixth and finally, we illustrate how a hermeneutic of imagination inspires and compels us to contend for justice.

A Hermeneutic of Imagination Encourages Reading with Peripheral Vision

Reading the Bible with imagination highlights that it was written to inspire its readers to contribute intentionally to human welfare. Reading the Bible with imagination encourages us to read it with peripheral vision.[3]

Peripheral Vision Attunes Us to the Concerns and Needs of Others

What is peripheral vision? A simple dictionary definition of *peripheral vision* is "side vision—what is seen on the side by the eye when looking straight ahead." It is part of a normal, wide-angle field of vision.

We can gain a better understanding of peripheral vision through considering its opposite, tunnel vision—when human eyesight is biologically impaired such that objects cannot be properly seen if they are not close to the center of the field of vision. Metaphorically, tunnel vision also describes people's limited ability to engage complex challenges; they tend to focus exclusively on a single or limited goal or point of view, their proposed solutions have a narrow focus, and their attitudes could be described as narrow-minded.

People who lose their peripheral vision describe the process as unpleasant and frightening: Losing your peripheral vision can feel like the world is closing in around you. A sense of foreboding arises because tunnel vision blinds us to the dangers that may lurk or even approach from just beyond our range of sight. This is exactly how many Christians feel today, we believe, because they have lost their peripheral vision as they read their Bibles and attempt to make sense of the world around them without a broadly informed theological framework. By contrast, a hermeneutic of imagination can restore readers' peripheral vision and bring into their perspective fresh possibilities for human flourishing that God has prepared—opportunities that are waiting just beyond a reduced field of vision.

This is not a new, risky, or dangerous attitude toward Scripture and the world. Rather, it is a return to the *normal*, the *natural* way of reading the Bible and observing the world. With peripheral vision intact, we can see the wider

3. The idea of reading the Bible with peripheral vision first saw the light of day in a presentation given at Denver Seminary as part of the annual Kent Mathews Lecture, October 2, 2017.

picture; we can spot dangers from afar and counter them. We gain a deeper understanding of the issues and opportunities. We feel more competent to tackle them appropriately. Of course, we can also see new opportunities and take advantage of them as they present themselves. Ultimately, we approach both the Bible and the world with a healthier dose of confidence.

Reading with peripheral vision, however, is not the same as so-called readings from the margin. Readings from the margin are well represented in Rasia S. Sugirtharajah's widely read volume *Voices from the Margin: Interpreting the Bible in the Third World* and a volume of collected essays edited by him: *Still at the Margins: Biblical Scholarship Fifteen Years after Voices from the Margin.*[4] Such marginal readings tacitly assume and inadvertently affirm that the "center" of reading the Bible is in Western Europe and North America and that those who practice reading at the center are predominantly white Europeans or North Americans, and mostly men. This is why biblical scholars from the majority world sometimes envision themselves "at the margin" of reading perspectives.

This perspective realistically portrays what has happened for centuries and has correctly identified the problem: The most influential readers and interpreters of the Bible have been Westerners, who all too often envisaged themselves as at the "center" of the world, of civilization, of the Christian world. However, the conceptualization of reading perspectives as "marginal" on the one hand or geographically and culturally centered in the West on the other is too static and outdated. It neglects the most important change of the past thirty years—the growing momentum of globalization.

Globalization is a process of interaction and integration among the people, companies, and governments of different nations, a process driven by international trade and investment and aided by information technology. And globalization also affects world religions like Christianity. This brief definition focuses on the economic drivers for globalization. For this reason, it falls short of describing the *cultural* impact of this process; it also fails to reflect that some of globalization's drivers emerge from a power shift in economics from North to South and from West to East. Additionally, this is paralleled by similar shifts in the global populations of Christians steadily toward the South and toward the East.

4. R. S. Sugirtharajah, *Voices from the Margin: Interpreting the Bible in the Third World* (Orbis Books, 1991); and R. S. Sugirtharajah, *Still at the Margins: Biblical Scholarship Fifteen Years after "Voices from the Margin"* (T&T Clark, 2008). Sugirtharajah's initial volume went through several revised editions, and a twenty-fifth anniversary edition demonstrates its ongoing impact and popularity: R. S. Sugirtharajah, *Voices from the Margin: Interpreting the Bible in the Third World*, 25th anniv. ed. (Orbis Books, 2016).

Taking the impact of globalization seriously, reading with peripheral vision is different from "marginal" readings on the one side and from "centrist" readings that are geographically and culturally situated in the West on the other. Rather, a hermeneutic of imagination helps us to take the geographical location and cultural identity of every reader and reading community anywhere in the world to be the center of that person's or that reading community's field of vision. Reading with peripheral vision starts with every single reader and reading community, wherever they are, as that person's or that community's vantage point—the geographical and cultural standpoint from where they take their bearings and define the center of their own field of vision, and from where they perceive the periphery of their field of vision. There is not one center but as many centers as there are readers. There is not one periphery but as many as there are readers.

In sum, a hermeneutic of imagination encourages all the Bible's readers, no matter where they are or what they perceive themselves to be ethnically or culturally, to expand their fields of vision and pay special attention to their peripheries. It is okay that the main concerns at the center of our field of vision remain important for us, but reading the Bible imaginatively stimulates us also to pay attention to our periphery. It encourages us *to read the Bible also with the interests of others in mind*. It encourages us to read the Bible with a special concern and affection for the vulnerable. It encourages us *to interpret and apply it for the benefit of others:* "Let each of you look not to your own interests, but to the interests of others" (Phil. 2:4).

Consequently, reading the Bible with an imaginatively expanded peripheral vision inspires us to learn from others whose center of vision differs from ours. Good starting points for such learning are the volumes *Scripture and Its Interpretation*, the global and ecumenical introduction to the Bible edited by Michael Gorman; and *Reading the Bible Around the World*, the student's guide to global hermeneutics edited by Federico Alfredo Roth and others. These contain chapters on Protestant, Roman Catholic, Orthodox, and Pentecostal interpretations of Scripture as well as chapters on African, Latino/a, and Asian and Asian American interpretations.[5]

To tackle the global challenges of the twenty-first century and beyond, the church needs a *global* vision, with as wide an angle of vision as possible. Global challenges need global solutions. The local church cannot envision these on its own, no matter how big it is, no matter where it is located. British

5. Michael J. Gorman, ed., *Scripture and Its Interpretation* (Baker Academic, 2017); and Federico Alfredo Roth, Justin Marc Smith, Kirsten Sonkyo Oh, Alice Yafeh-Deigh, and Kay Higuera Smith, eds., *Reading the Bible Around the World* (IVP Academic, 2022).

missiologist Lesslie Newbigin famously claimed that "the local church is the hope of the world." This motto has gained wide popularity in North America and elsewhere through Bill Hybels's use of it at Willow Creek's Global Leadership Summit in 2012. However, it is too narrow because it shrinks our field of vision to local concerns, a tunnel vision that perforce ignores Scripture's peripheral, global vision. The global church—with its wisdom, gained over centuries—is the hope of the world.

Peripheral Vision Helps Us Read Scripture as It Was Meant to Be Read

The Bible, all of it, was written with peripheral vision. A comprehensive survey of the entire Bible is highly desirable, but this lies beyond the scope of this chapter. Even so, a survey of the opening parts of the Old and New Testaments demonstrates the prominence of peripheral vision. If the opening parts of both Testaments were written with peripheral vision, then it is likely that the remainder of the Bible reflects the same perspective.

Peripheral Vision in the Gospels

The Gospels in the New Testament were written with peripheral vision. In our survey, we found a peripheral perspective in the genealogy of Jesus (Matt. 1), the social status of Jesus's parents (Luke 2), the early childhood of Jesus (Matt. 2:13–14), and the closest friends and followers of Jesus, the disciples (Matt. 4:18–22; 9:9; Luke 6:15; Acts 1:13). What is more, Jesus himself was considered a quasi-foreign outsider by people from his own culture (John 1:43–46), and the audiences and patients of Jesus also belonged to the social periphery (Matt. 8:1–4, 28–34; Mark 5:1–20; 8:22–26; 10:46–52; Luke 8:26–39, 43–48; John 8:1–11; 9). Jesus intentionally sought out the company of people at the periphery (Matt. 8:5–13; Mark 7:24–30; John 4; 12:20–32), and his parables also focus on the social periphery (e.g., Luke 10).

An imaginative reading of the so-called Jesus Manifesto in Luke 4 and an imaginative study of Jesus's eating habits support the conclusion that the Gospels were written with peripheral vision.

Peripheral vision in the Jesus Manifesto. Two forms of evidence suggest that in Luke 4 Jesus reads his Bible with peripheral vision.

First, when Jesus self-identifies with the messianic figure from Isaiah 61, he chooses a portion of the Bible that explicitly focuses on people at the periphery: "to bring good news to the poor . . . to proclaim release to the captives and recovery of sight to the blind, to set free those who are oppressed, to proclaim the year of the Lord's favor" (Luke 4:18–9). Jesus declares that he has been anointed with the Spirit of the Lord for the benefit of people at the periphery—the economically peripheral (the poor), the legally peripheral (the captives), the medically peripheral (the blind), and the socially peripheral (the oppressed).

Second, Jesus knows just how provocative, countercultural, and revolutionary his calling is. We can tell, because when his audience "all spoke well of him and were amazed at the gracious words that came from his mouth" (Luke 4:22), he realized that they were reading Isaiah 61 with an egocentric tunnel vision, with a focus on themselves. As they listened to his quotation, they saw themselves as "the poor" (in comparison with wealthier fellow Jews). They saw themselves as "the captives" and "the oppressed" (in the grip of the Roman Empire and its occupying forces). Consequently, Jesus challenges their reading strategy with provocative talk: "Doubtless you will quote to me this proverb: 'Doctor, cure yourself!' . . . No prophet is accepted in the prophet's hometown" (Luke 4:23–24). He anticipates their aggressive and violent rejection once they recognize that his calling is focused on people at their periphery. He then clarifies that he reads Isaiah 61 and the entire Bible with peripheral vision, explaining that it was meant to be read that way from the beginning: "But the truth is," he says, "there were many widows in Israel in the time of Elijah . . . yet Elijah was sent to none of them except to a widow at Zarephath in Sidon. There were also many with a skin disease in Israel in the time of the prophet Elisha, and none of them was cleansed except Naaman the Syrian" (4:26–27)!

We know that now Jesus's audience grasps the peripheral focus of his reading strategy, because they take offense. "When they heard this," we are told, "all in the synagogue were filled with rage." Then they get up, drive him out of the town, and lead him to a hill to throw him to his death (Luke 4:28–29)! The extremely violent response to Jesus's peripheral reading of Scripture can be explained only against his audience's inward-looking, egocentric, and ethnocentric reading strategy. Their tunnel vision made them read against the grain of Scripture.

Peripheral vision in the eating habits of Jesus. It is no exaggeration when a recent study of Jesus's ministry claims that he "ate his way through the Gospels."[6] Most importantly, Jesus ate so regularly with marginalized people—the "sinners and tax collectors," as they are often referred to—that Herbert Anderson and Edward Foley claim "they killed him because of the way he ate; because he ate and drank with sinners."[7]

6. Robert J. Karris, *Eating Your Way Through Luke's Gospel* (Liturgical Press, 2006); cf. also Mark Glanville, "Jesus Ate His Way Through the Gospels—Eaten with a Tax-Collector Recently?," *Mark Glanville* (blog), July 20, 2012, https://www.markglanville.org/blog/2012/07/20/jesus-ate-his-way-through-the-gospels-eaten-with-a-tax-collector-recently.

7. Herbert Anderson and Edward Foley, *Mighty Stories, Dangerous Rituals: Weaving Together the Human and the Divine* (Jossey-Bass, 2001), 155.

The paradigm example is the infamous meal with Matthew the tax collector, who in turn has invited many of his tax collector friends and a bunch of other people whose lifestyle was so unacceptable they were officially known as "sinners." Jesus's behavior is felt to be so outrageous that some Pharisees who witnessed the event challenge his disciples with the uncomfortable question "Why does your teacher eat with tax collectors and sinners?" (Matt. 9:11; cf. Mark 2:16 and Luke 5:30). Overhearing the exchange, Jesus replies, "Those who are well have no need of a physician, but those who are sick. . . . For I have come not to call the righteous, but sinners" (Matt. 9:12–13; cf. Mark 2:17 and Luke 5:31–32). In other words, Jesus's focus was on those at the religious and social periphery. On another occasion, Jesus goes one step further and invites himself into the home of Zacchaeus, the chief tax collector of Jericho, to stay the night and no doubt have a meal. Again his behavior is challenged: "He has gone to be the guest of one who is a sinner!" Jesus's response is similar to before: "The Son of Man came to seek out and save the lost" (Luke 19:7–10). His focus was on those at the periphery.

By contrast, on an occasion when Jesus is invited to a meal by a respected pillar of the community, a leader of the Pharisees, he notes the elitist atmosphere around the table and challenges his host and fellow guests: "When you give a banquet, invite the poor, the crippled, the lame, and the blind. And you will be blessed because they cannot repay you" (Luke 14:13–14). He then goes on to tell one of his famous parables, the one about the great dinner, which reflects Jesus's view on who will attend the great banquet in heaven. And he tells how the originally invited guests all made excuses and none of them came. In his disappointment, Jesus says, the owner of the house sends out new invitations: "Go out at once into the streets and lanes of the town and bring in the poor, the crippled, the blind, and the lame"—all people with what nowadays we call preexisting conditions (14:21). And when there is still room at the table—and there will always be room at God's table for more guests—he sends out additional invitations: "Go out into roads and lanes"—presumably outside the town—"and compel people to come in, so that my house may be filled!" (14:23). Note how the circle widens to include more and more among those at the periphery. Jesus ate and drank with the people at the margins of polite society; he sought out their company; he pursued the friendship and hospitality of people at the periphery.

In sum, this survey of the Gospels demonstrates that Jesus understood the Bible he read as having been written with peripheral vision and that he read it accordingly. Consequently, he conducted his ministry with special attention to those at the periphery. This was not lost on his followers, the writers of the

Gospels, or his enemies. Finally, it was also not lost on those at polite society's periphery, for they kept flocking to meet him wherever he went.

While there is not enough space in this chapter for an investigation of the entire New Testament, the evidence surveyed here suggests that the remainder of the New Testament was also written with peripheral vision and that it is meant to be read with peripheral vision.

Peripheral Vision in the Old Testament

The Old Testament materials that demonstrate the peripheral vision of its authors and actors are too numerous to cover in this chapter. Here too, therefore, we will focus on the beginning. Reading the creation stories (Gen. 1–3), the stories about the patriarchs (Gen. 12–50), and the drama of the exodus (Exod. 1–3) with imagination, we will discover that they were written with peripheral vision.

Peripheral vision in the creation stories. In Genesis 1–3, a foundational text for theological anthropology, human beings are created in the image of God (1:26–27). Genesis 1:1–2:3 presents a first creation story in which the whole earth is in view, and because it is all "very good" (1:31) yet wild and full of untamed animals and plants, humans are tasked not only to "be fruitful and multiply" but also to "fill the earth and subdue it and have dominion over . . . every living thing that moves upon the earth" (1:28). The narrative describes voluntary migration and intentional conquest to find a good, a very good, life. Human beings are *made* to migrate. But what does it mean that humans should not only fill the earth but also subdue it and have dominion over it? Genesis 1 simply does not give sufficient information for a satisfactory answer, thus prompting imaginative engagement.

Consequently, our attention is drawn to the next chapter, Genesis 2. It is commonly acknowledged that Genesis 2:4–25 presents a second creation story with a different style and emphases,[8] but together the two stories "provide a rich tapestry of creation theology."[9] In Genesis 2, humans are placed in a garden prepared for human habitation. It is a beautiful place, full of every good thing, abundance itself. The tasks that God gives humans here sound different from the tasks in the previous chapter: "The Lord God took the man and put him in the garden of Eden to till it and keep it" (2:15), as most modern translations put it. Yet the two Hebrew verbs, שׁמר and עבד, are

8. Bill T. Arnold, *Genesis*, New Cambridge Bible Commentary (Cambridge University Press, 2009), 54.

9. Arnold, *Genesis*, 51.

more naturally translated "to serve" and "to protect."[10] The narrative is one of nurture and preservation. Human beings are meant to care.

Reading the two creation stories with imagination prevents us from focusing on their differences, and it also prevents us from *reinterpreting* one in light of the other. The editors of Genesis juxtaposed them to prompt imaginative engagement. They are meant to *complement and enrich* each other.

According to Genesis 2, the human journey begins in a space designed for human flourishing, a perfectly prepared garden full of vegetation and habitation in perfect harmony. Humans were tasked with *serving and protecting* it (Gen. 2:15). However, when 1:28 and 2:15 are read together with imagination, the verbs "serve" and "protect" in 2:15 complement and enrich the meaning of the verbs "subdue" and "have dominion" in 1:28: When the two verses are read together with imagination, 2:15 unpacks the assignment in 1:28 to mean that humans are to *expand the borders of the garden* by caring for it, so that this place of beauty, bounty, and harmony would eventually extend to the ends of the earth even as humans multiply and fill the earth. The combined narrative in Genesis 1–2 reveals that the human purpose is one of *migration with care*, a conquest of love that overcomes obstacles to the flourishing of creation. Humans are to contribute to the common good by serving all living things. The very purpose of human existence is about movement from the center (the garden) to the periphery (to fill the earth), an outward movement with a benevolent purpose, a single-minded commitment to enhance, enrich, and include. Humanity was meant to have a peripheral vision from the start, to pursue dominion not for its own sake but for the welfare of all creation.

Peripheral vision in the lives of the patriarchs. Genesis 12–50 focuses on the life stories of the first four generations of the people of God called Israel—Abraham, Isaac, Jacob, and the ancestors of the twelve tribes, most notably Joseph. These texts consistently portray the patriarchs as nomads, economic migrants, and refugees.

In Genesis 12, Abram is called to migrate from his home, and in return he is promised a new home on foreign soil, numerous descendants, material and spiritual blessings, honor, and the privilege to become the source of material and spiritual blessings for others:

> Now the Lord said to Abram, "Go from your country and your kindred and your father's house to the land that I will show you. I will make of you a great nation, and I will bless you and make your name great, so that you will be a

10. Arnold, *Genesis*, 59.

> blessing. I will bless those who bless you, and the one who curses you I will curse, and in you all the families of the earth shall be blessed." (Gen. 12:1–3)

The call of Abram was a challenge to leave his home, to emigrate and leave his family and other cultural ties behind. It also was an invitation that held great promise of happiness, spiritual fulfillment, honor, fame, and the opportunity to benefit others: "so that you will be a blessing." Abram's migration was intended to be universally beneficial: "and in you all the families of the earth shall be blessed." Abram became a nomad and stranger not just for his own advantage but for the universal good. There was a peripheral vision at the very heart of his calling.

Jacob grasped by force, and ahead of time, what God had in store for him all along. Therefore, he was forced to flee from his own brother. He had to leave Canaan, the land of promise, to return to Haran and the family that Abram had left behind. There, being a foreigner now in his own country of origin, he became the victim of exploitation at the hand of his uncle Laban, a member of his own family (Gen. 27–31).

Joseph was trafficked into Egypt after being sold by his own brothers (Gen. 37:12–36)—a pattern that has all too often repeated itself in history. Large-scale slavery and human trafficking is possible only with the collaboration or neglect of those who should protect their kin. Upon his arrival on foreign soil, Joseph demonstrates high skill and becomes upwardly mobile (39:1–6). Yet he is accused of attempted rape, convicted, and imprisoned (39:6–20). He is accused of sexual misconduct, another component of the universal pattern of the exploitation of displaced humans the world over and throughout history. Eventually, however, the man at the very periphery of Egyptian society becomes its savior and joins the elite (39:21–41:57).

Then Joseph's family joins him in Egypt. His father and brothers with their families flee a famine in their homeland and seek refuge in a more prosperous country, hoping for survival and a better life (Gen. 42:1–47:28). They are welcomed with a generous relocation package, motivated by gratitude for the services rendered by Joseph and granted in anticipation of the immigrants' positive impact on the host country's economy.

Peripheral vision in the drama of the exodus. Through their forced migration and positive welcome, the people of God develop their identity as a growing family unit of opportunist migrants (nomads) in Canaan and then as economic refugees and legal immigrants in Egypt. While there is economic integration, there is no or little assimilation. They remain culturally and religiously distinct. Through a prolonged period, Israelites maintain their separate identity and become increasingly numerous, economically successful, culturally self-confident, and politically assertive (Exod. 1:1–8). Crucially, however, they remain at the cultural periphery of their host nation.

Over time, the strength of the Israelite community arouses jealousy, suspicion, and fear among its host culture (Exod. 1:9). This leads to resentment among the general population and coercive action on behalf of the government, which includes social engineering, repressive family planning, exploitation of labor, and publicly sponsored physical abuse at the hands of ordinary members of the host nation. Members of an ethnic minority are systematically pushed beyond the periphery of their host culture and into total exclusion. Time and the lack of cultural memory, as well as group emotions, play crucial roles (1:10–2:10).

Oppression, exploitation, and suppression continue for many years (Exod. 1:11–23). But God pays close attention to the fate of his people and eventually intervenes. Here are two key texts that demonstrate God's focus on the periphery of Egypt's social, economic, and religious life. Relevant words are italicized:

> The Israelites groaned under their slavery and cried out. Their cry for help rose up to God from their slavery. God *heard* their groaning, and God *remembered* his covenant with Abraham, Isaac, and Jacob. God *looked upon* the Israelites, and God *took notice* of them. (Exod. 2:23–25)

> Then the LORD said, "I have *observed* the misery of my people who are in Egypt; I have *heard* their cry on account of their taskmasters. Indeed, I *know* their sufferings, and I *have come down to deliver* them from the Egyptians and *to bring them up out of that land to a good and spacious land, to a land flowing with milk and honey*, to the country of the Canaanites, the Hittites, the Amorites, the Perizzites, the Hivites, and the Jebusites. *The cry of the Israelites has now come to me; I have also seen how the Egyptians oppress them.* Now go, *I am sending you* to Pharaoh to bring my people, the Israelites, out of Egypt." (Exod. 3:7–10)

These texts not only highlight God's careful attention to the plight of those at the periphery of their host culture but also emphasize that God took sides with them and acted redemptively on their behalf, even to the detriment of those who were supposed to be their hosts rather than their oppressors. God's attention was not on Egypt, the greatest nation on earth at the time, but on a small ethnic minority in need. God was, and is, concerned for those at the periphery.

In sum, an imaginative analysis of key texts from the beginning of the Old Testament reveals that they were written with concern for those at the periphery. The evidence suggests that the remainder of the Old Testament was also written with peripheral vision and that the Old Testament is meant to be read with peripheral vision.

Reading with Imagination Can Restore the Peripheral Vision at the Heart of Scripture

Short explorations of Old and New Testament texts demonstrate that the Christian Bible was written with a keen interest in people at the periphery of human society. The Bible was written with peripheral vision, and it invites us to read with peripheral vision. The Bible's own peripheral vision can inform, guide, and empower Christian readers today to read its pages with the interests of others in mind.

A peripheral vision in our reading of the Bible inspires us to look beyond our local circumstances and gives us confidence that we, today, have the resources we need to contribute to human welfare and make a difference. A peripheral vision emboldens us to move forward with confidence and self-assured generosity toward others who are different from us.

The church has been around for a long time. We are the longest-standing continually existing human organization in history. We have a larger number of intellectuals in our ranks than any other human organization, both historically and probably still currently. We have the deepest corporate experience and wisdom of any culture or large-scale human organization—an immense treasure that outstretches any present cultural identity. We have been networked both vertically (ecclesiastical hierarchy) and horizontally (church congregations in local vicinity or the same denomination) in every part of the world for centuries. We can move forward with a larger vision of what God can and will do through us, the church, in our time; and we can do so as part of a worldwide family of believers who can immensely enrich our perspective at every twist and turn of the path laid out before us.

The things we fear most are in God's control. We need to regain confidence from our peripheral reading of the Bible and from the history of the global church. This will empower us to live and act with generosity toward the other, no matter how threatening that other might seem.

Reading the Bible with peripheral vision is not an unusual or strange way of reading the Bible. Rather, this is how the Bible was meant to be read from the start. Reading the Bible with imagination gives us peripheral vision so we can divert our focus from ourselves and train it on those at or near the periphery of our field of vision—no matter where we are located. We will expectantly reach out to other branches of the Christian faith—from different continents, cultures, ethnic backgrounds, and denominational identities—to gather together a rich harvest of wisdom from others who believe differently in the one same God in whom we believe, for mutual enrichment.

Reading the Bible with peripheral vision will inspire us to read with a Christian imagination that is truly creative because it is illuminated by the Holy Spirit, who also works in others who are different from us. Reading the Bible with imagination helps us to develop our peripheral vision, and the broader horizon that emerges with it will help us Christians to be what we are meant to be—the light of the world and the salt of the earth (Matt. 5:13–14). Reading the Bible with imagination helps us to adopt a hermeneutic with a peripheral vision, and this hermeneutic promotes the role of justice to the level of prominence that it deserves in a hermeneutic of imagination.

Implications for a Hermeneutic of Imagination

As already stated, reading the Bible with imagination harnesses the moral imagination of the Old and New Testaments and puts it to work.[11] Eminent biblical ethicist Yiu Sing Lúcás Chan has demonstrated that Scripture gains its authority through its capacity to form communities whose behavior is consistent with God's will as revealed in its pages.

The more we recognize the Bible's authority, the more obedient we become to its demands. The more we live according to its moral and ethical demands, the more we reflect the extent of its authority to order our lives as individuals and as communities.[12] Conversely, a failure to align our actions with the

11. Cf. Houston, *Contending for Justice*, 228.

12. Yiu Sing Lúcás Chan, *The Ten Commandments and the Beatitudes: Biblical Studies and Ethics for Real Life* (Rowman & Littlefield, 2012), 17, citing Lisa Sowle Cahill, "Community and Universals: A Misplaced Debate in Christian Ethics," *Annual of the Society of Christian Ethics* 18 (1998): 3–12. Chan followed the lead of earlier groundbreaking work such as Bruce C. Birch and Larry L. Rasmussen, *Bible and Ethics in the Christian Life*, rev. and exp. ed. (Augsburg, 1989). The aim was to combine the interpretation of Scripture and ethics, to bridge the gap between the disciplines of biblical studies and moral theology. The profound impact of Chan's work can be traced in a volume of collected essays in dialogue with his writings and dedicated to his memory: Michael Cover, John S. Thiede, and Joshua Ezra Burns, eds., *Bridging Scripture and Moral Theology: Essays in Dialogue with Yiu Sing Lúcás Chan, S.J.* (Lexington, 2019). As James Keenan notes, Chan's work has made a convincing case that "the work of biblical ethics requires an inseparable double competency, namely the exegetical competency of the biblical theologian and the hermeneutical competency of the ethicist in applying the exegetical claims into a contemporary moral setting." James F. Keenan, SJ, "Hospitality: Interpreting Lúcás Chan's Work Through a Timely, Biblical Virtue from the Book of Ruth," in *Bridging Scripture and Moral Theology: Essays in Dialogue with Yiu Sing Lúcás Chan, S.J.*, ed. Michael Cover, John S. Thiede, and Joshua Ezra Burns (Lexington, 2019), 7.

divine will revealed in Scripture exposes our de facto rejection of its authority, official declarations to its inspired and authoritative nature notwithstanding. A hermeneutic of imagination reminds us that faith and obedience belong together in the Christian practice of reading the Bible.

Consequently, we begin to put into practice what we discussed at the end of chapter 4, when we argued for the primacy of love in a hermeneutic of imagination: Reading with imagination informs not only our beliefs but also how we feel about others and how we treat them. Orthodoxy and orthopraxy belong together. Practically, this means that imaginative interpretation must lead to imaginative application. What has been written with imagination must be interpreted with imagination, and what has been interpreted with imagination must be applied with imagination. To do this well, however, we need to explore how a hermeneutic of imagination encourages us to reimagine the relationship between the Old and New Testaments.

A Hermeneutic of Imagination Recalibrates the Relationship Between the Old and New Testaments

What Christians now call the Old Testament was, pure and simple, the Bible of Jesus.[13] All of it was the Scripture of Jesus, and it was the only Scripture he had. This is also true for the writers of what eventually would come to be known as the New Testament. John Goldingay rightly notes that what we now call the Old Testament was Jesus's scriptural authority:

> The First Testament provides the foundation for Jesus's moral teaching. Jesus goes on to declare, "You have heard that it was said. . . . But I tell you . . ." (Matt. 5:17–48). He is again "fulfilling" or "filling out" the First Testament, speaking like a prophet, helping people to see implications in the Scriptures that they might be avoiding, and inviting us to study what the Scriptures have to teach us about the way we should live.[14]

We agree with Goldingay's interpretation of Jesus's comment in Matthew 5:17, "Do not think that I have come to abolish the Law or the Prophets; I have come not to abolish but to fulfill." Jesus did not come to "fill up" what was lacking in the Law and the Prophets and make them full. Rather, he came to help us understand the full extent of God's desire for human flourishing,

13. John Goldingay, *Reading Jesus's Bible: How the New Testament Helps Us Understand the Old Testament* (Eerdmans, 2017), 1.

14. Goldingay, *Reading Jesus's Bible*, 2.

in contrast with interpretive traditions of his time that had watered it down by focusing on mere compliance.

Consequently, a hermeneutic of imagination helps us rediscover the importance of the Old Testament. Christian readings of the Bible have tended to value the New Testament more than the Old. They have tended to undermine the authority and validity of the Old Testament at the expense of the New. A dictum ascribed to Martin Luther, "Only what promotes Christ is valid for Christians," is an eloquent testimony to this effect. Typically, the Old Testament is read in the light of the New, to the extent that whenever Christians perceive tensions or disagreements between them, the New Testament trumps the Old. This demonstrates that "in Western cultures, at least, the phrase 'Old Testament' is also something of a slight; it rather implies that this collection of writings is antique and outdated by the 'New Testament.'"[15]

Against this background, our imaginative approach seeks to reclaim the importance of the Old Testament for Christian readings of the Bible, and we aim to achieve this by showing that the Old Testament is the *New* New Testament, in the sense that it is at least as relevant and important for modern Christians as the New Testament. The following reflections explore how the Old and New Testaments contribute to Christian formation in different ways.

A Hermeneutic of Imagination Reimagines the Old Testament as the New New Testament

The New Testament was written over a relatively brief period, one or two generations. The first writings were composed sometime after Easter and Pentecost, and the latest writings were completed perhaps as late as the first half of the second century. The New Testament was written within less than one hundred years after the events described in the Gospels.

Also, the various parts of the New Testament were written with the expectation of Jesus's return within the lifetime of their authors, or within the lifetime of their children at the latest. The expectation of Jesus's imminent return was based on an interpretation of Jesus's own words:

> Truly I tell you, there are some standing here who will not taste death before they see the Son of Man coming in his kingdom. (Matt. 16:28)

> And he said to them, "Truly I tell you, there are some standing here who will not taste death until they see that the kingdom of God has come with power." (Mark 9:1)

15. Goldingay, *Reading Jesus's Bible*, 1.

> Indeed, truly I tell you, there are some standing here who will not taste death before they see the kingdom of God. (Luke 9:27)

The most natural way of understanding these words was to take them as Jesus's prediction of his parousia, his second coming, to establish the kingdom of God as a physical reality, described in the final chapters of the book of Revelation and elsewhere. This expectation is also reflected in other parts of the New Testament, very likely because of the three Gospel texts.

In Acts 1:6–11, immediately before Jesus's ascension, his disciples express their expectation of an imminent establishment of the kingdom of God. "So when they had come together, they asked him, 'Lord, is this the time when you will restore the kingdom to Israel?'" (1:6). At the end of the episode, "While he was going and they were gazing up toward heaven, suddenly two men in white robes stood by them. They said, 'Men of Galilee, why do you stand looking up toward heaven? This Jesus, who has been taken up from you into heaven, will come in the same way as you saw him go into heaven'" (1:10–11).

In 1 Thessalonians 4:13–18, the letter's author comforts those who grieve the loss of loved ones, even though Jesus had not yet returned: "For this we declare to you by the word of the Lord, that we who are alive, who are left until the coming of the Lord, will by no means precede those who have died" (4:15). The need for comfort and theological clarification very likely arose because believers in Jesus had died before his return.

For this reason, the focus in most of the New Testament texts is on either the salvation of those who would come to believe in Jesus (e.g., Acts) or the social cohesion of the nascent Christian communities and the personal holiness of their members (the letters of the New Testament). Except for a few passages in the Gospels and the letter of James, the writings of the New Testament pay little to no attention to questions related to social injustice. A key text that reflects these sentiments is Romans 8:18: "The sufferings of this present time are not worth comparing with the glory about to be revealed to us [τὴν μέλλουσαν δόξαν ἀποκαλυφθῆναι εἰς ἡμᾶς]." And even those texts that do address questions related to social justice have typically been neglected in the church in favor of personal holiness and community cohesion. This attitude is prominently on display in Romans 13:1–7, which urges compliance with governing authorities under all circumstances.[16]

16. For a detailed discussion of the issues, see Knut M. Heim, "Proverbs in Dialogue with the New Testament," in *Reading Proverbs Intertextually*, ed. Katharine J. Dell and William Kynes, The Library of Hebrew Bible/Old Testament Studies 629 (Bloomsbury T&T Clark, 2018), 171–78.

The expectation was that Jesus would return imminently and end the suffering of the innocent by restoring universal justice through establishing God's kingdom. Since Jesus would return anytime soon and sort it all out, there was no need for his followers to address systemic injustices in the world. However, we now live almost two thousand years later, and Jesus has not returned yet. Reading the Bible with imagination addresses the problems associated with the interpretation of Jesus's pronouncement.

First, reading with imagination permits us to admit that Jesus was not speaking of the parousia in Matthew 16:28, Mark 9:1, and Luke 9:27, even though it sounded like that. Some interpreters think that he was speaking of the transfiguration (Matt. 17:1–8; Mark 9:2–8; Luke 9:28–36—note that all Synoptics place the transfiguration immediately after the pronouncements of Jesus), others of the resurrection (Matt. 28; Mark 16; Luke 24; John 20–21) or the ascension (Acts 1). Reading the texts with imagination enables us to engage with maturity with the complexities involved. Consequently, it permits us to admit that many of the early followers of Jesus understood him to speak of his parousia when he was not.

Second, our imaginative approach helps us to see that this misunderstanding does not undermine the veracity of Scripture. Even though matters related to systemic political, economic, and social injustice remained in the background of the New Testament writers' concerns, a hermeneutic of imagination resolves this problem because it enables us to rediscover the importance of the Old Testament for Christian faith and practice, including and especially regarding the duty to contend for justice.

By contrast with the New Testament, the Old Testament was written over a period of around one thousand years, and its writings focus on how to live as the people of God here and now and over time. The focus is on practical application of faith in community life. Therefore, a hermeneutic of imagination helps us to see that the Old Testament is the *New* New Testament, in the sense that it is directly relevant to all aspects of Christian faith and practice today, that it is at least as important for Christians as the New Testament. The two Testaments of the Christian Bible should not be played off against each other, as if one of them is more important than the other. They are both equally the Word of God, and they are both equally important. Understanding that the Old Testament is the *New* New Testament therefore helps us not only to read Old Testament texts with a keen appreciation for their importance today but also to avoid two pitfalls that have often plagued Christian practice.

First, we gain a more nuanced and wiser perspective on how to wait for the second coming of Christ. We will use an imaginative interpretation of the parable of the ten bridesmaids in Matthew 25:1–13 to illustrate this.

Jesus's conclusion to the parable, "Keep awake therefore, for you know neither the day nor the hour" (Matt. 25:13), has traditionally been understood *to emphasize that the groom might come earlier than expected* and that therefore one must be ready when he arrives. This has tended to reinforce the complacency regarding systemic political, economic, and social injustice here and now that we have already discussed above. However, both the foolish and the wise bridesmaids fall asleep, yet the wise bridesmaids are invited to join the groom for the wedding banquet, while the foolish ones are not (25:11–12)! What distinguishes them is that the wise bridesmaids are prepared for a possible *delay* in the groom's arrival. Therefore, the parable *emphasizes that the groom might come later than expected*, which is of course what has happened with the parousia. Consequently, Christians need to abandon their complacency regarding systemic political, economic, and social injustice.

Almost two millennia of church history ought to have taught us that we need to heed God's call upon his people in the Old Testament to maintain a just society or to restore it where things have gone wrong. Precisely because we know neither the day nor the hour of the bridegroom's arrival, we need to join the five wise bridesmaids. They took extra flasks of oil *in case the groom was delayed*. That is why they had fuel to trim their lamps and have them burning when he eventually did arrive. Reading the parable with imagination, we discover that keeping awake in Matthew 25:13 does not refer to a passive expectation for Jesus's imminent arrival that makes us complacent about prevailing conditions. Rather, keeping awake is about being prepared also for the possibility that his return may happen *later* than expected. The equivalent of the extra flasks of oil is our obedience to the ethical demands for justice in the Old and New Testaments. We do not wait until Jesus is about to arrive before we get busy with doing his will (cf. Matt. 7:21–23, 24–27; John 15:10, 12, 14, 17); rather, we are actively obedient now and remain faithful to our obligation to love our neighbor all the way to the end, however long it may take.

Second, we gain a more nuanced and wiser perspective on how to apply the Old Testament's ethical demands in Christian practice today. Here we find Chris Wright's concept of "the people of God" extremely helpful. In his *Old Testament Ethics for the People of God*, the term "people of God" includes Israel and the church together, and consequently his volume is a master class in how to apply the ethical demands of the Old Testament in Christian faith and practice today.[17] We will use an imaginative reading of the book of Isaiah to illustrate what we mean, with special reference to Isaiah 1:10–17.

17. Christopher J. H. Wright, *Old Testament Ethics for the People of God* (InterVarsity, 2004).

It is well-known that the first part of Isaiah, chapters 1–39, tends to emphasize divine judgment over the nation of Judah's sustained disobedience, while chapters 40–55, and to a certain extent chapters 56–66, are more conciliatory, emphasizing God's forgiveness and grace toward Judah. What has often gone unnoticed is how selective Christian applications of the book have been, both traditionally and in more recent exegetical practice. What Christians have tended to do is take the references to Judah and Israel literally when the texts in chapters 1–39 emphasize their disobedience and God's judgment, while they have tended to apply the references to Judah and Israel in chapters 40–66 that emphasize God's forgiveness and grace to themselves. As a result, Christian readings have tended to vilify Jews and to romanticize Christians.

By contrast, an imaginative reading of Isaiah will combine both Judah-Israel and the church under the designation "the people of God." This has tangible advantages. It makes an application of *all* Old Testament texts to Christian faith and practice more natural and organic. Consequently, even harsh passages like Isaiah 1:10–17 now also apply naturally to Christian faith and practice. When the prophet Isaiah addresses the people of Judah as "rulers of Sodom" and "people of Gomorrah," an imaginative reading will hear these words also as a verdict on the church. When verses 11–14 condemn Jewish worship as detestable to God, our imagination helps us to hear them also as an indictment of Christian worship. When verse 15 announces that God will not heed the prayers of Judah-Israel because the hands of Jews are full of blood, Christians are now confronted with the reality that God is not answering their prayers because their own hands are also soaked in blood. And when verses 15–16 appeal to the people of Judah-Israel to cease to do evil and to learn to do good, an imaginative engagement will help Christians hear these words as also addressed to themselves.

Finally, an imaginative look at verses 15–16: The verses are arranged in poetical parallel and chiastic flourish. The first verse begins with three legal demands, two commands related to purity laws ("wash yourselves," "make yourselves clean") and one related to social justice ("remove the evil of your doings from before my eyes"). This is then *rounded off* with a general and comprehensive summary statement that pertains to the law in general: "Cease to do evil." Arranged in reverse order, the second verse *begins* with a general and comprehensive summary statement that pertains to the prophets and the poetic literature: "Learn to do good." This is then explained in climactic fashion with four demands, rather than three. It is the escalation in number that shifts the emphasis in the prophetic utterance to its second part. We are moving from "cease to do evil" to "learn to do good," from the avoidance of wrong things to doing things right, from the prevention of wickedness to the active pursuit of righteousness, from not breaking the law to pursuing the ideals of God, from not harming our neighbor to loving them as ourselves. In short, we are shifting from legal compliance to moral excellence. We contend for justice.

The Importance of Imagination for Reading the Old Testament

In conclusion, while our claim that the Old Testament is the New New Testament is an intentionally over-the-top maxim for rhetorical effect, we hope to have made a compelling case for its importance for Christian faith and practice. In addition, we want to repeat four hermeneutical implications for the role of social justice in a hermeneutic of imagination that arise from my (Knut's) discussion of Romans 13:1–7 in conversation with Proverbs 24:10–12 and 25:26.[18]

First, New Testament texts need to be read in light of the Old Testament: "Doing nothing in the face of grievous evil is not an option for Christians who read their whole Bible."[19] Second, reading a text like Romans 13:1–7 in isolation from the Old Testament makes it "an unreliable guide in the face of complex ethical challenges,"[20] and the same is true when other New Testament texts are read without anchoring them in the Old Testament. Third, the example of Romans 13:1–7 in dialogue with texts from the book of Proverbs demonstrates that New Testament texts "can be read with great benefit in the light of Old Testament texts, even when intertextual connections were not in the mind of the New Testament author."[21] Fourth, a hermeneutic of imagination demonstrates that the dominant Christian model for reading the Old and New Testaments needs revision. The traditional reading strategy has gone in only one direction: reading the Old Testament in light of the New, with the New Testament relativizing the Old. An imaginative reading of the Bible, by contrast, will augment this reading strategy and make it a two-way street: Complex ethical problems can be overcome by reading the New Testament in light of the Old, with the Old Testament relativizing and nuancing the New.[22]

This is what we mean when we say that the Old Testament is the *New* New Testament. We read *both* Testaments in light of each other, and this new reading strategy promotes the role of social justice in a hermeneutic of imagination

18. Heim, "Proverbs in Dialogue with the New Testament," 177–78.
19. Heim, "Proverbs in Dialogue with the New Testament," 177.
20. Heim, "Proverbs in Dialogue with the New Testament," 177.
21. Heim, "Proverbs in Dialogue with the New Testament," 177.
22. Heim, "Proverbs in Dialogue with the New Testament," 177–78.

to the place of prominence that it deserves. We now turn to explore the implications for the role of social justice in a hermeneutic of imagination that arise from a monograph on the Old Testament's revolutionary ethics.

A Hermeneutic of Imagination Highlights the Central Role of Justice in the Old Testament

In this section, we build on Jeremiah Unterman's monograph *Justice for All: How the Jewish Bible Revolutionized Ethics*.[23] It demonstrates just how unique and important the Old Testament's contribution to human ethics is. It reveals why the Old Testament is such an inspirational and indispensable resource for a hermeneutic of imagination. And it illustrates why a hermeneutic of imagination compels us to contend for justice.

A comparison between Mesopotamian and biblical creation stories reveals a key innovation that the biblical creation accounts make to human flourishing.[24] For the first time, "men and women were created equally in the 'image of God' which in turn meant that human life was sacred," and consequently, "God's rest on the Sabbath was transformed into the first universal labor law."[25]

Unterman's volume also includes a substantial exploration of the implications of the God-Israel relationship revealed in the Sinai covenant in the books of Exodus and Deuteronomy for ethical conduct,[26] and it concludes: "The Sinai treaty thus gives rise to a new ethical concept in society: individual responsibility for the well-being and destiny of the community."[27] Summarizing the significance of the revelation of the law of Moses at Sinai, he explains the radical implications for human *individuals* and *communities*. The following quotations appear in one paragraph, but we break it into two for clarity's sake:

> Thus obedience or disobedience to the law in the Jewish Bible . . . becomes the determinant of the people's destiny. As such, law in the Jewish Bible takes on a much more important role than law in other societies. As with the Sinai treaty, for the first time in the ancient world, the individual is responsible for the fate of the community by his or her behavior. In reality, each individual now has a dual responsibility—as an individual and as a member of the nation.[28]

23. Jeremiah Unterman, *Justice for All: How the Jewish Bible Revolutionized Ethics*, JPS Essential Judaism Series (Jewish Publication Society, 2017).
24. Unterman, *Justice for All*, 1–14.
25. Unterman, *Justice for All*, 179.
26. Unterman, *Justice for All*, 15–40.
27. Unterman, *Justice for All*, 19.
28. Unterman, *Justice for All*, 24.

In the second half of the paragraph, Unterman develops the equally novel responsibility of the community for its individual members:

> The community whom the Bible addresses is now apprised of the extraordinary importance of each individual. So the community must take steps to ensure that its individuals obey the law. Additionally, this concern will be reflected in numerous Divine laws that enjoin the community and its members to care for the vulnerable elements of society. For the first time, the community becomes responsible for the fate of the individual. Thus is born the concept of communal responsibility.[29]

The Bible really did revolutionize ethics, yet unimaginative readings have emphasized, each in its own way, only one side of this coin. Some have emphasized individual responsibility, while others have emphasized communal responsibility, when a hermeneutic of imagination helps us to recognize that in the Bible these are two sides of the same coin. The responsibility of individuals for the community and the responsibility of the community for its individuals are cut from the same cloth.

In Leviticus 19, which, with Underman, we consider the "ethical pinnacle" of the Jewish Bible, the command to "love your neighbor as yourself" (v. 18) and the command to "love [the alien who resides among you] as yourself" (vv. 33–34) appear together. In addition, commands to leave "gleanings" in the fields for the poor and the alien (vv. 9–10) and not to be an idle bystander when someone else is in danger (v. 16) are unique among contemporary laws: "According to ancient Near Eastern law, one was only obligated not to do wrong. Only in the Bible did the law necessitate helping other members of society, whether one's fellows or the disadvantaged."[30]

Imaginative reading of the Bible recognizes, however, that Leviticus 19 and the commands we have just considered are not the ethical pinnacle of the Old Testament in the sense that they are more ethical than the rest; rather, they are its pinnacle in the sense that they express the underlying values and ethical norms that characterize all of it. Unterman demonstrates this with an in-depth exploration of the numerous biblical texts related to care for the widow, the orphan, the stranger, the poor, and the oppressed as well as the treatment of slaves.[31] The evidence is incontrovertible:

> The idea that the destiny of a society is determined by how its members behave towards the needy is a biblical intervention, and it prefigures the modern, ethical

29. Unterman, *Justice for All*, 24.
30. Unterman, *Justice for All*, 35.
31. Unterman, *Justice for All*, 41–84.

> conceptions of government, ranging from democracy to socialism, to create societies in which the needs of the impoverished will be met.[32]

Unterman's otherwise comprehensive study lacks a separate investigation of the historical books, the "Former Prophets" in the Jewish canon. The lack of in-depth engagement leads him to make the following generalization: "In the Former Prophets—Joshua, Judges, 1 and 2 Samuel, 1 and 2 Kings—the primary causes for national doom are the cardinal sins of worship of foreign gods and idolatry. Now, however, the prophets articulate a radical criterion: in the eyes of God, the destiny of the people is determined first and foremost by their ethical behavior," by which he means active care for the vulnerable members of society, obedience to God's ethical commands "to create a just, righteous, and caring society."[33]

Here we disagree with Unterman. Already in the historical books, the two main reasons for divine disapproval have been the worship of other gods and idolatry, as Unterman noted, but concern for the vulnerable is certainly present, and only slightly less prominent than the issue of idolatry. What the prophetic books have made clearer than before is that in God's eyes care for and protection of the vulnerable in society not only aims to prevent their maltreatment but also crucially includes positive care for them when they cannot help themselves and protecting them against the powerful who might oppress and exploit them. Active opposition against any maltreatment when the powerful seek to take advantage of the vulnerable becomes especially prominent in the prophetic books (cf., e.g., our discussion of Isa. 1:16–17 above; see also Prov. 25:26). Unterman's study demonstrates the centrality of care for the vulnerable members of society in the Old Testament. Consequently, contending for justice must be central to a hermeneutic of imagination.

Unterman's extended review of biblical materials that urge providing for the vulnerable in society—the foreigner, the poor, widows, orphans, and slaves—pays special attention to the treatment of foreigners and the poor.[34] He notes:

> An examination of the treatment of the resident alien and the poor—the most underprivileged members of society—reveals that the Torah, unlike all other ancient Near Eastern legal collections, *creates a host of laws on their behalf.* The resident alien was transformed into a divinely, legally protected member

32. Unterman, *Justice for All*, 84.
33. Unterman, *Justice for All*, 108.
34. Unterman, *Justice for All*, 41–84.

> of society with wide-ranging benefits and significant parity with the average citizen. The result is the elimination of xenophobia.[35]

Regarding the poor, he notes:

> Each member of society is obligated to care for and sustain the poor, which includes the widow and the orphan. *New laws are established for their benefit*, which are unattested even by the most ethical considerations of the ancient Near Easter wisdom literature.[36]

Furthermore,

> a survey of prophetic texts uncovered a revolutionary message: religious ritual is both secondary to ethics and dependent upon moral behavior for its validity. The superior importance of obedience to God's ethical commandments is for the purpose of creating a just, righteous, and caring society. Therefore, ethical behavior becomes the determining factor in national destiny.[37]

In other words, contending for justice—loving our neighbor as ourselves—becomes more important than religious observance. We cannot genuinely love God unless we also care for the vulnerable—that is, love them as ourselves.

We agree with Unterman's conclusion, which highlights the uniqueness of the biblical materials:

> In contrast to all the rest of the literature of the ancient Near East, the biblical texts in which these ethical advances are found all posit a good, just, caring God who created the world and humankind and chose to reveal His will to the people of Israel and their prophets. Truly, the Torah itself displays awareness of its ethical uniqueness in the ancient world, as Moses is quoted in Deuteronomy 4:7–8, "For . . . what great nation has laws and statutes as righteous as all this teaching that I set before you this day?"[38]

In conclusion, social justice plays a central role in the Old Testament. A hermeneutic of imagination resists the temptation to relativize this truth because the emphasis of the New Testament is elsewhere (see above) and thus compels us to contend for justice because the God who inspired the Bible is righteous and just.

35. Unterman, *Justice for All*, 180 (emphasis added).
36. Unterman, *Justice for All*, 180 (emphasis added).
37. Unterman, *Justice for All*, 180.
38. Unterman, *Justice for All*, 181–82.

A Hermeneutic of Imagination Trains Our Focus on God's Righteousness and Justice

When we read Scripture with imagination, we are inspired to adopt God's passion for righteousness and justice, to imitate and embody his qualities of goodness, love, righteousness, and justice.

Joze Krašovec puts it like this: "God's work of creation and salvation for the good of Israel, humanity, and the world is a manifestation of the nature of God's being."[39] A hermeneutic of imagination helps us appreciate that both God's acts of judgment and his acts of mercy and forgiveness—actions that seem to be in tension with each other—not only are just but also flow naturally from who he is:

> Only the supreme being is able to judge righteously and justly, which means that in the final analysis both God's punishment and his forgiveness and mercy are expressions of absolute justice. When God has reasons for forgiveness and mercy, he acts out of the inner compulsion of being loyal to his own essential nature.[40]

For this reason, a hermeneutic of imagination helps us understand the role of justice by combining two fundamental theological realities: the nature of God and the nature of human beings. "The positive purpose of God, manifested in the acts of creation and salvation, is asserted in a world that reflects the constant tension between good and evil in a situation of human need and the search for solutions."[41] For beings who are created in God's image, therefore, the record of God's self-revelation in the Bible is a natural resource for imaginative reflection on social justice, and such reflection must include an honest evaluation of the human condition, admitting that human individuals and human societies fall short of God's ideals.

Even so, a hermeneutic of imagination helps us to remain hopeful for a solution: "The Hebrew Bible reveals and records the consequences of human guilt, provides a justification of punishment, and states the conditions of forgiveness." Although humans deserve judgment for their failures, God's resolution is relational: "Forgiveness is a matter of an intimate relationship between God and his creation—humankind." Crucially, however, God's forgiveness does not undermine his fundamental righteousness: "That God's disapproval of human wickedness is as intense as his approval of righteousness

39. Joze Krašovec, *God's Righteousness and Justice in the Old Testament* (Eerdmans, 2022), 411.

40. Krašovec, *God's Righteousness and Justice*, 409.

41. Krašovec, *God's Righteousness and Justice*, 412.

is profound."[42] It is our hermeneutic of imagination that helps us to reconcile both sides of this puzzling equation.

As Craig Bartholomew observes, in the ancient Near East, "justice and law were the provenance of the king rather than of the gods."[43] In the Old Testament, by contrast, the law was given by the God of Israel:

> The Bible avoids representing the king as legislator. The one lawgiver is God. That idea was unparalleled novelty in the ancient Middle East, where only the king made laws. The Torah has no real parallel in those ancient civilizations. The God of Israel replaces the Oriental king in the role of lawgiver. Hence the predicates attributed to the pharaoh in Egypt are reserved for God alone in Israel.[44]

Two comments are in order. First, this corroborates Unterman's claim that the Bible's ethics, reflected most prominently in its laws, is revolutionary and unique in its socioreligious context. What is more, other genres of the Old Testament also reflect God's central role in establishing a just society, and the biblical witness has played a fundamental role in the formation of modern ideas about social justice: "Biblical texts in various literary genres have a strong influence on the formation of a sense of justice, empathy, and the justification of human rights in the modern humanities in theory and in application of law."[45] Second, while the king is not the lawgiver in the Old Testament, the king represents God (Pss. 72 and 101) and certainly is responsible for upholding the law given by God: "It is an abomination to kings to do evil, for the throne is established by righteousness" (Prov. 16:12); "If a king judges the poor with equity, his throne will be established forever" (Prov. 29:14). Regarding Psalms 72 and 101, Karen Durant comments: "Just as God is the rescuer of the poor in these psalms, in Psalm 72 it is the king who is the rescuer of the poor" and "The king in Psalm 101 pledges to live and rule ethically in ways that are a reflection of God's own power and conduct."[46] Imaginative reflection helps us appreciate the intricate relationship between divine imperative and human responsibility.

In the highly imaginative poetry of Psalm 82:3–4, for example, the following four characteristics of just governance emerge: (1) providing justice for the

42. Krašovec, *God's Righteousness and Justice*, 412, 413.

43. Craig G. Bartholomew, *The Old Testament and God: Old Testament Origins and the Question of God* (Baker Academic, 2022), 386.

44. Rémi Brague, *The Law of God: The Philosophical History of an Idea*, trans. Lydia G. Cochrane (University of Chicago Press, 2007), 49, quoted in Bartholomew, *Old Testament and God*, 386–87.

45. Krašovec, *God's Righteousness and Justice*, 416.

46. Karen Elizabeth Durant, "Imitation of God as a Principle for Ethics Today: A Study of Selected Psalms" (doctoral thesis, University of Birmingham, 2010), 116, 122, https://etheses.bham.ac.uk//id/eprint/1184/2/Durant_10_PhD.pdf.

weak and fatherless; (2) maintaining the rights of the afflicted and destitute; (3) rescuing the weak and needy; (4) delivering such vulnerable people from the hand of the wicked.[47]

What is more, Psalm 82:5 engages our imagination when it claims that systemic injustice threatens the very fabric of creation, that "all the foundations of the earth are shaken." Bartholomew rightly concludes that this "alerts us unequivocally to the vital importance of law and justice in any society if it is to be healthy and to promote human flourishing."[48] And so the texts of the Old Testament aim to appeal to our imaginative capacities to shape and develop human character; they "develop a natural sense of justice and empathy in the pursuit of basic human rights for everyone."[49] And a hermeneutic of imagination prompts us to go beyond the obvious and helps us to understand that care for the vulnerable of necessity entails opposition against those who would oppress and exploit them, "the wicked" in the language of Psalm 82:4. Consequently, "the relationship between a formalistic and personal understanding of the application of law in social life is critical,"[50] and we need imagination to appreciate this. Reading texts like this with imagination reveals that social justice is at the center of biblical revelation and that it reflects the very nature of God. It motivates, even compels, us to "contend for justice." This is one of the fundamental insights of liberation theology: "God takes the side of the poor because he is the God of righteousness and justice."[51] Bartholomew comments, "Yhwh is the God of justice, and as such he exercises what Catholics refer to as a preferential option for the poor."[52] A hermeneutic of imagination helps us understand that these insights are not mere opinions current among special interest groups but foundational insights into the very nature of God as revealed in Scripture.

A Hermeneutic of Imagination Compels Us to Contend for Justice

We need to read Scripture with imagination if we want to embody and implement its passion for justice. Genuinely imaginative readings will inspire us to uphold the justice envisioned in the text.

47. Bartholomew, *Old Testament and God*, 464.
48. Bartholomew, *Old Testament and God*, 465.
49. Krašovec, *God's Righteousness and Justice*, 417.
50. Krašovec, *God's Righteousness and Justice*, 417.
51. Gordon Spykman et al., eds., *Let My People Live: Faith and Struggle in Central America* (Eerdmans, 2005), 229, quoted in Bartholomew, *Old Testament and God*, 465.
52. Bartholomew, *Old Testament and God*, 465.

The biblical vision for a just world, exemplified in text after text, works as a stimulus for our imagination. The biblical texts inspire us to *contend* for justice, not just engage in wishful thinking about it. They "project an image of a world of justice and non-violence which convinces us that such a thing is possible and encourages us to work towards it."[53] And a hermeneutic of imagination helps us to recognize this and inspires us to implement it in our own lives and in the lives of the communities for whom we interpret the Bible. Contending for justice implies a willingness to fight its opposite: "The moral imagination of the Old Testament still has the power to break open the ideologies of our own world. It is indeed the Old Testament's moral imagination which is its permanent contribution to the struggle for human community."[54]

As imaginative readers of the Bible, we learn that we are meant to be "vehicles of the justice of God."[55] And as members of a worldwide Christian community of faith, we are not alone. All of us can become involved, and each of us is responsible for doing so. In the words of Walter Houston:

> Social justice concerns social relationships, but it is only capable of becoming a reality through the commitment of individuals. There is a stimulus to the moral imagination of the individual felt through reading and reflecting on the Bible, which affects attitude, concern and habitus. However, such a stimulus is only effective if the individual works within a community concerned for the transformation of social life and economic relationships, and willing to work alongside those struggling for justice worldwide, primarily the victims of injustice.[56]

A hermeneutic of imagination inspires and compels us to contend for justice. We are responsible for doing so, all of us. When we take up the task, we are not alone. And our efforts will not be in vain: "The disciples of Jesus are those called in the present-day world to serve the victims of injustice by putting into practice the Bible's values of justice."[57] This is what it means to love God with all our heart, mind, and soul, and to love our neighbor as ourselves.

But how does a hermeneutic of imagination inspire and compel us to contend for justice? Is it just the acquisition of knowledge from the words in Scripture? Or is something more taking place when we read Scripture imaginatively? We will explore these questions in the conclusion.

53. Houston, *Contending for Justice*, 229.
54. Houston, *Contending for Justice*, 227.
55. Houston, *Contending for Justice*, 230.
56. Houston, *Contending for Justice*, 230.
57. Houston, *Contending for Justice*, 230.

Conclusion

The first part of our conclusion explores how a hermeneutic of imagination releases the transformative power of Scripture, for it invites us to read the Bible in a way that *actually* depends on the Holy Spirit. The second part applies a hermeneutic of imagination to Psalm 23:2, drawing on key insights from the preceding chapters. It illustrates why reading the Bible with imagination is such an exciting adventure of the mind that is at once theologically rewarding, intellectually compelling, and transformative. The third and final part consists of concluding reflections that invite you to join us on the journey.

A Hermeneutic of Imagination Attunes Us to the Transformative Power of Scripture

The Holy Spirit appears frequently throughout Scripture, in both the Old and New Testaments.[1] The Holy Spirit is essential for a hermeneutic of imagination. Yet even well-known biblical scholars who identify as Pentecostal or charismatic tend to find it hard to explain what role the Holy Spirit plays in how they interpret the Bible.[2] In *Listening to the Spirit in the Text*, for example, eminent New Testament scholar Gordon Fee emphasizes understanding the original sense, and the emphasis is on the Spirit's communication in the Scriptures rather than the Spirit's guidance in its interpretation.[3]

1. John R. Levison, *Filled with the Spirit* (Eerdmans, 2009); and John R. Levison, *A Boundless God: The Spirit According to the Old Testament* (Baker Academic, 2020).

2. Craig S. Keener, "Pentecostal Biblical Interpretation / Spirit Hermeneutics," in *Scripture and Its Interpretation*, ed. Michael J. Gorman (Baker Academic, 2017).

3. Gordon D. Fee, *Listening to the Spirit in the Text*, 2nd ed. (Eerdmans, 2001). Cf. also the essays on the Holy Spirit in Scripture collected in Craig S. Keener and L. William Oliverio, eds., *The Spirit Throughout the Canon: Pentecostal Pneumatology* (Brill, 2022).

In the first part of this conclusion, we explore how a hermeneutic of imagination unleashes Scripture's transformative power, looking at three areas: the role of the Holy Spirit in the Bible itself, the role of the Holy Spirit in a hermeneutic of imagination, and (briefly) the role of prayer for the Holy Spirit to inspire such a hermeneutic of imagination.

The Role of the Holy Spirit in the Bible

"The Word of God not only expresses the *power* of God; it also conveys the *presence* of God."[4] Reading the Bible with imagination can help us to experience the Bible as "a living document, filled with the power and presence of God."[5] In this chapter, we propose that a hermeneutic of imagination leads to reading the Bible through a Pentecostal lens.[6]

Sometimes the impression is created that Pentecostals are only those Christians who exercise the supernatural gifts of the Holy Spirit—performing miraculous healings or praying and speaking in tongues. By contrast, those who do not exercise the gifts of the Holy Spirit are considered traditional, non-Pentecostal Christians. Here, however, we want to emphasize that *all* Christians, whether they exercise these supernatural gifts or not, are "Pentecostal" in the sense that the power of the Holy Spirit is available to them to some degree. It is not an either-or in which either you are a Pentecostal or you are not. Rather, all Christians experience the power of the Holy Spirit on a continuum, regardless of whether they perceive or experience this power as supernatural.

Even so, Christians with *life-changing* experiences of the Holy Spirit are most likely to experience the transformative power of Scripture. Not only do they experience divine guidance in decision-making, not only do they experience illumination in their study of the Bible, but they also grow spiritually in faith, hope, and love over time (1 Cor. 13). What is especially remarkable about them is that they have the gifts *and* the fruit of the Holy Spirit: They have received the supernatural gifts of the Holy Spirit, and they enjoy cultivating the supernatural fruit of the Holy Spirit, such as love, joy, peace, patience, kindness, and so on (Gal. 5:22–23).

All Christians have the capacity to read the Bible with imagination, and to benefit spiritually and practically from doing so. However, those who have

4. Cheryl Bridges Johns, *Re-Enchanting the Text: Discovering the Bible as Sacred, Dangerous, and Mysterious* (Baker Academic, 2023), 128 (emphasis added).

5. Johns, *Re-Enchanting the Text*, 20, with reference to how Pentecostal Christians tend to read the Bible.

6. Johns, *Re-Enchanting the Text*, 21.

already been shaped more profoundly by their reading are more likely to experience further growth as they continue to read. Even so, anybody who reads the Bible has the capacity to experience transformation, and this capacity increases "in proportion to readers' growth in holiness and conformity to Christ."[7]

This is because the Bible has an inherent capacity to bring its readers "in living and life-giving contact with the divine realities mediated by the sacred text."[8] In their comprehensive study of how the Bible can do this, William Wright and Francis Martin examine, in the form of case studies, the impact that the Bible had on four prominent Christian saints, Saint Antony of Egypt, Saint Augustine, Saint Francis of Assisi, and Saint Thérèse of Lisieux. They conclude their fascinating phenomenological study with the following observations:

> Sacred Scripture can put people in living and life-giving contact with the divine realities it mediates. By putting people in cognitive contact with the realities it mediates, the biblical text puts people in contact with the divine mystery, which those realities bear. Although much of what the Bible speaks of is historically past, the divine mystery that the biblical realities bear is eternal and can be encountered in the present moment. The Holy Spirit acts upon the discourse of the prophets and apostles, making it apt for mediating the divine mystery and making it present to people. Witness from both Scripture and the tradition also recognizes the action of the Holy Spirit within people to give them the gift of understanding. This is the gift of penetrating insight into these divine realities and faith experience of their truth and power.[9]

The Bible is designed by the Holy Spirit to mediate the self-revelation of God, by making God present to those who read it and by exerting a transformative power upon them that enables them to experience that presence as a positive dynamic reality in their lives. In the following paragraph, Wright and Martin make the same point:

> Although the biblical realities are temporally past, the mystery that they bear is divine: it is eternal and thus ever present. These divine mysteries are available to people in their present moment through Scripture, but a living encounter with

7. William M. Wright IV and Francis Martin, *Encountering the Living God in Scripture: Theological and Philosophical Principles for Interpretation* (Baker Academic, 2019), 247.

8. Francis Martin, "Introduction to Acts," in *Acts*, ed. Francis Martin, Ancient Christian Commentary on Scripture: New Testament 5 (IVP Books, 2006), xxiii, quoted in Wright and Martin, *Encountering the Living God in Scripture*, 1.

9. Wright and Martin, *Encountering the Living God in Scripture*, 243.

> these divine mysteries requires both the action of the Holy Spirit and readers properly disposed towards the Spirit's action in them.[10]

For this to happen, however, the Bible's readers should have certain spiritual and moral dispositions, including a proper disposition toward the work of the Holy Spirit.[11] According to Wright and Martin, these also include active participation in the life of the church, repentance and humility, piety, personal application, obedience, and persevering faith and love (on the latter, see also chap. 6).[12] But how does reading with imagination foster a proper disposition toward the work of the Spirit?

Here a reorientation regarding the Holy Spirit's work is needed, for in many conceptualizations of the inspiration of Scripture, the Bible is seen only as "an inspired *product*."[13] It is considered a historical artifact that is "inerrant in all it affirms," and its inspiration is something that happened only in the distant past, when the autographs of the biblical texts were composed by their original authors and editors.[14] When traditional theories of inspiration and biblical authority reflect on the reading and interpretation of Scripture, they employ the term "illumination."[15] This term aims to portray a separate agency of the Holy Spirit, and its effect is mainly on the reader of Scripture who—in the act of reading—experiences the Holy Spirit shining light on scriptural content as he or she reads, thereby giving deeper insight. The Bible remains an object of contemplation, and it is the contemplating subject whose *ratio* is enhanced to gain deeper insight into the meaning and significance of the biblical text that lies dormant in its pages. By contrast, a hermeneutic of imagination has a higher view of Scripture and proposes a higher view of biblical inspiration because it leads us to read the Bible through a Pentecostal lens.

The Role of the Holy Spirit in a Hermeneutic of Imagination

Through imagination the Bible makes the divine realities of which it speaks present to those who read it. It not only narrates God's self-revelation but

10. Wright and Martin, *Encountering the Living God in Scripture*, 8.

11. Wright and Martin, *Encountering the Living God in Scripture*, 8, 243.

12. Wright and Martin, *Encountering the Living God in Scripture*, 244.

13. John Webster, *Holy Scripture: A Dogmatic Sketch*, Current Issues in Theology (Cambridge University Press, 2003), 33.

14. See, e.g., article 10 of the Chicago Statement on Biblical Inerrancy, in Robert C. Sproul and Norman L. Geisler, *Explaining Biblical Inerrancy: The Chicago Statements on Biblical Inerrancy, Hermeneutics, and Application with Official ICBI Commentary* (Bastion, 2013), 8.

15. Cf. the exposition of the Chicago Statement on Biblical Hermeneutics, in Sproul and Geisler, *Explaining Biblical Inerrancy*, 37.

also has the power to mediate it.[16] Reading it with imagination enables us to adopt a posture whereby we open ourselves to experience this reality inductively, through the effects that the Bible has on us as we read it. Reading with imagination helps us discover that there are at least two more levels of inspiration where the Holy Spirit is active.

The first is in the formation of Scripture. The Holy Spirit took an active role in the *canonization* of Scripture. It was not merely an act of discernment by the church that led to the identification of textual products that were inspired at their inception; rather, the canonization of Scripture was a response on the church's behalf *to the ongoing work of inspiration through the Holy Spirit, who continued to minister God's powerful presence* as the church kept reading those texts.[17] And this ongoing work of inspiration continues to help readers today experience Scripture's transformative power, as the Holy Spirit continues the same ministry.

The second is in the reading of Scripture itself. The Holy Spirit continues to "be active and present in the inscripturated Word," to use Johns's memorable formulation.[18] The Bible as the written Word of God continues to be a "Spirit-empowered agent."[19] Consequently, "the purposes of God manifest in the Bible express the very presence of the Trinity and not merely information about God."[20] It is the Holy Spirit who directly addresses the Bible's readers through every word they read that makes this personal encounter with God possible, whenever they read it or listen to it.[21] The Bible communicates God's power and presence. Wright and Martin capture this timeless aspect of the Bible's inspired nature:

> Through his Word, God exercises his power and brings about various effects, such as in creating and governing the world and in the course of salvation history. God also exercises his power when his Word is proclaimed in inspired human discourse, spoken or written. The Word of God also has associations with various forms of presence. God reveals himself to people through his Word, and we can say that God becomes present to people in the mode of being known . . . through his Word.[22]

16. Wright and Martin, *Encountering the Living God in Scripture*, 248.
17. Cf. Johns, *Re-Enchanting the Text*, 135.
18. Johns, *Re-Enchanting the Text*, 124.
19. N. T. Wright, *The Last Word: How to Read the Bible Today* (HarperCollins, 2013), 67, quoted in Johns, *Re-Enchanting the Text*, 125.
20. Johns, *Re-Enchanting the Text*, 122.
21. Johns, *Re-Enchanting the Text*, 122.
22. Wright and Martin, *Encountering the Living God in Scripture*, 245.

Through the active agency of the Holy Spirit in our reading, the Bible becomes "a place where the pneumatic imagination flourishes."[23] Reading the Bible, we come face-to-face with the living God, and a hermeneutic of imagination helps us to become aware of this: "Scripture is more than a static entity. It is an 'en-spirited' closed canon existing in service of dynamic and ongoing revelation." Reading the Bible with imagination thus "creates a space where the veil between the supernatural and the natural world becomes transparent."[24] It allows the Holy Spirit to "impress the truth and reality of the divine mystery" and to "provide a faith experience and intimate understanding of that mystery."[25] The same insight is also captured in Henri de Lubac's understanding of biblical inspiration:

> It is not only the sacred writers who were inspired one fine day. The sacred books themselves are and remain inspired. . . . The Spirit immured himself in it, as it were. He lives in it. His breath has always animated it. . . . It is full of the Spirit.[26]

It is not we who illuminate Scripture through our reading but Scripture that illuminates us through the Holy Spirit's active intervention, so that the eyes of our hearts become enlightened (Eph. 1:18), and "our reading and studying of Scripture becomes an act of worship, an experience of fellowship" with God.[27] Reading the Bible with imagination also endows our hearts with ears, and through our reading we can enjoy the wonderful synesthetic experience of hearing the very voice of God in our hearts as we contemplate his words on the page with our eyes. We encounter the reality of God's presence in the transforming power of Scripture, for we now experience firsthand that it is indeed "living and active and sharper than any two-edged sword," because it pierces *us* and divides *our* soul from spirit, separates *our* joints from marrow, and judges the thoughts and intentions of *our* heart (Heb. 4:12). As Wright and Martin put it in the conclusion to their examination of Hebrews 4:12–13: "God speaks to people through Scripture in their present moment, and through Scripture, God works powerfully in them at the deepest level of their being."[28] Returning to the vision of Scripture being God-breathed, we see that a hermeneutic of imagination helps us to remember that the Holy

23. Johns, *Re-Enchanting the Text*, 144.

24. Johns, *Re-Enchanting the Text*, 141.

25. Wright and Martin, *Encountering the Living God in Scripture*, 247.

26. Henri de Lubac, *Medieval Exegesis*, trans. Mark Sebanc and E. M. Macierowski, 3 vols. (Eerdmans, 1998–2009), 1:81–82, quoted in Wright and Martin, *Encountering the Living God in Scripture*, 221.

27. Johns, *Re-Enchanting the Text*, 145.

28. Wright and Martin, *Encountering the Living God in Scripture*, 99; see also 79–85.

Spirit breathed God's message into the Scriptures at their inception, and it helps us to experience how the Holy Spirit breathes that same message through the Word of God into our hearts and minds as we hear and read its words today.

The characterization of Scripture as "living and active" in Hebrews 4:12 thus allows us "to understand the Word of God as deeply related to God's own being and powerful activity in the world," inviting us to recognize the Bible as "a special means by which God is powerfully present and active" in us as we read.[29] Every time we read the Bible with imagination, therefore, we have an opportunity for a *theophanic encounter*, and if we let God's Word do what it does best, our reading will be as dramatic and transformative as any theophany we read about in Scripture. The Bible exists in service of the Spirit's work to facilitate genuine encounters between us and the God who addresses us with its words.[30]

Reading with imagination thus helps us to adopt a posture toward Scripture that is conducive to strengthening our conviction about its inspired nature because we experience it inductively, because we continually enjoy its capacity to help us experience God's benevolent presence, and because we consistently experience how it transforms us. "Scripture is not just a record of past events from which people of later generations can learn; it is also a vehicle for present encounter with the Word of God in its power."[31] With these wonderful insights in mind, we now turn briefly to the role of prayer in a hermeneutic of imagination.

The Role of Prayer for Unlocking Scripture's Full Potential

As we have seen, the Holy Spirit continues to inspire the Bible; it remains a vehicle for encountering God's powerful presence. Readers can be "affected and changed through the prayerful reading" of Scripture.[32] Reading with imagination is a form of theological interpretation, and there is built-in synergy between spirituality and vigorous academic study. We agree with Craig Bartholomew and Matthew Emerson's reflections on the benefits of theological interpretation: "If we are handling the Word through which God addresses his people, then there ought to be a deeply existential ethos to theological interpretation. In our view there is no antithesis between prayer and the most rigorous exegesis, and these elements will be inseparable in

29. Wright and Martin, *Encountering the Living God in Scripture*, 82.
30. Johns, *Re-Enchanting the Text*, 161.
31. Wright and Martin, *Encountering the Living God in Scripture*, 216.
32. Wright and Martin, *Encountering the Living God in Scripture*, 4.

theological interpretation."[33] We explored this important insight in more detail in chapter 7, where we argued that imagination helps and encourages us to conduct our academic study of Scripture theologically and to conduct our theological study of the Bible academically.

The imaginative understanding of biblical inspiration presented above provides a powerful incentive for reading and studying the Bible prayerfully. It is a virtuous circle, for prayer invites the active intervention of the Holy Spirit to enhance our imagination. As we benefit from the Spirit's supernatural assistance, we unlock more and more of the Bible's potential to bring us face-to-face with God's powerfully transformative presence. Continuing the circle, prayerful imagination transforms our academic study of the Bible into an aesthetically inspiring, intellectually stimulating, emotionally rewarding, theologically rich, and spiritually transformative adventure of the mind. And as we experience the Bible's transformative power more and more, we develop close, deep, lusciously savored, highly imaginative, and pleasurable readings of the biblical texts that release their potential for problem-solving and human flourishing today.[34] Come join us, we are going to have so much fun doing this together!

How, then, should we pray? In line with the key imaginative insight of chapter 4, a hermeneutic of imagination inspires us to pray to the Holy Spirit to help us understand how a given biblical text inspires us to grow in love for God, neighbor, and self. It also inspires us to petition the Holy Spirit to help us apply what we read so that others experience the way Scripture has inspired our love for them, in turn prompting them to grow in love for God, neighbor, and self. Whenever this happens, the transformative power of Scripture will be on full display for all to see. It is our hermeneutic of imagination's most verdant fruit.

In the remainder of the chapter, we now apply the various aspects of imagination we have explored in this volume to an imaginative reading of Psalm 23:2, to illustrate what changes when we read Scripture with a hermeneutic of imagination.

33. Craig G. Bartholomew and Matthew Y. Emerson, "Theological Interpretation for All of Life," in *A Manifesto for Theological Interpretation*, ed. Craig G. Bartholomew and Heath A. Thomas (Baker Academic, 2016), 257.

34. Our formulation is inspired by a phrase from Dobbs-Allsopp's introduction to his reading of Ps. 133 in his magisterial volume on biblical poetry, F. W. Dobbs-Allsopp, *On Biblical Poetry* (Oxford University Press, 2015), 326–49. His reading of Ps. 133 forms an admirable example of the kinds of imaginative readings that we hope to inspire through our own work here.

Reading Psalm 23:2 with a Hermeneutic of Imagination: An Intellectually Compelling, Theologically Rewarding, and Spiritually Transformative Adventure of the Mind

This final part of our conclusion applies a hermeneutic of imagination to Psalm 23:2, drawing on insights from the preceding chapters.[35] Consider it your personal invitation to join us on the adventure of reading the Bible with imagination, a quest that is at once intellectually compelling, theologically rewarding, and transformative.

Psalm 23 is one of the most well-known and well-studied portions of Scripture. Consequently, if we succeed in offering a close, deep, lusciously savored, highly imaginative, and pleasurable reading of the psalm that goes beyond existing attempts, we hope to have demonstrated that a hermeneutic of imagination can provide added value to the work of interpretation. We hope that our example makes a credible case for the importance of applying a hermeneutic of imagination to all of Scripture.[36]

Throughout our discussion, we will be in conversation with a brief article on Psalm 23 published by Heim in 2016 and with a book-length study of the psalm by Richard Briggs from 2021—a thorough treatment by a skilled interpreter that at times comes close to what we envisage when we read with imagination.[37]

Reading Psalm 23:2 in Dialogue with Richard Briggs

The following paragraphs are not a comprehensive reading of all aspects of the psalm but a reading of one verse in dialogue with Richard Briggs's comprehensive study of the poem. His work is uniquely fitting for this purpose because, in our opinion at least, it represents the best and most thorough reading of the psalm based on traditional exegetical methods and hermeneutical models, with the added benefit that Briggs is more aware of the benefits of imaginative engagement with the psalm than any other recent interpreter

35. Our interpretation expands on an imaginative reading of the psalm that appeared in print in 2016: Knut M. Heim, "Psalm 23 in the Age of the Wolf," *Christianity Today* (January/February 2016), 60–63.

36. In doing so, we follow the example of Dobbs-Allsopp, who concluded his magisterial study on biblical poetry with a "close, deep, lusciously savored, highly imaginative" reading of Ps. 133, using it "as a cashing out of my efforts to think through the several facets of biblical poetics on offer throughout this book," as he put it (Dobbs-Allsopp, *On Biblical Poetry*, 5, 326). (Our add-on "pleasurable" comes from the dust jacket.)

37. Richard S. Briggs, *The Lord Is My Shepherd: Psalm 23 for the Life of the Church*, Touchstone Texts (Baker Academic, 2021).

we are aware of. The following quotation from Briggs's introduction to his volume illustrates what we mean:

> We will seek a full, imaginative, and serious engagement with the psalm's words and phrases, its images and its own imaginative vision, in order that we might hear it in all its widescreen wonder.[38]

In fact, Briggs's volume is peppered with similar, if isolated, statements that highlight the benefits of imagination.[39] Briggs is already on the right track, and it shows in the quality of his work. Even so, the following dialogue with Briggs on verse 2 will demonstrate that a more comprehensive hermeneutic of imagination can bring us further still. So, while much of the conversation focuses on areas where we aim to improve on Briggs's work, we want to avoid the impression that we fundamentally disagree with him. The opposite is true; when we critique his work, we do so on the basis of a relatively high level of satisfaction.

With these preliminary considerations in place, we now turn to a reading of verse 2 in Psalm 23 that illustrates the positive contribution of a hermeneutic of imagination to biblical interpretation.

We begin with the short affirmation, "I won't want," that completes verse 1. Briggs notes that it is worth asking "in what sense one lacks nothing or will not lack." His answer: "Clearly not in every conceivable sense." He then goes on to clarify this claim: "The person who prays Psalm 23:1 has confidence that God is a God who meets needs and who is not caught unawares by one's difficulties." The verse "points to letting YHWH decide what it is that I need, in the process of ensuring that whatever it is, I will not lack it." He concedes that this is still not an experience of absolute and unlimited provision, but he brushes this concession away with the explanation that "Psalm 23 is partly in the business of training my sense of need to be better attuned to what God provides."[40] In other words, "the sheep of the shepherd are not guaranteed

38. Briggs, *The Lord Is My Shepherd*, 2–3, citing R. W. L. Moberly, *The Theology of the Book of Genesis*, Old Testament Theology (Cambridge University Press, 2009), 197; and R. W. L. Moberly, *Old Testament Theology: Reading the Hebrew Bible as Christian Scripture* (Baker Academic, 2013), 285, whose language of "full imaginative seriousness" inspired Briggs's own approach.

39. E.g., "The process I have been describing is a hermeneutical engagement with Scripture that seeks a second naivete—that sense of coming fresh (naively) to the text with eyes alert and with critical insight harnessed to know what to look for and what to appreciate in an imaginative and serious reading of *what the text says*" (Briggs, *The Lord Is My Shepherd*, 4). "Capturing the imaginative vision of those who attend to the text has at least some chance" (18) to nourish preaching of the psalm for the life of the church.

40. Briggs, *The Lord Is My Shepherd*, 73.

permanent good health or food. But they will experience such needs in a context of care."[41]

So far, so good. We do not fundamentally disagree with any of Briggs's interpretive moves. In the final analysis, however, Briggs does not see a problem in the psalmist's claim at all: "Only a failure to grasp the poetry as the open-ended celebration of thankfulness for provision would find Psalm 23:1 to be a statement of overconfidence or wilful lack of realism."[42]

And this is where we disagree. Our hermeneutic of imagination can take us further. As we discussed in chapter 2 above, the interpretive instincts of Bible scholars can tempt them to explain away problematic aspects in biblical texts before fully appreciating their imaginative potential. Here, we believe, Briggs has fallen prey to this very temptation.

By contrast, the statement was far more unusual and thought-provoking in its original context of composition and reception than later readers have noticed. The patently false claim that the "sheep" will not lack *anything*, implicit and salient through the awkward omission of an object after the verb, was meant to fire the hearers' and the readers' imaginations, prompting them to ask questions like, How can this possibly be true?

The claim's counterintuitive nature and over-the-top quality *was meant to be perceived*, its hyperbolic unrealism intentionally accentuated to raise curiosity and "hook" readers and their audiences. How can the poet claim that his relationship with the deity will cause him to lack nothing, when in reality—as Briggs and others are quick to note—it is plainly obvious that human life is full of challenges, obstacles, and dangers? Our response is that the psalm's opening was not inviting "culpable passivity" by inducing a false sense of security, as Pink Floyd's song "Sheep" would have it.[43] Rather, it triggered instant objections and thus *invited imaginative critical engagement through skeptical exploration* right from the start. We shall discover the powerful poetic impact of this as we turn to our verse, which we read quite differently from Briggs and other traditional interpreters.

Verse 2 introduces two pastoral images, both apparently related to the sheep's sustenance, food and water. The traditional interpretation is captured well by Briggs: "We should see these as two pictures that begin to offer examples of what it means to be cared for by the shepherd of verse 1."[44]

41. Briggs, *The Lord Is My Shepherd*, 74.

42. Briggs, *The Lord Is My Shepherd*, 74.

43. See Briggs, *The Lord Is My Shepherd*, 8–9; and esp. Heim, "Psalm 23 in the Age of the Wolf," 62.

44. Briggs, *The Lord Is My Shepherd*, 75.

The opposite is, in fact, the case. And ancient audiences, familiar as they were with the behavior of sheep, would also have seen it that way. Our imaginative translation of the verse (see chap. 6) helps us make the case: "In pastures of green he *makes* me lie down; toward waters of stillness he *steers* me" (the italicized words are crucial for interpretation). The causative *hiphil* form of the first verb, the shepherd "makes" the sheep lie down, rather than letting it lie down of its own accord, has often been discussed. Briggs follows the traditional way of dealing with the apparent incongruity, explaining it away: "I do wonder whether the word 'makes' brings with it today connotations of insistence that are unhelpful. The image is rather that the shepherd has brought me to a place where I lie down; this is provision, and only in a distant second-sense compulsion."[45] And yet, this is what the text actually says!

By contrast, a hermeneutic of imagination invites us to explore whether there is significance in the textual challenge of the apparent incongruity (see chap. 2) and to engage more imaginatively with the psalm's figurative language (see chap. 3), particularly the shepherd-and-sheep metaphor in the poem. We begin with my (Heim's) reflections on how ruminants behave:

> Sheep are ruminants—vegetarian animals with a special digestive system. First, they cut with their teeth the grass they feed on and then swallow it whole. The food is then predigested in the stomach and eventually regurgitated. The sheep then lie down and keep the regurgitated food, "cud," in their mouths and chew on it at length—a process called "chewing the cud."
>
> Chewing the cud is a demanding task, and ruminants typically lie down and lapse into a semiconscious state. At this stage, they are particularly vulnerable to predators. This is why ruminants wander to and fro between "feeding grounds"—the green pastures of verse 2—and "resting grounds." The feeding grounds are where predators expect them to be. So ruminants tend to eat hurriedly before withdrawing again to various hideaways.[46]

Knowledge of relevant animal behavior—including behavior contingent on their digestive system—becomes instrumental for discerning how the psalm's language was intended to be understood by the original audience. Lying down in green pastures is contrary to the natural behavior of sheep because it would put them in mortal danger, and that is why the shepherd has to *force* the animal to do it!

45. Briggs, *The Lord Is My Shepherd*, 76. David Clines makes the same interpretive move: David J. A. Clines, "Translating Psalm 23," in *Reflection and Refraction: Studies in Biblical Historiography in Honour of A. Graeme Auld*, ed. Robert Rezetko, T. H. Lim, and W. B. Aucker, Supplements to Vetus Testamentum 113 (Brill, 2006), 70.

46. Heim, "Psalm 23 in the Age of the Wolf," 62.

But why would the shepherd want to do something that we now know to be so counterintuitive, and why does the psalmist showcase his shepherd's strange behavior? What function could this detail have in a psalm whose overall aim is to convey the poet-sheep's trust in his God-shepherd and inspire the same in his audience? We will return to these questions after considering the remainder of verse 2.

We have translated the second verb in the verse with "steers" (rather than the traditional "guides" or "leads") to reflect the verb's *piel* form, which suggests a more intense action than a *qal* form of the verb would have indicated. It reflects just enough intentionality to suggest that the sheep, left to its own devices, would not have chosen to go near the still waters of the psalm and needed at least some prodding by the shepherd to get there.

Here, again, knowledge of nature and sheep behavior is essential for discerning what the author intended to convey. An accurate interpretation hinges on two pieces of information that were obvious to the psalm's original audiences but are unfamiliar to most modern readers: Sheep are not good swimmers, and "still" waters tend to be sufficiently deep to put sheep in danger of drowning. We will reflect briefly on these two points.

First, sheep are not good swimmers. One seasoned sheep farmer notes, "While sheep certainly do not enjoy swimming and they're not particularly good at it, they can indeed swim if they fall into water. Sheep will swim if they have to in order to survive."[47] However, several circumstances make swimming an immensely dangerous exercise for sheep. Chief among these are the following:

- The water makes the sheep's wool coat so heavy that it has difficulty continuing to swim and becomes submerged, or it stops it from being able to haul itself out of the water.
- The sheep is pregnant.
- The body of water that the sheep is trying to traverse is too large.
- There is a fast current and the animal is caught up in it. The weight of wet wool would make this even more likely.
- The wool is long and gets caught on objects in the water, making it impossible for the sheep to continue swimming and escape.
- The sheep becomes exhausted and cannot continue swimming. The weight of wet wool can make this happen quite quickly.[48]

47. "Can Sheep Swim?," Raising Sheep, accessed September 4, 2024, https://www.raisingsheep.net/can-sheep-swim. See that article for information on the swimming ability of sheep and how they behave near water.

48. "Can Sheep Swim?"

These observations demonstrate that water deep enough to soak a sheep's wool poses a serious threat to its survival. Deep water is extremely dangerous for sheep. This leads us to our next reflection.

Second, still waters run deep. As the adage says, "still waters run deep." Anyone who has approached a shallow brook in the countryside will be familiar with the sensation of hearing it before it comes into view. This is because water in a shallow stream runs up against obstacles like rocks and pebbles that disturb the water's flow and turn the brook into a constant stream of micro-waterfalls that make the water bubble up and gurgle, thus creating the pleasant sounds typical of such waters.

By contrast, there is so much water above the various obstacles on the riverbed of deeper waterways that these obstacles rarely if ever disturb the water's surface, and hence the flow remains undisturbed and quiet on the deeper water's surface. It is this natural phenomenon that inspired the adage. For this reason, when the poet in verse 2 of our psalm draws attention to the fact that the shepherd steers his sheep persona toward waters that are "still," he is thinking not of peaceful provision but of mortal danger.

The sheep farmer mentioned earlier notes why sheep may be wary of "still" waters:

> Sheep don't have depth perception. This means that they cannot tell how deep water is. However, they can see if there is any movement in water, and they will especially avoid going into water that is moving. That is because of the fact they can be so quickly swept away by currents in the water.[49]

To be sure, the reference to "movement in the water" is not to the quick-moving gurgling of shallow brooks but to currents in "still" water. Equally, even though sheep do not have depth perception, they are of course able to distinguish between a shallow, gurgling brook and water that is deep enough to be "still" and thus potentially dangerous. If this sheep farmer is correct, then *any* water that runs still will be considered deep and dangerous by sheep.

While the psalm's pastoral imagery has always caught the imagination of its audiences, we believe that unfamiliarity with these two important pieces of information has misled audiences to conjure an unrealistic pastoral idyll of provision and peaceful safety that is simply not there.

By contrast, relevant knowledge about natural phenomena and animal behavior inspires a truly imaginative reading that suggests an altogether different

49. "Can Sheep Swim?" This article includes several excellent pictures that illustrate what kind of water sheep tend to traverse, including how they tend to proceed when they do it.

scenario: Already in verse 2, the villain of verse 4 casts his shadow on the pastoral scene; the sheep feeds already "in the presence of my enemies" (v. 5).[50]

Before we return to our earlier question as to why the psalmist would want to showcase that his shepherd has such a high tolerance for risk, a possible objection to our imaginative reading of the psalm deserves our attention. It is simply this: So what? We respond that our aim has not been to "knock out" the traditional interpretations of the verse until our interpretation is "the last one standing," to use Briggs's memorable formulations.[51] Even though we expended considerable energy on demonstrating the plausibility and even likelihood of our reading of verse 2, we have not removed the text "from the realms of joy or reassurance and [left] it stranded . . . under learned discussions of shepherding practices." Neither have our imaginative reflections led to that "most disheartening of scholarly observations: that our familiar and much loved translations [and interpretations, we might add] are mistaken, that the text never really said *that*, and so forth."[52] Rather, what we hope to have achieved in our imaginative attention to Hebrew grammar, figurative language, knowledge of riparian mechanics, and knowledge of animal physiology and behavior is "a vivifying of the imagination so that we can pay better attention to the text."[53]

In our final reflections, we will answer the questions raised earlier: Why does it matter that the psalmist showcases his shepherd's high tolerance for risk? Why is it that our imaginative reading, for all its novelty and difference, does not render traditional interpretations of the verse and the psalm obsolete? The best way of answering those question is to witness how Abby Hopkins, one of our students, responded during a lecture on Psalm 23 in the spring semester of 2021. She was visibly moved by the lecture's content and upon request reflected in writing on her experience a few days later:

> **Psalm 23 Reflection**
> The way Psalm 23 has typically been presented throughout my life has often felt inauthentic. With pictures of serenity and stillness, the text has often led me to muster up disingenuous feelings of peace while I hope for circumstances to change, for the open meadows and still waters to be set before me. I often found the Psalm to be in conflict with reality. However, when I was first presented

50. For an imaginative exploration of v. 4 and the entire psalm, see Heim, "Psalm 23 in the Age of the Wolf," 62–63.

51. See Briggs, *The Lord Is My Shepherd*, 6.

52. Briggs, *The Lord Is My Shepherd*, 2.

53. Briggs, *The Lord Is My Shepherd*, 55. Briggs credits Kenneth Bailey with having achieved just that in Kenneth E. Bailey, *The Good Shepherd: A Thousand-Year Journey from Psalm 23 to the New Testament* (SPCK, 2015).

> with an imaginative reading of the text that fully embraced the metaphor of the shepherd guiding his sheep, my understanding of Psalm 23 and its theological implications completely shifted.
>
> When I picture myself as the sheep and envision the open pastures and still waters, I enter into circumstances that my instincts desire to flee from. These are two places where sheep are endangered by predators and the realistic possibility of death, not peaceful, calming scenes as we often assume. This is not a promise that God will lead us into ease with no potential for harm. Rather, God might lead us into dangerous, intimidating, or fearful circumstances. However, the great truth of the Psalm is that He goes before us and offers protection by never leaving our side. There is no room to fear when we are surrounded by death and evil because we know the shepherd who guides us, which is emphasized in verse four. This metaphor is further illustrated and deepened when Jesus places himself into the role of the shepherd in John 10. We do not have a shepherd who is unaccustomed to evil, danger, and fear, but one who willingly entered into those things for our sake. Therefore, no matter what circumstances we are led into, even those that bring death, we are comforted by the rod and staff of our shepherd who sympathizes with our weaknesses and never leaves us on our own.[54]

The student acknowledges in the first paragraph that her exposure to traditional interpretations of the verse (and of the psalm as a whole) "often felt inauthentic," causing her "to muster up disingenuous feelings" and to find the psalm "to be in conflict with reality."

Once she encountered an interpretation of the psalm guided by a hermeneutic of imagination, however, she reports that "my understanding of Psalm 23 and its theological implications completely shifted." The remainder of her reflections, the entire second paragraph, eloquently narrate how her new insights enabled her to inhabit the world of the psalm and make it her own in a more realistic, authentic, and wholesome form that deepened her trust and confidence in God as a truly good shepherd even and especially when the going gets tough.

Concluding Reflections

This brings us to a vantage point allowing us to glimpse the exciting intellectual and theological opportunities that present themselves when we engage Scripture with a hermeneutic of imagination. The invitation to join us on this journey does not prescribe a singular method or formula for engaging with the Bible. Instead, we have opened the door to a broader hermeneutical framework that situates the act of imaginative reading as an opportunity for deeper

54. Abby E. Hopkins, personal communication, March 3, 2022. Used with permission.

engagement with the sacred text. What you see before you is a map that enables you to chart your own personal journey into close, deep, lusciously savored, highly imaginative, even pleasurable readings of Scripture—your pathway into an adventure of the mind that is at once theologically rewarding, intellectually compelling, emotionally liberating, and personally transformative.

On the preceding pages we have shared with you the multifaceted nature of imagination as we have experienced it on our own journey, positioning it not merely as a creative tool but as a critical mode of engagement that amplifies your understanding of Scripture. We know, because we have been there. This type of reading challenges conventional approaches by highlighting underappreciated nuances, stimulating theological insight through a deeper exploration of metaphor and figurative language, and attuning readers to the emotional resonances embedded in the text. With a hermeneutic of imagination, reading the Bible need no longer be a passive exercise in which you trod along behind your scholarly tour guide. Rather, reading with imagination allows you to inhabit the world of Scripture for yourself, in your own unique way. You turn from being a tourist into a citizen; you become an active participant who fully inhabits God's Word as the biblical texts call forth all your faculties—physical, intellectual, emotional, spiritual—to inhabit them ever more fully.

Further, exploring the Bible with imagination is an inherently theological enterprise. Through our imagination we allow the Holy Spirit to become our guide on a path with divine encounters at every twist and turn. The Spirit leads us to see Scripture as more than just an ancient document. We now experience it as a place of regular encounter with God. God is our host who invites us into dynamic, life-giving conversations as we explore every nook and cranny of Scripture, making it our new home. Prayer, then, is indispensable for such imaginative reading, allowing God to unlock the full potential of the Bible's meaning. It helps us to understand ever more fully how a given biblical text inspires us to grow in love for God, neighbor, and self. It also helps us apply what we read so that others experience the way Scripture has inspired our love for them, in turn prompting them to grow in love for God, neighbor, and self.

Finally, we hope that you already know that this volume is not exhaustive. Rather, it is a launching point. A hermeneutic of imagination does not prescribe fixed boundaries. Rather, it serves as a vantage point, as a point of entry into the vast terrain of Scripture, to begin exploring the beautiful, breathtaking depths of Scripture with renewed creativity and insight. The field of biblical studies will benefit as this approach gains momentum, inspiring scholars and ordinary readers alike to venture beyond traditional interpretations and into the fertile imaginative landscapes of Scripture. The Bible, written with imagination, invites us to read it with imagination.

Selected Bibliography

Abraham, Anna, ed. *The Cambridge Handbook of the Imagination*. Cambridge University Press, 2020.

Abrams, M. H. *A Glossary of Literary Terms*. 7th ed. Heinle & Heinle, 1999.

Acolatse, Esther E. *Powers, Principalities, and the Spirit: Biblical Realism in Africa and the West*. Eerdmans, 2018.

Aldrich, Virgil C. "Visuelle Metapher." In Haverkamp, *Theorie der Metapher*.

Alonso Schökel, Luis. *A Manual of Hebrew Poetics*. Subsidia Biblica 11. Pontificio Istituto Biblico, 1988.

Alter, Robert. *The Art of Biblical Narrative*. Basic Books, 1981.

Andersen, Francis I., and David Noel Freedman. *Micah: A New Translation with Introduction and Commentary*. 1st ed. The Anchor Bible 24E. Doubleday, 2000.

Anderson, Herbert, and Edward Foley. *Mighty Stories, Dangerous Rituals: Weaving Together the Human and the Divine*. Jossey-Bass, 2001.

Andrews, James A. *Hermeneutics and the Church: In Dialogue with Augustine*. University of Notre Dame Press, 2012.

Apte, M. L. *Humor and Laughter: An Anthropological Approach*. Cornell University Press, 1985.

Aristotle. *Art of Rhetoric*. Translated by J. H. Freese. Harvard University Press, 2020.

Arnold, Bill T. *Genesis*. New Cambridge Bible Commentary. Cambridge University Press, 2009.

Attardo, Salvatore. "The General Theory of Verbal Humor." In Attardo, *Routledge Handbook of Language and Humor*.

Attardo, Salvatore, ed. *The Routledge Handbook of Language and Humor*. Routledge, 2017.

Attardo, Salvatore, and Victor Raskin. "Linguistics and Humor Theory." In Attardo, *Routledge Handbook of Language and Humor*.

Attardo, Salvatore, and Victor Raskin. "Script Theory Revis(it)ed: Joke Similarity and Joke Representation Model." *Humor: International Journal of Humor Research* 4, no. 3 (1991): 293–347.

Auerbach, Erich. *Mimesis: The Representation of Reality in Western Literature*. Translated by Willard R. Trask. Princeton University Press, 1953.

Augustine. *On Christian Teaching*. Translated by Roger P. H. Green. Oxford University Press, 2008.

Avis, Paul. *God and the Creative Imagination: Metaphor, Symbol and Myth in Religion and Theology*. Routledge, 1999.

Bacon, Francis. *The Philosophical Works of Francis Bacon*. Edited by J. M. Robertson. Routledge, 1905.

Bailey, Kenneth E. *The Good Shepherd: A Thousand-Year Journey from Psalm 23 to the New Testament*. SPCK, 2015.

Baloian, Bruce Edward, ed. *New International Dictionary of Old Testament Theology and Exegesis*. Vol. 4. Paternoster, 1996.

Bartholomew, Craig G. *The Old Testament and God: Old Testament Origins and the Question of God*. Baker Academic, 2022.

Bartholomew, Craig G., and Matthew Y. Emerson. "Theological Interpretation for All of Life." In Bartholomew and Thomas, *Manifesto for Theological Interpretation*.

Bartholomew, Craig G., and Heath A. Thomas, eds. *A Manifesto for Theological Interpretation*. Baker Academic, 2016.

Bartlett, John R. "Archaeology." In Rogerson and Lieu, *Oxford Handbook of Biblical Studies*.

Bergen, Benjamin K. *Louder Than Words: The New Science of How the Mind Makes Meaning*. Basic Books, 2012.

Berlin, Adele, Marc Zvi Brettler, and Michael A. Fishbane, eds. *The Jewish Study Bible*. Oxford University Press, 2004.

Birch, Bruce C., and Larry L. Rasmussen. *Bible and Ethics in the Christian Life*. Rev. and exp. ed. Augsburg, 1989.

Boda, Mark J. *The Heartbeat of Old Testament Theology: Three Creedal Expressions*. Acadia Studies in Bible and Theology. Baker Academic, 2017.

Brague, Rémi. *The Law of God: The Philosophical History of an Idea*. Translated by Lydia G. Cochrane. University of Chicago Press, 2007.

Briggs, Richard S. *The Lord Is My Shepherd: Psalm 23 for the Life of the Church*. Touchstone Texts. Baker Academic, 2021.

Broomhall, Marshall. *The Bible in China*. The British and Foreign Bible Society, 1934.

Brown, William P. *A Handbook to Old Testament Exegesis*. Westminster John Knox, 2017.

Brown, William P. *Sacred Sense: Discovering the Wonder of God's Word and World*. Eerdmans, 2015.

Brown, William P. *Seeing the Psalms: A Theology of Metaphor*. Westminster John Knox, 2002.

Cahill, Lisa Sowle. "Community and Universals: A Misplaced Debate in Christian Ethics." *Annual of the Society of Christian Ethics* 18 (1998): 3–12.

Carey, Greg. "Rhetorical Criticism." In *The New Cambridge Companion to Biblical Interpretation*, edited by Ian Boxall and Bradley C. Gregory. Cambridge Companions to Religion. Cambridge University Press, 2023.

Chan, Yiu Sing Lúcás. *The Ten Commandments and the Beatitudes: Biblical Studies and Ethics for Real Life*. Rowman & Littlefield, 2012.

Charry, Ellen T. *God and the Art of Happiness*. Eerdmans, 2010.

Cheung, Andy. "Foreignising Bible Translation: Retaining Foreign Origins When Rendering Scripture." *Tyndale Bulletin* 63, no. 2 (2012): 257–73.

Childs, B. S. *Biblical Theology of the Old and New Testaments: Theological Reflection on the Christian Bible*. SCM, 1992.

Childs, B. S. *Introduction to the Old Testament as Scripture*. SCM, 1979.

Childs, B. S. *Isaiah: A Commentary*. Old Testament Library. Westminster John Knox, 2001.

Childs, Brevard S. *Biblical Theology in Crisis*. Westminster, 1970.

Childs, Brevard S. *The Book of Exodus: A Critical, Theological Commentary*. The Old Testament Library. Westminster, 1974.

Clines, David J. A. "Translating Psalm 23." In *Reflection and Refraction: Studies in Biblical Historiography in Honour of A. Graeme Auld*, edited by Robert Rezetko, T. H. Lim, and W. B. Aucker. Supplements to Vetus Testamentum 113. Brill, 2006.

Coulson, Seana. *Semantic Leaps: Frame-Shifting and Conceptual Blending in Meaning Construction*. Cambridge University Press, 2001.

Cover, Michael, John S. Thiede, and Joshua Ezra Burns, eds. *Bridging Scripture and Moral Theology: Essays in Dialogue with Yiu Sing Lúcás Chan, S.J.* Lexington, 2019.

Davis, Paige E. "Imaginary Friends: How Imaginary Minds Mimic Real Life." In Abraham, *Cambridge Handbook of the Imagination*.

Deane-Drummond, Celia. *Wonder and Wisdom: Conversations in Science, Spirituality and Theology*. Darton, 2006.

Deane-Drummond, Celia. *Wonder and Wisdom: Conversations in Science, Spirituality, and Theology*. Templeton Foundation, 2006.

de Lubac, Henri. *Medieval Exegesis*. Translated by Mark Sebanc and E. M. Macierowski. 3 vols. Eerdmans, 1998–2009.

de Waard, Jan, and Eugene Nida. *From One Language to Another: Functional Equivalence in Bible Translating*. Nelson, 1986.

Dewrell, Heath D. "Child Sacrifice in Ancient Israel." *Ancient Near East Today* 5, no. 12 (December 2017), http://www.asor.org/anetoday/2017/12/child-sacrifice-ancient-israel.

Dewrell, Heath D. *Child Sacrifice in Ancient Israel*. Explorations in Ancient Near Eastern Civilizations 5. Eisenbrauns, 2017.

Dobbs-Allsopp, F. W. *On Biblical Poetry*. Oxford University Press, 2015.

Donner, Herbert, ed. *Gesenius: Hebräisches und aramäisches Handwörterbuch über das Alte Testament*. Vol. 18. (Springer, 2013).

Durant, Karen Elizabeth. "Imitation of God as a Principle for Ethics Today: A Study of Selected Psalms." Doctoral thesis, University of Birmingham, 2010. https://etheses.bham.ac.uk/id/eprint/1184/2/Durant_10_PhD.pdf.

Erickson, Amy. *Jonah: Introduction and Commentary*. Illuminations. Eerdmans, 2021.

Fee, Gordon D. *Listening to the Spirit in the Text*. 2nd ed. Eerdmans, 2001.

Fischer, Irmtraud. *Gotteskünderinnen: Zu einer geschlechterfairen Deutung des Phänomens der Prophetie und der Prophetinnen in der Hebräischen Bibel*. Kohlhammer, 2002.

Fischer, Irmtraud. *Rut*. Herders Theologischer Kommentar zum Alten Testament. Herder, 2001.

Fischer, Irmtraud. *Women Who Wrestled with God: Biblical Stories of Israel's Beginnings*. Liturgical Press, 2000.

Fishbane, Michael. *Biblical Interpretation in Ancient Israel*. Oxford University Press, 1985.

Floss, Johannes P. "Form, Source, and Redaction Criticism." In Rogerson and Lieu, *Oxford Handbook of Biblical Studies*.

Gilot, Françoise, and Carlton Lake. *Life with Picasso*. Reprint ed. New York Review Books, 2019.

Gironzetti, Elisa. "Prosodic and Multimodal Markers of Humor." In Attardo, *Routledge Handbook of Language and Humor*.

Goldingay, John. *Reading Jesus's Bible: How the New Testament Helps Us Understand the Old Testament*. Eerdmans, 2017.

González-Andrieu, Cecilia. *Bridge to Wonder: Art as a Gospel of Beauty*. Baylor University Press, 2012.

Good, Edwin M. "Jonah: The Absurdity of God." In *Irony in the Old Testament*. SPCK, 1965.

Gorman, Michael J., ed. *Scripture and Its Interpretation*. Baker Academic, 2017.

Gosetti-Ferencei, Jennifer Anna. *The Life of Imagination: Revealing and Making the World*. Columbia University Press, 2018.

Gray, Alison. *Psalm 18 in Words and Pictures*. Biblical Interpretation. Brill, 2013.

Guidi, Annarita. "Humor Universals." In Attardo, *Routledge Handbook of Language and Humor*.

Guite, Malcolm. *Faith, Hope and Poetry: Theology and the Poetic Imagination*. Routledge Studies in Theology, Imagination and the Arts. Routledge, 2017.

Hart, David Bentley. *The New Testament: A Translation*. Yale University Press, 2017.

Haverkamp, Anselm, ed. *Theorie der Metapher: Studienausgabe*. Wissenschaftliche Buchgesellschaft, 1983.

Hays, Richard B. *Echoes of Scripture in Paul*. Yale University Press, 1989.

Heim, Knut M. *Ecclesiastes*. Tyndale Old Testament Commentaries 18. InterVarsity, 2019.

Heim, Knut M. *Ecclesiastes*. Zondervan Exegetical Commentary on the Old Testament. Zondervan Academic, 2025.

Heim, Knut M. "The (God-)Forsaken King of Psalm 89: A Historical and Intertextual Enquiry." In *King and Messiah in Israel and the Ancient Near East*. Journal for the Study of the Old Testament Supplement Series. Sheffield University Press, 1998.

Heim, Knut M. "Humor and Performance in Ecclesiastes 7:23–8:1." In *Biblical Humor and Performance*, edited by Peter S. Perry. Biblical Performance Criticism. Cascade Books, 2023.

Heim, Knut M. "Of Leeches, Lizards, and Lions: The Humorous Function of Animal Talk in Proverbs 30." In *Human Interaction with the Natural World in Wisdom Literature and Beyond: Essays in Honour of Tova L. Forti*, edited by Mordechai Cogan, Katharine J. Dell, and David Glatt-Gilad. The Library of Hebrew Bible/Old Testament Studies 720. Bloomsbury T&T Clark, 2023.

Heim, Knut M. "The Perfect King of Psalm 72—an 'Intertextual' Inquiry." In *The Lord's Anointed: Interpretations of Old Testament Messianic Texts*, edited by P. E. Satterthwaite, Richard S. Hess, and Gordon J. Wenham. Eerdmans, 1995.

Heim, Knut M. "Proverbs in Dialogue with the New Testament." In *Reading Proverbs Intertextually*, edited by Katharine J. Dell and William Kynes. The Library of Hebrew Bible/Old Testament Studies 629. Bloomsbury T&T Clark, 2018.

Heim, Knut M. "Psalm 23 in the Age of the Wolf." *Christianity Today* (January/February 2016): 60–63.

Heim, Knut M. "Wordplays." In *Dictionary of the Old Testament: Wisdom, Poetry and Writings*, edited by Tremper Longman III and Peter Enns. IVP Academic, 2008.

Held, Shai. "A Response to My Respondents." *Canadian-American Theological Review* 9 (2020): 43–54.

Holbert, John C. "Deliverance Belongs to YHWH! Satire in the Book of Jonah." *Journal for the Study of the Old Testament* 21 (1981): 59–81.

Houston, Walter J. *Contending for Justice: Ideologies and Theologies of Social Justice in the Old Testament*. The Library of Hebrew Bible/Old Testament Studies 428. T&T Clark, 2006.

Jacobson, Roman. "Der Doppelcharakter der Sprache und die Polarität zwischen Metaphorik und Metonymik." In Haverkamp, *Theorie der Metapher*.

Jauss, Hannelore. *Der liebebedürftige Gott und die Gottbedürftige Liebe des Menschen: Ursprung und Funktion der Rede von der Liebe des Menschen zu Gott als alttestamtentlicher Beitrag zur Gotteslehre*. Beiträge zum Verstehen der Bibel 25. Lit Verlag, 2014.

Johns, Cheryl Bridges. *Re-Enchanting the Text: Discovering the Bible as Sacred, Dangerous, and Mysterious*. Baker Academic, 2023.

Jones, Max, and Sam Wilkinson. "From Prediction to Imagination." In Abraham, *Cambridge Handbook of the Imagination*.

Karris, Robert J. *Eating Your Way Through Luke's Gospel*. Liturgical Press, 2006.

Keenan, James F., SJ. "Hospitality: Interpreting Lúcás Chan's Work through a Timely, Biblical Virtue from the Book of Ruth." In Cover, Thiede, and Burns, *Bridging Scripture and Moral Theology*.

Keener, Craig S. "Pentecostal Biblical Interpretation / Spirit Hermeneutics." In Gorman, *Scripture and Its Interpretation*.

Keener, Craig S., and L. William Oliverio, eds. *The Spirit Throughout the Canon: Pentecostal Pneumatology*. Brill, 2022.

Kind, Amy. "Philosophical Perspectives on Imagination in the Western Tradition." In Abraham, *Cambridge Handbook of the Imagination*.

Koehler, Ludwig, Walter Baumgartner, and Johann J. Stamm, *The Hebrew and Aramaic Lexicon of the Old Testament: Study Edition*, trans. and ed. Mervyn E. J. Richardson, 2 vols. Brill, 2001.

Koukouti, Maria Danae, and Lambros Malafouris. "Material Imagination: An Anthropological Perspective." In Abraham, *Cambridge Handbook of the Imagination*.

Krašovec, Joze. *God's Righteousness and Justice in the Old Testament*. Eerdmans, 2022.

Lakoff, George, and Mark Johnson. *Metaphors We Live By*. University of Chicago Press, 2003 (paperback edition 1980).

Lakoff, George, and Mark Johnson. *Philosophy in the Flesh: The Embodied Mind and Its Challenge to Western Thought*. Basic Books, 1999.

Lakoff, George, and Mark Turner. *More Than Cool Reason: A Field Guide to Poetic Metaphor*. University of Chicago Press, 1989.

Lamb, David. "Compassion and Wrath as Motivations for Divine Warfare." In *Holy War in the Bible: Christian Morality and an Old Testament Problem*, edited by Heath Thomas, Jeremy A. Evans, and Paul Copan. IVP Academic, 2013.

Lancaster, Mason D. *Hosea's God: A Metaphorical Theology*. Ancient Israel and Its Literature 48. SBL Press, 2023.

Larking-Galiñanes, Cristina. "An Overview of Humor Theory." In Attardo, *Routledge Handbook of Language and Humor*.

Leech, Geoffrey N. *A Linguistic Guide to English Poetry*. English Language Series. Longman Harlow, 1973.

Lefcourt, H. M. *Humor: The Psychology of Living Buoyantly*. Kluwer Academic, 2001.

Legaspi, Michael C. *The Death of Scripture and the Rise of Biblical Studies*. Oxford Studies in Historical Theology. Oxford University Press, 2011.

Levison, John R. *A Boundless God: The Spirit According to the Old Testament*. Baker Academic, 2020.

Levison, John R. *Filled with the Spirit*. Eerdmans, 2009.

Linafelt, Tod. "Why Is There Poetry in the Book of Job?" *Journal of Biblical Literature* 140, no. 4 (2021): 683–701.

Littlemore, Jeanette. *Metonymy: Hidden Shortcuts in Language, Thought and Communication*. Cambridge University Press, 2015.

Martin, Francis. "Introduction to Acts." In *Acts*, edited by Francis Martin. Ancient Christian Commentary on Scripture: New Testament 5. IVP Books, 2006.

Mathews, Jeanette. *Prophets as Performers: Biblical Performance Criticism and Israel's Prophets*. Wipf & Stock, 2020.

McClellan, David. *Marxism and Religion: A Description and Assessment of the Marxist Critique of Christianity*. Macmillan, 1987.

McDiarmid, Ian. "Underdetermination and Indeterminacy: What Is the Difference?" *Erkenntnis* 69 (2008): 279–93.

Medved, Goran. "The Fatherhood of God in the Old Testament." *Kairos—Evangelical Journal of Theology* 10, no. 2 (2016): 203–14.

Middleton, J. Richard. *Abraham's Silence: The Binding of Isaac, the Suffering of Job, and How to Talk Back to God*. Baker Academic, 2021.

Mitchell, Margaret M. "Rhetorical and New Literary Criticism." In Rogerson and Lieu, *Oxford Handbook of Biblical Studies*.

Moberly, R. W. L. *Old Testament Theology: Reading the Hebrew Bible as Christian Scripture*. Baker Academic, 2013.

Moberly, R. W. L. *The Theology of the Book of Genesis*. Old Testament Theology. Cambridge University Press, 2009.

Morse, Holly, and Katherine E. Southwood. Introduction to *Psalms and the Use of the Critical Imagination: Essays in Honour of Professor Susan Gillingham*, edited by Holly Morse and Katherine E. Southwood. The Library of Hebrew Bible/Old Testament Studies 710. T&T Clark, 2022.

Morton, J. "Anthropology." In *Encyclopedia of Humor Studies*, edited by Salvatore Attardo. Sage, 2014.

Muffs, Yochanan. *Love and Joy: Law, Language, and Religion in Ancient Israel*. Jewish Theological Seminary of America; Harvard University Press, 1992.

Muilenberg, James. "Form Criticism and Beyond." *Journal of Biblical Literature* 88 (1969): 1–19.

Müller, Reinhard, and Juha Pakkala. *Editorial Techniques in the Hebrew Bible: Toward a Refined Literary Criticism*. Resources for Biblical Study 97. SBL Press, 2022.

Nanay, Bence. "Perception and Imagination: Amodal Perception as Mental Imagery." *Philosophical Studies* 150 (2010): 239–54.

Nida, Eugene A. *Good News for Everyone: How to Use the Good News Bible (Today's English Version)*. Word, 1977.

Oppenheim, A. L. "Babylonian and Assyrian Historical Texts." In *Ancient Near Eastern Texts Relating to the Old Testament*, edited by J. B. Pritchard. Princeton University Press, 1969.

Oring, E. "Between Jokes and Tales: On the Nature of Punch Lines." *Humor: International Journal of Humor Research* 2, no. 4 (1989): 349–64.

Perry, Peter S. "And Now for Something Completely Different: An Introduction to Humor and Biblical Performance." In Perry, *Biblical Humor and Performance*.

Perry, Peter S., ed. *Biblical Humor and Performance: Audience Experiences That Make Meaning*. Biblical Performance Criticism 20. Cascade Books, 2023.

Raabe, Paul R. "Deliberate Ambiguity in the Psalter." *Journal of Biblical Literature* 110 (Summer 1991): 213–27.

Radday, Yehuda Thomas. "On Missing the Humour in the Bible: An Introduction." In *On Humour and the Comic in the Hebrew Bible*, edited by Yehuda Thomas Radday and Athalya Brenner-Idan. Journal for the Study of the Old Testament Supplement 92. Almond Press, 1990.

Raskin, Victor. *Semantic Mechanisms of Humor*. Reidel, 1985.

Reiss, Katharina, and Hans J. Vermeer. *Towards a General Theory of Translational Action: Skopos Theory Explained*. Translated by Christiane Nord. Routledge, 2014.

Renfrew, C., and P. Barn. *Archaeology: Theories, Methods and Practice*. Thames & Hudson, 1996.

Reno, R. R. *The End of Interpretation: Reclaiming the Priority of Ecclesial Exegesis*. Baker Academic, 2022.

Rhoads, David. Foreword to Perry, *Biblical Humor and Performance*.

Rhoads, David. "Performance Criticism: An Emerging Methodology in Second Testament Studies—Part I." *Biblical Theology Bulletin* 36 (2006): 118–33.

Richards, Ivor Armstrong. "Die Metapher (1936)." In Haverkamp, *Theorie der Metapher*.

Richards, Ivor Armstrong. *The Philosophy of Rhetoric*. Oxford University Press, 1936.

Rogerson, J. W., and Judith M. Lieu, eds. *The Oxford Handbook of Biblical Studies*. Oxford University Press, 2006.

Rohrbaugh, Richard L. *The New Testament in Cross-Cultural Perspective*. Cascade Books, 2007.

Roth, Federico Alfredo, Justin Marc Smith, Kirsten Sonkyo Oh, Alice Yafeh-Deigh, and Kay Higuera Smith, eds. *Reading the Bible Around the World*. IVP Academic, 2022.

Rowland, Christopher. "Social, Political, and Ideological Criticism." In Rogerson and Lieu, *Oxford Handbook of Biblical Studies*.

Salovey, Peter, Marja Kokkonen, Paulo N. Lopes, and John D. Mayer. "Emotional Intelligence: What Do We Know?" In *Feelings and Emotions: The Amsterdam Symposium*, edited by Antony S. R. Manstead, Nico Frijda, and Agneta Fischer. Cambridge University Press, 2004.

Schiewer, Gesine Lenore. *Studienbuch Emotionsforschung: Theorien—Anwendungsfelder—Perspektiven*. Wissenschaftliche Buchgesellschaft, 2014.

Schroer, Silvia, and Thomas Staubli. *Body Symbolism in the Bible*. Translated by Linda M. Maloney. Liturgical Press, 2001.

Schwarz-Friesel, Monika. *Sprache und Emotion*. 2nd ed. Universitäts-Taschenbuch. Francke, 2013.

Scott, James C. *Domination and the Arts of Resistance: Hidden Transcripts*. Yale University Press, 1990.

Sherwood, Yvonne. *A Biblical Text and Its Afterlives: The Survival of Jonah in Western Culture*. Cambridge University Press, 2000.

Smith, Ralph L. *Micah–Malachi*. Word Biblical Commentary 32. Word, 1984.

Soskice, Janet. *Metaphor and Religious Language*. Oxford University Press, 1989.

Sperber, D., and D. Wilson. *Relevance: Communication and Cognition*. Blackwell, 1986.

Sproul, Robert C., and Norman L. Geisler. *Explaining Biblical Inerrancy: The Chicago Statements on Biblical Inerrancy, Hermeneutics, and Application with Official ICBI Commentary*. Bastion, 2013.

Spykman, Gordon, Guillermo Cook, Michael Dodson, Lance Grahn, Sidney Rooy, and John Stam, eds. *Let My People Live: Faith and Struggle in Central America*. Eerdmans, 2005.

Still, J., and M. Worton, eds. *Intertextuality: Theories and Practices*. Manchester University Press, 1990.

Sugirtharajah, R. S. *Still at the Margins: Biblical Scholarship Fifteen Years after "Voices from the Margin."* T&T Clark, 2008.

Sugirtharajah, R. S. *Voices from the Margin: Interpreting the Bible in the Third World*. Orbis Books, 1991.

Sugirtharajah, R. S. *Voices from the Margin: Interpreting the Bible in the Third World*. 25th anniv. ed. Orbis Books, 2016.

Tate, W. Randolph. *Biblical Interpretation: An Integrated Approach*. 3rd ed. Baker Academic, 2013.

Thomas, Nigel J. T. "Mental Imagery." *Stanford Encyclopedia of Philosophy*, 2021. https://plato.stanford.edu/entries/mental-imagery.

Tov, Emanuel. *Textual Criticism of the Hebrew Bible*. 2nd rev. ed. Fortress, 2001.

Unterman, Jeremiah. *Justice for All: How the Jewish Bible Revolutionized Ethics*. JPS Essential Judaism Series. Jewish Publication Society, 2017.

van der Kooij, Arie. "Textual Criticism." In Rogerson and Lieu, *Oxford Handbook of Biblical Studies*.

Venuti, Lawrence. *The Scandals of Translation: Towards an Ethics of Difference*. Taylor & Francis, 1998.

Venuti, Lawrence. *The Translator's Invisibility: A History of Translation*. 2nd ed. Routledge, 2008.

Vygotsky, Lev S. "Imagination and Creativity in Childhood." *Journal of Russian and East European Psychology* 42, no. 1 (1930): 7–97.

Wacker, Marie-Theres. "Feminist Criticism and Related Aspects." In Rogerson and Lieu, *Oxford Handbook of Biblical Studies*.

Warnock, Mary. *Imagination*. Faber & Faber, 1976.

Webster, John. *Holy Scripture: A Dogmatic Sketch*. Current Issues in Theology. Cambridge University Press, 2003.

Webster, John. *Word and Church: Essays in Christian Dogmatics*. 2nd rev. ed. Bloomsbury T&T Clark, 2016.

Wegner, Paul D. *A Student's Guide to Textual Criticism of the Bible: Its History, Methods and Results*. IVP Academic, 2006.

Wheelwright, Philip. "Semantics and Ontology." In *Metaphor and Symbol*, edited by L. C. Knights and B. Cottle. Colston Papers 12. Butterworth's Scientific Publications, 1960.

Wilckens, Ulrich. *Der Brief an die Römer (Röm 12–16)*. Evangelisch-Katholischer Kommentar zum Neuen Testament VI/3. Neukirchener Verlag, 1989.

Wolff, Hans Walter. *Anthropology of the Old Testament*. Translated by Margaret Kohl. SCM, 1974.

Wolff, Hans Walter. *Jonah and Obadiah*. Translated by Margaret Kohl. Hermeneia. Augsburg, 1986.

Wright, Christopher J. H. *Old Testament Ethics for the People of God*. InterVarsity, 2004.

Wright, N. T. *The Last Word: How to Read the Bible Today*. HarperCollins, 2013.

Wright, William M., IV, and Francis Martin. *Encountering the Living God in Scripture: Theological and Philosophical Principles for Interpretation*. Baker Academic, 2019.

Yus, Francisco. *Humour and Relevance*. Topics in Humor Research 4. Benjamins, 2016.

Yus, Francisco. "Relevance-Theoretic Treatments of Humor." In Attardo, *Routledge Handbook of Language and Humor*.

Zittoun, Tania, Vlad Glăveanu, and Hana Hawlina. "A Sociocultural Perspective on Imagination." In Abraham, *Cambridge Handbook of the Imagination*.

Scripture Index

Old Testament

Genesis

Exodus

Leviticus

Numbers

Deuteronomy

Judges

Ruth

1 Samuel

2 Samuel

1 Kings

Ezra

Nehemiah

Psalms

Subject Index